# Palgrave Studies in Political History

Series Editors
Henk te Velde and Maartje Janse
Leiden University
Leiden, The Netherlands

Hagen Schulz-Forberg
Aarhus University
Aarhus, Denmark

The contested nature of legitimacy lies at the heart of modern politics. A continuous tension can be found between the public, demanding to be properly represented, and their representatives, who have their own responsibilities along with their own rules and culture. Political history needs to address this contestation by looking at politics as a broad and yet entangled field rather than as something confined to institutions and politicians only. As political history thus widens into a more integrated study of politics in general, historians are investigating democracy, ideology, civil society, the welfare state, the diverse expressions of opposition, and many other key elements of modern political legitimacy from fresh perspectives. Parliamentary history has begun to study the way rhetoric, culture and media shape representation, while a new social history of politics is uncovering the strategies of popular meetings and political organizations to influence the political system. Palgrave Studies in Political History analyzes the changing forms and functions of political institutions, movements and actors, as well as the normative orders within which they navigate. Its ambition is to publish monographs, edited volumes and Pivots exploring both political institutions and political life at large, and the interaction between the two. The premise of the series is that the two mutually define each other on local, national, transnational, and even global levels.

More information about this series at
http://www.palgrave.com/gp/series/15603

Remieg Aerts • Carla van Baalen
Henk te Velde
Margit van der Steen • Marie-Luise Recker
Editors

# The Ideal of Parliament in Europe since 1800

## palgrave
macmillan

*Editors*

Remieg Aerts
Faculty of Humanities
University of Amsterdam
Amsterdam, The Netherlands

Carla van Baalen
Center for Parliamentary History
Radboud University
Nijmegen, The Netherlands

Henk te Velde
Institute for History
Leiden University
Leiden, The Netherlands

Margit van der Steen
Netherlands Research School
Political History
Huygens Institute for the History of
the Netherlands
Amsterdam, The Netherlands

Marie-Luise Recker
Goethe University
Frankfurt am Main, Hessen, Germany

Leiden University
Leiden, The Netherlands

Palgrave Studies in Political History
ISBN 978-3-030-27704-8        ISBN 978-3-030-27705-5   (eBook)
https://doi.org/10.1007/978-3-030-27705-5

This Palgrave Macmillan imprint is published by the registered company Springer Nature
Switzerland AG.
The registered company address is: Gewerbestrasse 11, 6330 Cham, Switzerland

# PREFACE

In 2013 the European Information and Research Network on Parliamentary History (EuParl.net) organized the international conference 'The Ideal Parliament: Perception, Interpretation and Memory of Parliaments and Parliamentarism in Europe'. The conference took place in The Hague, 30 May–1 June 2013. Experts from different parts of Europe presented their views on the ideal of parliament in the nineteenth, twentieth and twenty-first century. Most of these presentations are included in this volume, in an adapted form, and completed with an introduction on the central theme, and some concluding observations.

We are grateful to Kate Delaney (language correction), Irene Helsen (editorial assistance) and Paul Reef (index) for their invaluable help and support.

| | |
|---|---|
| Amsterdam, The Netherlands | Remieg Aerts |
| Nijmegen, The Netherlands | Carla van Baalen |
| Frankfurt am Main, Germany | Marie-Luise Recker |
| Amsterdam and Leiden, The Netherlands | Margit van der Steen |
| Leiden, The Netherlands | Henk te Velde |

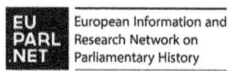

EU PARL .NET  European Information and Research Network on Parliamentary History

# Contents

# Notes on Contributors

**Remieg Aerts** is Professor of Dutch History at the University of Amsterdam, the Netherlands.

**Marnix Beyen** is Professor of Political History at the research group Power in History of the Centre for Political History at Antwerp University, Belgium.

**András Cieger** is senior researcher at the Institute of History of the Hungarian Academy of Sciences in Budapest, Hungary.

**Wim de Jong** is postdoctoral researcher and research coordinator at Open University, the Netherlands.

**Jure Gašparič** is senior researcher at the Institute of Contemporary History in Ljubljana, Slovenia.

**Adéla Gjuričová** is research fellow and the head of the working group on Parliaments in Transition at the Institute of Contemporary History of the Czech Academy of Sciences in Prague, Czech Republic.

**Kálmán Pócza** is senior research fellow at the Hungarian Academy of Sciences, the National University of Public Service, and associate professor in the Department of Political Science at the Pázmány Péter Catholic University in Budapest, Hungary.

**Thomas Raithel** is Adjunct Professor of Modern History at the Ludwig Maximilian University in Munich and a staff historian at the Leibniz Institute for Contemporary History Munich, Berlin, Germany.

**Marie-Luise Recker** is Professor Emeritus of Modern History at the Goethe University in Frankfurt am Main, Germany.

**Andreas Schulz** is Professor of Modern History at the J. W. Goethe-Universität Frankfurt am Main in Frankfurt am Main and the secretary general of KGParl (Kommission für Geschichte des Parlamentarismus und der Politischen Parteien), Germany.

**Jens Späth** is assistant professor at Saarland University, Germany.

**Henk te Velde** is Professor of Dutch History at Leiden University, the Netherlands.

**Carla van Baalen** is Director of the Centre for Parliamentary History and Professor of Parliamentary History at Radboud University, Nijmegen, the Netherlands.

**Joop Th. J. van den Berg** is Professor Emeritus of Parliamentary History at the universities of Leiden and Maastricht, the Netherlands and former member of the Eerste Kamer (Dutch Senate).

**Margit van der Steen** is managing director of the Netherlands Research School Political History, Amsterdam and Assistant Professor of Dutch History at Leiden University, the Netherlands.

**Stephanie Zloch** is head of the research group on Migration and Education at the Georg Eckert Institute for International Textbook Research in Braunschweig, Germany, and research fellow at the Technical University in Dresden, Germany.

# LIST OF FIGURES

# CHAPTER 1

# The Ideal of Parliament in Europe Since 1800: Introduction

*Remieg Aerts and Joop Th. J. van den Berg*

No other political institution may have been the subject of criticism for so long as parliament. Official figures show that national parliaments in the European Union score low rates of political trust, a poor 30 per cent on average.[1] Yet no political institution seems so close to the heart of democratic government as parliament. As national assembly and popular representation, it has been the key political power in almost all modern states in the last two centuries. Parliaments come in all shapes and sizes: some adhere to the Westminster model, others belong to the consociational model, some have two large parties, while other parliaments host a number of smaller parties. There are parliaments with 50 or with 700 representatives, and with one Chamber or with two Houses. Some parliaments have more powers, others have fewer. But there hardly are modern states

R. Aerts (✉)
Faculty of Humanities, University of Amsterdam, Amsterdam, The Netherlands
e-mail: R.A.M.Aerts@uva.nl

J. T. J. van den Berg
University of Leiden, Leiden, The Netherlands

University of Maastricht, Maastricht, The Netherlands

© The Author(s) 2019
R. Aerts et al. (eds.), *The Ideal of Parliament in Europe since 1800*,
Palgrave Studies in Political History,
https://doi.org/10.1007/978-3-030-27705-5_1

1

without some form of parliament. Even authoritarian or dictatorial states for the sake of formality retain a parliament of sorts.

This demonstrates the vitality and power of the idea of 'parliament'. It is the symbol of political legitimacy as such. Parliament has become a *Leitidee*, a guiding concept. The idea of parliament is normative: it is actually an ideal, or an *Idealtypus*.[2] It is so in four different ways. In the first place, parliament stands for the political idea of popular representation as legislative power, in a constitutional state on a democratic basis. In the second place, parliament embodies both the ideal and the practice of politics as reasonable deliberation and careful consideration of opposing social interests on a higher level. It hosts the loyal opposition and represents the process of binding decision-making by means of a generally accepted protocol. Thirdly, many parliaments are closely related to national history, the formation of the national state or the self-image of the political class. Next to the monarch, or even in his place, they have become the symbolic centre or locus of national government.

The fourth aspect of the parliamentary ideal seems paradoxical. As a good deal of parliamentary tradition was formed in the nineteenth century, an ideal type of rituals, manners and style tacitly became a standard early on. In the process parliament became firmly associated with liberalism and bourgeois culture. This association nourishes a widespread 'discourse of nostalgia' that affects the evaluations of parliaments time and again. Each generation entertains the illusion that parliamentary life used to be loftier in bygone days. The ideal of parliament, however, always includes several inherent tensions, for instance that between the requirements of representation and those of proper deliberation. These and other innate tensions are a source of disaffection, which is essential to the ideal as such.

This book examines this intrinsically complex, multifaceted and contested ideal of parliament. The chapters collected in this volume present the evolution of the ideal of parliamentary government, or the 'parliamentarization' of politics in Europe since 1800. They also discuss the reception and valuation of parliament as an institution, in particular the ambivalent dynamics springing from the intricate ideal type of a parliament, which is supposed to be reasonable, deliberative, representative and efficient to the utmost and simultaneously. In more than one way, parliament is a complex institution per se. The ideal of parliament itself brings forth a great deal of disillusion about the practice of parliamentary government.

This volume is based on the papers delivered at a conference on the ideal of parliament in The Hague in 2013, which was convened by the European Information and Research Network on Parliamentary History (EuParl.net).[3] It is the mission of EuParl.net to bring together initiatives and results of research in the field of parliamentary history. In recent years, a good deal of innovative research has been done on parliament as an institution and on parliamentary culture. Political scientists study numerous aspects of the system of parliamentary government. In particular the German 'Studien zum Parlamentarismus' constitute a steadily growing series of monographs and collections of articles from political science, law and contemporary history.[4] In the present volume, however, the focus is not on parliamentary history in the traditional sense, or on the study of the powers and workings of contemporary parliaments. Instead, its subject matter is parliament as an idea, as a specific culture of doing politics and as a practice of representation, deliberation and procedure. This book is about parliament as an historical institution, its culture, public perception, evaluation and resilience.

This approach fits in with the volumes of the German series 'Parlamentarische Kulturen in Europa', published by the Kommission für Geschichte des Parlamentarismus und der politischen Parteien.[5] In a way this book forms the mirror image of the recent volume *Parlamentarismuskritik und Antiparlamentarismus in Europa*, about the repertoire, the media, the theatres, the actors and the practices of criticism, rejection and denunciation of parliamentary government.[6] A Europe-wide and in-depth historical analysis of parliamentarism as a key concept in modern political cultures also was the subject of the volume *Parliament and Parliamentarism. A Comparative History of a European Concept* (2016).[7] As the French verb 'parler' indicates, language, deliberation and rhetoric lay at the heart of parliamentarism. Discursive practices received due attention in recent literature, in particular in *Parliament and Parliamentarism* (2016) in *Das Parlament als Kommunikationsraum* (2012) and in *Parliamentarism and Democratic Theory* (2015), about the important role of parliament and parliamentarism in the history of modern democracies as 'cultures of political debate'.[8] Taking the Westminster model as his ideal type, the eminent Finnish social scientist Kari Palonen, in his *Parliamentary Thinking. Procedure, Rhetoric and Time* (2018), amply discusses such key elements of parliamentarism as representation, procedure, deliberation and the rhetorical repertoire.[9]

It has become clear from the above-mentioned publications that parliamentarism is a common European legacy, which as a matter of fact also includes the United States. It emanated from classical, mediaeval and early modern forms and traditions of power sharing, separation of powers, deliberation and representation. From the late eighteenth century, four aspects or functions of parliamentarism evolved: representation, deliberation, sovereignty and the relation with the government, the head of state or the executive power.[10] Actually, not all these four aspects were part and parcel of the concept or of the institution per se. Deliberation and procedure were never absent, but the discussion about representation, the meaning of sovereignty and the aspiration to attain a balance with or an ascendancy over the executive were part of the ongoing 'project' of parliamentarism. This was a nonlinear process, with ruptures and drawbacks. Its pace and its results differed widely in all the parts of Europe.

Be that as it may, it still was a common European development. In the course of the nineteenth and twentieth centuries, the ideal of parliamentarism even spread to other parts of the world, in the wake of western colonialism and decolonization. The history of parliament and parliamentarism is an outstanding example of political and cultural transfer. The architecture and design, the powers, the procedures and the evaluation of parliaments are transnational phenomena. In many ways the British and French parliaments served as an example to other polities. In this volume they are given due attention, without being the main substance. Instead this book shows which part smaller polities and parliaments in Central, Eastern and Southern Europe took in this transnational exchange of ideals, forms and experiences from the beginning of the nineteenth century. It so happened that the Scandinavian countries are not included, despite their long parliamentary tradition. By and large though they would fit in with the developments described here.[11]

The aspects of the ideal of parliament will be presented in three parts. In the first part, 'Establishing Parliaments', five chapters describe the rise of parliament as a political institution and the transfer of parliamentary ideals, models and practices in the nineteenth century. 'Crises of Expectations' is the subject of the second part. Three chapters show how the high expectations of parliamentary democracy in newly established states after the First World War gradually subsided into dissatisfaction. The four chapters of the third part, however, attest to the 'Resilience of Parliament' in the half century after the Second World War, that is to say the strength of the ideal of parliament and its power to incorporate criticism and to make good use of it.

## THE IDEAL OF PARLIAMENT

Since the Middle Ages or early modern history, many European polities had diets or some other form of general assembly of estates, provinces or counties in a Reichstag, Landtag or Estates-General. So there was a long tradition of representing interests with the king or the local ruler, in an orderly negotiation procedure taking place in a fixed location, a town or a building. New, however, was the transformation of such diets into a popular, national representation at the turn of the eighteenth to the nineteenth century, based on the novel concept of the nation or the people as a moral body on an equal level to or even superior to the king. This new ideal of a parliament as a national and popular representative body originated in the American and French revolutions. Partly it adjusted the older model of the British Parliament, which shared power in a 'mixed government' admittedly since 1689, but actually functioned as a squirarchy.[12]

Despite the democratic experiments at the end of the eighteenth century, it was only after 1813, from 1848 and the 1870s onwards, that the idea of constitutional government and national representation gradually gained force to become the general standard. As Andreas Schulz points out in his chapter on Germany in this book, a basically moral pretension to speak for 'the people' transformed into a political claim to represent sovereignty as such. In some countries this parliamentary 'self-empowerment' took place through gradual stages of expansion, while in others that process went by fits and starts, in a bumpy dynamics of revolution and reaction.[13] Nevertheless, parliament everywhere evolved from a rather modest and upper-class representation with the monarch into an electorally broader-based authority next to the king, or reducing the monarchy to a new, primarily symbolic dignity, or even becoming the centre of power, as in France after 1871. Towards the end of the nineteenth century, the majority of European countries had a parliamentary government, no longer a monarchical rule.

Like the constitutionalizing process, the spread of parliamentary government has been a transnational phenomenon.[14] Constitutions and parliaments above all intended to represent and to express their polity, the national tradition and the national state. Their names referred to the former diets or appealed to national memories: Cortes, Staten-Generaal,

Landtag, Reichstag, Rigstag, Folketing, Vouli. But actually the new national parliaments and constitutions were the outcome of an ongoing process of interchange, borrowing, reproduction and adaptation. In his contribution to this volume, Henk te Velde unfolds how 'parliament' eventually became the general designation for a variety of bodies of popular representation.[15]

To other countries, Parliament in Westminster and the French Assemblée Nationale more or less served as models of what a parliament could be, with regard to procedures, powers and order of the meetings. For a while the advanced Belgian constitution and the National Assembly of 1831, the subject of Marnix Beyen's chapter, also acted as examples for newly founded national states in Eastern Europe.[16] Jens Späth in his contribution demonstrates the influence of the early Cádiz Constitution (1812) and the Cortes on the formation of representative institutions in Portugal, the Two Sicilies, Sardinia and Latin American states. András Cieger's chapter shows in detail how in Hungary the constitutional arrangement and parliamentary government of 1848 and 1867 were the result of a skilful piecing together of foreign examples and national tradition.

The rise of parliamentary government and the firm establishment of parliament as an authoritative institution is a fascinating process of self-styling and self-assertion. Their 'representative claim' presumed the creation of a discourse of legitimacy and the idea of a 'political nation'.[17] The Spanish Cortes, the Belgian Assemblée Nationale and the German Frankfurter Parlament factually constituted the national polity that they asserted to represent. Also in established states, which were not the result of a revolution, parliaments needed to define their position vis-à-vis the nation, the monarch and the executive. They had to develop procedures and practices and to learn to deal with opposition, political strife, party politics and change of government. They evolved a parliamentary language for deliberation, compromise, persuasion, authority and mobilization.[18] Andreas Schulz's contribution to this volume, about the short-lived but influential Frankfurter Parlament, highlights this 'making of a parliament'.

## DESIGNING AN IDEAL: THE ARCHITECTURE OF PARLIAMENTS

Nineteenth-century parliaments were faced with the task of making themselves visible to the nation. The examples of the Cortes, the Belgian and the French national assemblies, the Frankfurter Parlament and even the very much established British Parliament show that they invested in press coverage, theatrical display, public relations, visual culture, ceremony and a display of dignity. Although this volume does not include a chapter about the meaning of parliamentary architecture, the parliamentary buildings may be the best illustration of the spread of the ideal of parliament. In their ambition to present themselves as the centre of political power, the national polity and the new authority vis-à-vis the king, the parliaments reached for the classical rhetoric of power architecture.[19]

All the nineteenth-century parliaments provided themselves with a palace, mostly former royal lodgings or distinguished government buildings, churches or monasteries, which were allotted a new purpose. The National Assembly of the revolutionary Batavian Republic and afterwards the Dutch Second Chamber moved into the Binnenhof and settled into the former ballroom of the ousted Stadholder William V.[20] The French Chambre des Députés, afterwards the Assemblée Nationale, took up its residence in the Palais Bourbon, while the Italian parliament made its abode in the former papal Palazzo di Montecitorio. The Belgian Chambre des Députés, successor to the National Congress that founded Belgium as an independent state in 1831, took its seat in the former building of the Estates-General of the United Kingdom of the Netherlands, but converted it into a genuine 'Palace of the Nation'.[21] The symbolic dash for power already inherent in the expression 'palace of the people', or 'the nation', was grievously felt by nineteenth-century royalists and conservatives.

In the second half of the nineteenth century, many parliaments manifested their rising status through the erection of prestigious new buildings, when the old lodgings were no longer satisfactory or got damaged by fire. That was the right moment to give expression to the idea of national representation, history, and the relation to the executive and the head of state through the selection of a location, a style, a size, a lay-out and a decoration programme. After 1834 Westminster had to be rebuilt, in Madrid a new Palacio de las Cortes was erected after 1843, and in Bern the Swiss Confederation presented itself with an impressive Bundeshaus from 1852 onwards. The Norwegian Storting was provided with a new palace in 1866. On the Viennese Ringstrasse, the Hohe Haus made its appearance from 1874 onwards, and in the German Empire the monumental Reichstag was realized in 1884. About the same time imposing and characteristic new parliament buildings were established in Athens, Budapest and Stockholm.

In part the grandeur of the parliamentary palaces was defined by their location. Both the former palaces or monasteries that were given a new function and the newly designed buildings exploited the rhetorical opportunities of the site to the full. They display themselves majestically on a hilltop, or at a site of historical significance, or situated on a vast square or alongside the main river of the capital city. The buildings always are elevated above street level, visually enhanced through a basement and a flight of steps. The Palais Bourbon, housing the French Assemblée, imposingly stands on the quay of the Seine. Barry's neo-gothic Westminster Palace impressively stretches alongside the Thames. The spectacular Hungarian parliament building, inspired by the British Houses of Parliament, overlooks the Danube river and is deliberately situated across from the royal Castle Hill. The monumental Swedish Riksdagshuset (1897) dominates the Helgeandsholmen island and rivals the royal palace on the neighbouring island. The huge complex of the Bundeshaus in Bern has the spacious Bundesplatz on its front side and towers above the Aare and the lower part of the city behind it, as if it is on display on a panoramic terrace. The Austrian parliament has a raised lie on the spacious Ringstrasse. The Greek Vouli, whose new house was built in 1875, moved into the former royal palace on the vast Syntagma Square in 1929.

The location was selected not merely for reasons of visibility and standing. A good number of parliament buildings were erected on sites of historical importance, such as ancient strongholds of power or national *lieux de mémoire*. In most cases the parliament buildings are consciously sited next to or opposite the royal or presidential palace, or the seat of the government. In many bicameral parliaments, the Lower House and the Senate are lodged in separate buildings or in different halls across from each other under the same roof. Only in the Netherlands, in Switzerland and in Denmark did parts of the legislative, the executive, the bureaucracy or even the judiciary used to be lodged in the same block of buildings.[22]

The transnational character of the ideal of parliament plainly manifests itself in the architectural styles chosen. In view of their ambitions to represent the nation, in a century ridden with nationalism, it may surprise that the parliament buildings of the nineteenth century, whether in Europe or in overseas countries that were once under colonial rule, come in only about three styles. The ample majority of parliament buildings have a neo-classicist appearance. The Assemblée Nationale in Paris, the Paleis der Natie in Brussels, the bright Palacio de São Bento in Lisbon, the Palacio de las Cortes in Madrid, the Hohe Haus in Vienna and both the former and the present seat of the Greek Vouli look like classical temples. The German Reichstag, the Danish Folketing and the Swedish Riksdagshuset have the rather heavy and pompous exterior of neo-baroque architecture.[23]

When Westminster was rebuilt in the 1840s, it was deliberately decided to choose a British national and historical style: neo-gothic or neo-Elizabethan. Charles Barry designed a building that was as refined as it was monumental. About half a century later, Imre Steindl, the architect of the Hungarian parliament building, chose the same neo-style, in an even more luxuriant execution. Although the Országház, the 'House of the Nation', was intended to become the outstanding expression of Hungarian nationality and history, Steindl and his patrons held the view that only the ageless monumentality of the neo-gothic and neo-renaissance styles—both foreign to Hungarian cultural history—could render the building a lasting dignity.[24] The majority of designs of new parliament buildings were conventional varieties of the internationally current neo-styles: classicism, renaissance and baroque. This repertoire of styles could be used for all sorts of prestige architecture, such as government buildings, stock exchange buildings, museums, theatres and opera houses. Paradoxically the age of cultural nationalism lacked a repertoire of national architectural styles able to fulfil the need for monumentality and prestige. The parliaments provided for the display of the national identity and the historical legacy in lavish decoration programmes, both on the exterior and in the interior of the building.

The transnational repertoire of parliamentary architecture is also shown by the fact that the assembly hall, too, is limited to three designs. The first is the 'Westminster model', that is the oblong hall with opposing grandstands. The second, and most common, type is the semicircular hall or mounting amphitheatre. The third type is the school-classroom model.[25] As the British and the French parliaments served as a model to many other states, in Europe and the Commonwealth, the first and particularly the second types were copied almost everywhere. The popularity of the semicircular theatre hall is usually explained as a result of the accidental availability of such halls at the time or by reason of such practical advantages as audibility and a flexible display of party-political diversity. In the course of time, this type prevailed, including in the design of new parliament buildings. However, the lay-out of the parliamentary assembly hall can also be interpreted as a symbolic representation of a new post-monarchical political order in which the 'political body' moved from the king to the parliament.[26]

## CRISIS OF EXPECTATIONS

The ideal of parliament became firmly established in the course of the nineteenth century. But in the wake of this success, a first round of criticism arose, directed at the bourgeois and liberal character of the parliamentary order. In the 1870s social-interest groups began to organize themselves in formal political parties, backed by a rapidly expanding press. As the expectations with regard to the government, politics and politicians rose, the claim of the bourgeois, liberal parliaments to represent the people came under attack. In most countries there was a wide gap between the electoral *pays légal* and the *pays réel*. With the formation of socialist, republican, conservative or confessional parties, parliaments themselves became both the object and the arena of a political conflict about the role of the state, the political agenda or the needs of society. At the same time, the shortcomings of the parliamentary practices, such as the sluggishness, the lack of decisiveness and the difficult relationship with the executive power, became the subject of criticism.[27]

This criticism was linked in two ways with the ideal of parliament. On the one hand, gaining access to parliament raised high expectations with social groups that had not been politically represented before. When practical results and the prospects for carrying out substantial reform proved disappointing, a crisis of expectations accompanied their integration into parliament. On the other hand, the former political elites, who little by little saw themselves reduced to a minority, developed a 'discourse of nostalgia' in which they continued to judge parliamentary practices by the standards of a bygone notable, bourgeois-liberal parliamentary culture that had been an idealized picture anyway.

After the First World War, the prospects for parliamentary government seemed favourable. In many countries the extension of the vote or the introduction of universal suffrage connected parliamentary government with actual democracy. The collapse of the authoritarian and aristocratic old regimes in 1918 and the victory of the United States, the United Kingdom and France made democracy the new standard within parliamentary government. The newly established nation-states that resulted from the dissolution of the Habsburg, the Russian and the Turkish empires and the settlements of the Paris Peace Conference (1919–1920) were all set up as parliamentary democracies, and in most cases as republics.

A moderate enthusiasm for parliamentary democracy was not simply a reaction to the failure and collapse of the old political and social regime.

At first, the new system offered ample room to the imagination and the interpretation of what parliamentary democracy could be. This aspect is highlighted by the contribution of Stephanie Zloch about the Second Polish Republic (1918–1939). Again, as in the nineteenth century, though in a new way, parliamentary democracy could be connected with the idea of the nation. Now parliament was thought of as a house for a diverse nation, a national meeting place. Parliamentary democracy was the recognition for the common effort of the population during the war and the representation of the commitment of all social classes, ethnic communities and women to the national project. Parliament could also be imagined as a bearer of national memories of an older past.

In the majority of West European countries, too, parliamentary government evolved to full democracy through universal suffrage in the wake of the First World War. Almost nowhere was that development advanced by great enthusiasm for the prospect of mass democracy. In part it was the outcome of a long struggle of competing social and political groups, while others saw it as a deserved recognition for the collective effort of the population in the war. Granting universal suffrage was a means to avert a socialist revolution and an illustration of the dwindling power of traditional elites over politics and society. As parliamentary democracy was more an outcome or a second-best solution than an ideal, it would always experience an undercurrent of criticism and meet with competition from alternative forms of government, for instance suggestions of a corporatist order.

Universal suffrage reopened the issue about the difference between 'true democracy' and representative government that had already come into the open in the French revolution. Supporters of parliamentary government, having the dignified and detached parliament of the nineteenth century in mind, found it hard to digest that in the emerging mass party democracy, the House was being colonized by well-organized social-interest groups. To radical social and democratic parties, however, parliament would remain too much of a nineteenth-century, bourgeois-liberal instrument of control and domination.

In the 1920s the success of parliamentary democracy in the newly formed states in Central and Eastern Europe was seriously hampered by a number of problems.[28] The dissolution of the Habsburg Empire resulted in the creation of Austrian and Hungarian rump-states and the Czechoslovakian and Yugoslavian combination-states. The outcome of the war and the peace settlements of the Paris Conference not only bred frustration and disillusionment in substantial parts of society, it also opened up a Pandora's box of conflicts over ethnic minorities. Furthermore, there were serious disproportions in social-economic power and property, conservative social structures proved to be tenacious, and a civil society still remained underdeveloped. In the interwar years, a general problem of parliamentary government was its inability to effectively manage the growing tasks and responsibilities of the modern state. Initially parliaments were designed as an instrument of control, to curb the power of the executive. They were much less equipped for the active, co-managerial role they now had to assume.[29] As a consequence, many polities, having a multitude of deeply divided political parties in parliament, had to contend with frequent changes of government and with difficulties in forming a government. Parliaments were subject to the censure that they impeded the government by their sluggish procedures, their composition or party discord. These problems became pressing after 1930, when the economic crisis seemed to call for strong governments. Now even the supporters of parliamentary democracy began to vent criticism of the attitudes, the quality and the instruments of parliamentarism.

From 1925 on, but in most countries after 1930, the ideal of parliament became subject to severe criticism, on two levels. Nationalists, fascists, communists and other radicals rejected parliamentary democracy and the politics of deliberation as such. Other critics, while approving of the system, often expressed their dissatisfaction with the inadequacy of parliamentary practice. In both instances parliament itself could be used as the stage for such stricture.

As Kálmán Pócza shows in his chapter about the Hungarian parliament in the interwar years, two types of discourse can be distinguished in the dissatisfaction with parliamentary practice. The first was the traditional repertoire of 'crisis and decline'. In this discourse of nostalgia, parliament always was measured against an ideal vision of how politics and parliament ought to be. This implicit standard was the supposedly independent, liberal and notable parliament of the third quarter of the nineteenth century. The other discourse of criticism indicated that the level of expectations and demands people had regarding parliamentary democracy was rising. The system, however, was not up to these expectations and demands. In either case the parliamentary ideal itself burdened the assessment of the actual practice. The ideal stood in the way of a more realistic appreciation.

As is well known, in 1921, in the first wave of enthusiasm for parliamentary democracy after the First World War, there were 21 countries that had adopted parliamentary government on a more or less democratic basis. By 1940 only nine were left. Probably the best-known case is the fate of the Reichstag of the Weimar Republic. In his contribution Thomas Raithel shows the negative dialectics of normative, idealized expectations, on the one hand, and depreciatory criticism of parliament, on the other, by the members of the Reichstag themselves. In the long run, this constant internal impairment of the image of parliamentary politics corroded its legitimacy and prepared the way for authoritarian government.

## THE RESILIENCE OF PARLIAMENT

After the misery of the Second World War and the hard experience of fascist and national-socialist dictatorship, parliamentary democracy was allowed a new opportunity to establish itself as a humane and efficient political system. It gained the public confidence due to the moral example of the victor states, the United States and the United Kingdom, the economic recovery through the Marshall Plan, and the new Atlantic alliance which implied an ideological opposition to authoritarian communism. Basically, the Northwest European countries, and also Germany, Austria and Italy, could resume their prewar or older parliamentary traditions. As Marie-Luise Recker demonstrates in her contribution, after 1945 the three states that emerged from the former totalitarian dictatorships returned to the period of their most liberal and democratic constitutional experiences, in the nineteenth century or the early 1920s.

In the post-war era, most European polities adopted a rather disciplined, pragmatic, technocratic and managerial form of parliamentary democracy.[30] Their citizens had modest demands with regard to liberties and political participation. Parliamentary government became the standard for a proper democracy. Right-wing, authoritarian organizations lost all attraction, and socialism and communism no longer emphatically presented themselves as an alternative for liberal parliamentary democracy. During the Nazi occupation, socialists and communists had pledged themselves to the cause of national independence and democracy. After the war they participated in the realization of social democracy and the welfare state.

How obvious the idea of parliament had become is demonstrated by the socialist 'people's democracies' that were being formed under Soviet direction in Central and East Europe in 1948–1949. Even under communist single-party rule, the GDR, Poland, Czechoslovakia, Hungary,

Yugoslavia, Romania and Bulgaria maintained parliaments of sorts. In her chapter in this volume Adéla Gjuričová reveals in which forms parliament retained a function in Czechoslovakia after 1949 and since 1989. During the communist decades, parliament, due to its association with bourgeois-liberal politics and political pluralism, was replaced by a semi-official 'representative assembly' without legislative power. Its task was to provide for 'policy without politics'. In this way a parliamentary body survived, which in stages managed to 're-parliamentarize' itself in the course of the 1960s. Through a process of federalization the parliamentary model even was applied to several levels of government. In the 1980s the federal parliament more or less acquired the function of a non-Party addressee for appeals, petitions and letters from society. Thus, after the 1989 Velvet Revolution, the federal parliament seemed the only institution that could accomplish the political transition in a legitimate and procedural way.

In the meantime parliaments in the Northwest European democracies had been faced with a renewed 'crisis of expectations' in the 1960s, just as they seemed permanently and firmly established in the heart of the political system. In the emerging welfare states, the post-war sparing, restrained and technocratic form of democracy was felt as unsatisfactory. Some strains of this new wave of criticism called the credibility or even the legitimacy of parliament as democratic representation into question, while others complained about its performance. Around 1970 the ideal of parliament would appear to give way to the ideal of direct and extra-parliamentary democracy, which actually implied a thorough and general democratization of all aspects of social and private life, beyond the confines of political institutions. Leftist activists, protesters, political movements, journalists and political scientists now pictured parliamentary government as an outdated and deficient form of representation and as a tool in the hands of capitalism, the 'military-industrial complex' and other vested interests.

Disturbingly at first sight, this putative crisis of democracy actually demonstrated that parliamentary democracy had become fully grown. Only the standards of representation and good democracy had been raised: civic participation and a high voter turnout had become criteria of assessment. In his chapter about Dutch politics in the 1960s and 1970s, Wim de Jong reveals the remarkable resilience of the parliamentary model in this alleged 'crisis of democracy'.[31] Amidst the public turmoil, the parliament in The Hague managed to incorporate major points of social criticism, social movements and the call for further democratization. By establishing the office of the *ombudsman*, originally a Swedish institution, it manifested its receptivity to day-to-day social problems. More importantly still, parliament found that its own basic values of deliberation, dialogue and procedural decision-making became adopted as a model in the implementation of democracy in schools, universities and work councils.

The resilience and strength of the ideal of parliament became also apparent in the return or the establishment of parliamentary democracy in the Baltic states and the Central and Eastern European states after 1989. As Jure Gašparič shows in his chapter on Slovenia, the new democracies could draw inspiration and models from the West European parliamentary legacy, and partly from their national past. Besides, in the first years the revived or restored parliaments derived considerable prestige from their role in the transition from socialist satellite states to independent national states. Almost all parliaments maintained the buildings they were seated in, as they had no pressing need to restyle themselves.[32] Although parliaments in the region have lost much of their lustre since, and public confidence in the institute has decreased as a consequence of the ever recurring crises of expectations, they have managed to establish themselves in a normal role. In three decades, parliamentary government, however diverse, has become the standard practice in all the Central and Eastern European polities, even if there may be a tendency towards forms of authoritarian political leadership in recent years.

In the second half of the twentieth century, the architecture of new parliamentary buildings again reflected the evolution of the ideal of parliament. The nineteenth-century palaces intended to display monumentality, dignity and national identity, which was expressed by the use of historicist neo-styles. After 1945 discussions about the designs and realizations of new parliamentary buildings still manifested a clear awareness of their 'symbolic intent', that is the need to convey political values and to present parliamentary life to the public.[33] The difference is that those values and their presentation point to a new ideal, that is, the expression of modernity, in two forms: first, as efficiency, professionalism and public management; second, as democratic ethos, inclusion and transparency, represented by open buildings with glass walls, ceilings or domes, and a pleasing suggestion of accessibility. Examples of this new interpretation of the ideal of parliament are the Bundestag buildings in Bonn (1949, 1983–1992), the new Second Chamber in The Hague (1980–1991), Norman Foster's remodelling of the historically charged Reichstag building in Berlin and the Scottish parliament in Edinburgh (1999–2004).[34]

## A COMPLICATED IDEAL: THE THREE-FACED PARLIAMENT

Inadvertently both the people's representatives and the public have an idealizing, normative and often nostalgic picture of parliament in mind. That ideal burdens the evaluation of everyday practice. Sometimes the institution cannot meet the high expectations of political change, while at other moments its members display a pettiness or rudeness in manners that seems inappropriate in such a dignified house. Although parliaments generally enjoy a good deal of respect as an institution, the public appreciation of everyday politics is much lower. It is difficult indeed to raise sympathy for the practice of parliamentary work, as it is intricate, opaque, ostensibly tardy and therefore ungrateful. Most of the time, citizens do not get to see the dignity of the institution, but rather the bickering and the petty gains or losses of party politics. The ideal of parliament suffers from the fact that each parliament in workaday practice actually consists of three institutions being housed under the same roof. The first is parliament as an arena. The second is parliament as a marketplace. The third is parliament as an institute: the House.[35] The problem is that these three forms entail different, even contradictory values, attitudes, expressions and expectations.

Usually parliament looks like an arena of party politics and party conflict. Relations with the political parties outside the House are close, and the language is that of political ideology. Discussion in the arena is not so much an exchange of arguments with the purpose of convincing the opponents as an opportunity to give account of the party's convictions and of its reasons for the policy choices it has made. The majority party or party coalition in office backs the government, while the opposition routinely criticizes the government's policies and looks for little cracks in the united majority front. Parliament as an arena is a theatre in which everyone plays his allotted role, rather than a stage for open debate.

A second, much less visible form parliament can assume is that of the marketplace. This refers to the networks of interest representation. Lobby organizations seek to influence debate and decision-making through parties and individual members of parliament. In some cases these interests may converge with the ideology, the aims or the policies of political parties, but most lobbies and interests do not directly mesh with the ideological side of politics. This whole system of special-interest promotion operates in and outside parliament and can put parliamentary politics under great strain. It can even give birth to new political movements and party formations. What matters is that this kind of interest representation weaves strands of cross-cutting loyalties in parliament. It tends to de-ideologize politics. In non-ideological parliaments or parliaments with relatively limited party-political pressure, such as the European Parliament, the marketplace function is predominant or at least matches the arena function. With the role of political parties dwindling, as appears to be a general development, the marketplace function, with its pragmatic, technocratic and somewhat hidden nature, seems to become more important. As a form of functional representation, though, it is at odds with electoral representation.

At times the third form comes to the fore, when parliament as a whole or groups or parties within the House display a heightened awareness of their rights and the dignity of the institute. Frustrated backbenchers may rise up against their leaders, calling upon their rights as individual MPs and defending their personal mandate against party discipline. For parliaments not only have to safeguard their powers against the king or the government, they also ought to defend individual members and small parties against the majority. At intervals the House acknowledges the need to investigate its own performance and the effects and effectiveness of earlier policies. It does not always take a scandal to set this process of reflection in motion, in the form of a parliamentary inquiry or by establishing an external committee. Parliamentary committees, designated to undertake such an investigation, usually operate on a non-party-political and non-special-interest basis. In these cases, parliament as a House retakes its classical rights, beyond party loyalty or the influence of vested interests, and chooses to behave like an independent institution, if necessary acting against those in office. It may be observed that such public hearings and inquiries by parliamentary committees go together with a significant rise in public trust. Apparently, citizens appreciate their representatives in this scrutinizing but non-partisan role. Besides, parliamentary hearings make a good spectacle and enhance the visibility of parliament.

With regard to the three institutional roles, the European Parliament is an interesting case in point. As a House, defending and extending its rights, and as a well-organized marketplace, the EP has managed to become an authoritative and a highly influential body within the European Union. Like the parliaments of the nineteenth century, it had to carve out its position and powers. The problem, though, is that the EP mainly produces 'policy without politics'.[36] As a parliament, it is not really an arena, as it hosts only low-profile political parties, lacks a direct relation to the preferences of a European electorate, and has no majority party or parties corresponding with the political persuasion of the European Commission, which is not supposed to have a political profile anyway. Being a successful institute otherwise, the EP remains a deficient parliament due to the fact that it is not a political arena.

At the same time, however, the arena function is waning in the national parliaments, too. Political parties and ideologies have lost much of their attraction and mobilizing power. Identity politics, single-issue movements and populist parties have the effect of furthering political fragmentation, while decision-making about big financial, economic, social and environmental issues tends to move away from the national level to supranational bodies or authorities. The pressure of the financial markets and credit-rating agencies confines the room for national policies. To compensate for the loss of real power, parties in national parliaments appear to enhance their representative role, by voicing the day-to-day needs and problems of their voters. As a result, the national political arena increasingly tends to produce 'politics without policy'. Thus, in the end, the arena function erodes the relevance of parliament, while it was meant to be the core of the idea of parliament.

The institutional triad of arena, marketplace and House affects the appreciation of parliament. There is an obvious tension between the three functions. The arena and the marketplace determine the success of parliament as regards its democratic, managerial and representative functions, but the picture of tasteless bickering and unprincipled bargaining is harmful to the image of the House. The increasing visibility of the business of parliament works against its appreciation by the public. Each parliament experiences the tension between 'policy without politics'—the illusion of technocracy, causing a lack of interest and public support—and 'politics without policy', the mere expressive form of representation, lacking a clear direction and weak in results. To the public eye, the House, giving account of its own decisions, and calling the government to account for its acts and faults, may seem to come closest to the ideal of parliament. It is obvious, though, that parliaments cannot do without their arena and marketplace functions.

As an institution, parliament cannot live on its past and historical dignity. Yet, the ideal of parliament is a legacy and an asset that constitute a strong 'representative claim': parliaments still embody the values of democracy, deliberation, diversity, weighing up pros and cons, articulating and voicing public interests, and legitimate decision-making through careful procedure. Recent publications emphasize that the force and conviction by which parliaments and officials make this democratic claim will determine its success.[37] The ideal itself is a strength in a highly performative process.

## NOTES

1. *Standard Eurobarometer 88 (Autumn 2017). Public Opinion in the European Union*, 12: Europeans and trust in political institutions 2004–2017.
2. Cf. K. Palonen, *Parliamentary Thinking: Procedure, Rhetoric and Time* (Cham: Palgrave Macmillan, 2018) 17–39; K. Palonen, 'Political Theories of Parliamentarism' in P. Ihalainen, C. Ilie and K. Palonen (eds.), *Parliament and Parliamentarism. A Comparative History of a European Concept* (New York and Oxford: Berghahn, 2018) 219–227.
3. https://euparl.net/; the conference was made possible by a grant from the Netherlands Organization for Scientific Research (NWO).
4. *Studien zum Parlamentarismus* (Baden-Baden: Nomos Verlag); in this series, among other relevant titles: W.E. Patzelt and S. Dreischer (eds.), *Parlamente und ihre Zeit* (Baden-Baden: Nomos, 2009); W.E. Patzelt (ed.), *Parlamente und ihre Evolution. Forschungskontext und Fallstudien* (Baden-Baden: Nomos, 2012).
5. A. Schulz and A. Wirsching (eds.), *Parlamentarische Kulturen in Europa. Das Parlament als Kommunikationsraum* (Dusseldorf: Droste Verlag, 2012); J. Feuchter and J. Helmradt (eds.), *Parlamentarische Kulturen vom Mittelalter bis in die Moderne: Reden—Räume—Bilder* (Dusseldorf: Droste Verlag, 2013); A. Gjuricova et al. (eds.), *Lebenswelten der Abgeordneten in Europa 1860–1990* (Dusseldorf: Droste Verlag, 2014).
6. M.-L. Recker and A. Schulz (eds.), *Parlamentarismuskritik und Antiparlamentarismus in Europa* (Dusseldorf: Droste Verlag, 2018).
7. Ihalainen, Ilie and Palonen (eds.), *Parliament and Parliamentarism*.
8. K. Palonen and J.M. Rosales (eds.), *Parliamentarism and Democratic Theory. Historical and Contemporary Perspectives* (Opladen, Berlin, Toronto: Barbara Budrich Publishers, 2015) 11; A. Schulz and A. Wirsching (eds.), *Parlamentarische Kulturen in Europa. Das Parlament als Kommunikationsraum* (Dusseldorf: Droste Verlag, 2012).
9. Palonen, *Parliamentary Thinking*.
10. P. Ihalainen, C. Ilie and K. Palonen, 'Parliament as a Conceptual Nexus' in Ihalainen, Ilie and Palonen (eds.), *Parliament and Parliamentarism*, 1–16, esp. 6–8.
11. U. Jacobsen and J. Kurunmäki, 'The Formation of Parliamentarism in the Nordic Countries from the Napoleonic Wars to the First World War' in

Ihalainen, Ilie and Palonen (eds.), *Parliament and Parliamentarism*, 97–114.

12. The history of representative bodies and traditions in: Ihalainen, Ilie and Palonen (eds.), *Parliament and Parliamentarism*; B. Manin, *The Principles of Representative Government* (Cambridge: Cambridge University Press, 1997); J. Keane, *The Life and Death of Democracy* (London etc.: Simon & Schuster, 2009); M.A.R. Graves, *The Parliaments of Early Modern Europe* (Harlow and London: Longman, 2001); D. Gerhard (ed.), *Ständische Vertretungen in Europa im 17. und 18. Jahrhundert* (Göttingen: Vandenhoeck & Ruprecht, 1969); H.G. Koenigsberger, *Monarchies, States-General and Parliaments in the Netherlands in the fifteenth and sixteenth centuries* (Cambridge: Cambridge University Press, 2001); H. Hofmann, *Repräsentation. Studien zur Wort- und Begriffsgeschichte von der Antike bis ins 19. Jahrhundert* (Berlin: Duncker & Humblot, 1974); H.F. Pitkin, *The Concept of Representation* (Berkeley, Cal.: University of California Press, 1967); M. van Gelderen and Q. Skinner (eds.), *Republicanism. A shared European Heritage I. Republicanism and Constitutionalism in Early Modern Europe* (Cambridge: Cambridge University Press, 2002); P. Rosanvallon, *La démocratie inachevée. Histoire de la souveraineté du peuple en France* (Paris: Gallimard, 2000).

13. H. Spoormans, *'Met uitsluiting van voorregt'. Het ontstaan van liberale democratie in Nederland* (Amsterdam: SUA, 1988) identifies four types or paths in the historical development of parliamentary government.

14. H. Dippel, 'Modern Constitutionalism. An introduction to the History in Need of Being Written' in *Tijdschrift voor Rechtsgeschiedenis* 73 (2005) 153–170; D. Willoweit and U. Seif (eds.), *Europäische Verfassungsgeschichte* (Munich: C.H. Beck, 2003); W. Daum et al. (eds.), *Handbuch der europäischen Verfassungsgeschichte im 19. Jahrhundert II. 1815–1847* (Bonn: Dietz Verlag, 2012); website The Rise of Modern Constitutions 1776/1849: www.modern-constitutions.de. See also Henk te Velde, 'Political Transfer. An Introduction' in *European Review of History* 12 (2005) 205–221.

15. Also see H. Boldt, 'Parlament, parlamentarische Regierung, Parlamentarismus' in O. Brunner, W. Conze and R. Koselleck (eds.), *Geschichtliche Grundbegriffe. Historisches Lexikon zur politisch-sozialen Sprache in Deutschland* 4 (Stuttgart: Klett-Cotta, 1978) 649–676; Ihalainen, Ilie and Palonen (eds.), *Parliament and Parliamentarism*, part one.

16. J. Gilissen, 'Die Belgische Verfassung von 1831–ihr Ursprung und ihr Einfluss' in Werner Conze (ed.), *Beiträge zur deutschen und belgischen Verfassungsgeschichte im 19. Jahrhundert* (Stuttgart: Klett-Cotta, 1967) 38–69.

17. M. Saward, *The Representative Claim* (Oxford: Oxford University Press, 2010).
18. Schulz and Wirsching (eds.), *Parlament als Kommunikationsraum;* Ihalainen, Ilie and Palonen (eds.), *Parliament and Parliamentarism,* part two.
19. About political architecture in general: Charles T. Goodsell, 'The Architecture of Parliaments: Legislative Houses and Political Culture' in *British Journal of Political Studies* 18 (1988/3) 287–302; N.S. Roberts, 'Grand Designs: Parliamentary Architecture, Art, and Accessibility' in *Political Science* 61 (2009/2) 75–86; D. Sudjic and H. Jones, *Architecture and Democracy* (London and Glasgow: Lawrence King Publishers, 2001); I. Flagge (ed.), *Architektur und Demokratie* (Stuttgart: Krämer Verlag, 1992); Stephan Paulus, '"Das Baulige Herz der Demokratie". Parlamentsarchitektur im öffentlichen Raum' in Schulz and Wirsching (eds.), *Parlament als Kommunikationsraum,* 389–422; B. Brincker and A.S. Leoussi, 'Anthony D. Smith and the role of art, architecture and music in the growth of modern nations: a comparative study of national parliaments and classical music in Britain and Denmark' in *Nations and Nationalism* 24 (2018) 312–326.
20. D. Smit, *Het belang van het Binnenhof. Twee eeuwen Haagse politiek, huisvesting en herinnering* (Amsterdam: Prometheus, 2015); J. Oddens, *Pioniers in schaduwbeeld. Het eerste parlement van Nederland, 1796–1798* (Nijmegen: Vantilt, 2012).
21. M. Beyen and R. Röttger, 'Het streven naar waardigheid. Zelfbeelden en gedragscodes van de volksvertegenwoordigers' in E. Gerard et al. (eds.), *Geschiedenis van de Belgische Kamer van Volksvertegenwoordigers 1830–2002* (Brussel, 2003) 337–383.
22. www.christiansborgpalace.dk; www.folketinget.dk; Smit, *Het belang;* A. Minta and B. Nicolai (eds.), *Parlamentarische Repräsentationen. Das Bundeshaus in Bern im Kontext internationaler Parlamentsbauten und nationaler Strategien* (Bern: Peter Lang Publishers, 2014).
23. Information about parliament buildings worldwide, see 'Plenum. Places of Power. A wiki on National Parliament Buildings Worldwide': www.places-of-power.org; see also 'Encyclopaedia of Romantic Nationalism in Europe': https://ernie.uva.nl
24. Sudjic and Jones, *Architecture and Democracy,* 52.
25. A review of all the assembly halls in the world in: David Mulder van der Vegt and Max Cohen de Lara, *Parliament* (Rotterdam: XML, 2016).
26. Ph. Manow, *In the King's shadow. The Political Anatomy of Democratic Representation* (Cambridge: Cambridge University Press, 2011) chapter 2; H. te Velde, *Sprekende politiek. Redenaars en hun publiek in de parlementaire Gouden Eeuw* (Amsterdam: Prometheus, 2015) 15–18.

27. See Recker and Schulz (eds.), *Parlamentarismuskritik*.
28. M. Mazower, *Dark Continent. Europe's Twentieth Century* (London: Penguin, 2001) chapter 1; about anti-parliamentarianism, see: R. Aerts, 'An Unrewarding Task. Criticism of Parliament and Anti-parliamentarianism: a Historical Review' in Recker and Schulz (eds.), *Parlamentarismuskritik*, 25–42; J. Gijsenbergh, 'Contesting Complaints about Parliamentarism in Western Europe (1918–1939)' in Ihalainen, Ilie and Palonen (eds.), *Parliament and Parliamentarism*, 117–140.
29. Mazower, *Dark Continent*, 20–25.
30. M. Conway, 'Democracy in Postwar Western Europe: the Triumph of a Political Model' in *European History Quarterly* 32 (2002) 59–84; Mazower, *Dark Continent*, chapter 9; J.-W. Müller, *Contesting Democracy. Political Ideas in Twentieth-Century Europe* (New Haven and London: Yale University Press, 2013).
31. See also J. Gijsenbergh et al. (eds.), *Creative Crises of Democracy* (Bern etc.: Peter Lang Publishers, 2012).
32. Paulus, '"Baulige Herz"', 412–416.
33. D. Judge and C. Leston-Bandeira, 'The Institutional Representation of Parliament' in *Political Studies* 66 (2018) 154–172, esp. 158.
34. Sudjic and Jones, *Architecture and Democracy*, 94–109 and 141–177; Paulus, '"Bauliche Herz"', 394–411; Smit, *Het belang*, 213–273; Judge and Leston-Bandeira, 'Institutional Representation', 159 and 163.
35. About forms and modes of parliamentary practice: J.Th.J. van den Berg, 'Het parlement: één instelling, drie instituties' in: J.Th.J. van den Berg, J.L.W. Broeksteeg and L.F.M. Verhey (eds.), *Het parlement. Staatsrechtconferentie 2006* (Nijmegen: Wolf Legal Publishers, 2007); J.Th.J. van den Berg, 'Eén parlement in vier gedaanten' in W.J. van Noort et al. (eds.), *Organiseren op een breukvlak. Zes opstellen over organisaties in verleden, heden en toekomst* (Amsterdam: SISWO, 1993); A. King, 'Modes of Executive-Legislative Relations: Great Britain, France and West-Germany' in *Legislative Studies Quarterly* 1 (1976/1) 11–36; R.B. Andeweg and J. Thomassen, 'Modes of Political Representation: Towards a new Typology' in *Legislative Studies Quarterly* 30 (2005/4) 507–528.
36. V. A. Schmidt, *Democracy in Europe: the EU and National Polities* (Oxford: Oxford University Press, 2006).
37. Saward, *Representative claim*; Judge and Leston-Bandeira, 'Institutional representation'; Schmidt, *Democracy*.

# PART I

# Establishing Parliaments

# CHAPTER 2

# Between National Character and an International Model: Parliaments in the Nineteenth Century

## *Henk te Velde*

Historians are used to seeing the nineteenth century as an age of parliamentary expansion. Until a couple of decades ago, most histories of parliamentarianism focused on the progressive development of ministerial responsibility, the growing power of the executive and the extension of the suffrage.[1] The interwar period, on the other hand, has usually been seen as a time of 'crisis' of parliamentary government. However, crises had already appeared during the nineteenth century. At the end of that century, the idea of a crisis of parliament was already prominent.[2] Even in what many people would assume to be the golden age of liberal parliaments, the 1850s and 1860s, the future of parliamentary government looked rather bleak. It is not an exaggeration to call the situation of the mid-nineteenth century a forgotten crisis of parliamentary government. It was a real low point. Britain was the only prominent example of parliamentary government left in Europe. In the first half of the nineteenth century, during the Restoration and the July monarchy, France had been the other shining

H. te Velde (✉)
Leiden University, Leiden, The Netherlands
e-mail: H.te.Velde@hum.leidenuniv.nl

R. Aerts et al. (eds.), *The Ideal of Parliament in Europe since 1800*,
Palgrave Studies in Political History,
https://doi.org/10.1007/978-3-030-27705-5_2

model of parliamentary government, but after 1848, Napoleon III reduced the parliament to insignificance. The parliament continued to exist, but its constitutional power dwindled. In most German states, there was no powerful parliament anyway. Small countries such as Belgium, let alone the Netherlands with its unfamiliar language, were often overlooked by commentators. Only the great powers were seen as possible models, and Great Britain was the only great power with a proper parliament.

By looking closely at the forgotten crisis of parliaments in the middle of the nineteenth century, we will be able to discover a change in the perception and perhaps even the nature of parliaments between the beginning and the end of the nineteenth century. 'Parliaments' started as the property of a few privileged nations: Britain and France whose parliaments were seen as national institutions that reflected the national culture. By the end of the nineteenth century, parliaments had developed into rather formal institutions, primarily regarded as legal and constitutional rather than national and cultural organizations. By then, even though they retained their national characteristics, they had become exportable commodities, but perhaps at the expense of some of their more substantive qualities. In order to highlight this evolution, we will start in the 1860s.

## PARLIAMENTS AND NATIONAL CHARACTERS

In his famous *The English Constitution* of 1867, Walter Bagehot compares Britain to the United States. The United States had a parliament, but it had, in fact, a presidential form of government, quite different from proper parliamentary government. France was even worse. The parliament or 'assemblies' of the existing Empire of Napoleon III were, according to Bagehot, 'shams', 'suitable appendages to an Empire which desires the powers of despotism without its shame'. A couple of years later, in 1872, Bagehot wrote a preface for the second edition of his book. In the meantime Napoleon III had been overturned, his empire was gone, and a new and powerful parliament had been installed. The behaviour of this parliament, however, confirmed Bagehot's opinion that the French national character was not suited for parliamentary government. As soon as French MPs heard something they did not like, Bagehot said, they did not just 'clamour', but started to 'scream, and to scream as only Frenchmen can'. Bagehot had witnessed the disorderly proceedings of the 1848 French parliament in Paris, and the Assembly that was sitting in Versailles was the same: 'there was not an audience willing to hear'.[3] According to Bagehot, parliamentary government was apparently a matter of national character and only the British or English character was fit for that system. Parliamentary government was not an export product.

For Bagehot and other commentators, 'national character' was a self-evident category of analysis, and they naturally reified French revolutionary politics as a trait of the national character and a kind of permanent inhibition to the parliamentary mode of politics. That a society needs certain qualities to be able to support a parliamentary system is not such a strange idea, but the British were so convinced of the importance of national character, that they often believed that only the British character was fit for the parliamentary system, in particular in the mid-nineteenth century.[4] On the occasion of the inauguration of the new parliament buildings in 1852, the *Illustrated London News* wrote that Britain, with 'some trifling exceptions', had 'the only free Parliament in Europe', 'the model and envy of nations'. Did the British really regard their parliament as a model—that could be copied—or rather as a unique part of the British national heritage? According to *The Times*, Britain, as a 'model of representative government', was left to 'stand alone in its glory'.[5] A model could not be inimitable; otherwise it would not be a model. 'Parliament' was the name of the representative institution of Great Britain, but was it really the name of a category to which many other institutions (still) belonged?

These remarks raise the questions to what extent, in what form and at what time parliamentary government became a model that was available for copying. In trying to answer these questions for the nineteenth century, I would like to make two distinctions, one between parliamentary regulations and parliamentary culture, and the other between the elite parliament of the Restoration period and the democratic parliament of the end of the nineteenth century.

Nineteenth-century representative bodies often consciously chose names other than parliament. Most countries used expressions reminiscent of their own national traditions, such as Cortes (Spain), Landtag (German states), Staten-Generaal or States General (the Netherlands) or Folketing (Denmark, since 1849). This was a reflection of the national orientation of nineteenth-century politics which should, of course, not be taken at face value. Representative institutions were presented as indigenous, national systems, but this could disguise a process of copying foreign elements. The most famous case in point is the adoption of British rules during the French Revolution. Both the British MP and legal reformer Samuel

Romilly and the utilitarian philosopher and political theorist Jeremy Bentham provided Count Mirabeau, the most prominent French politician of the beginning of the Revolution, with an overview of the largely unwritten parliamentary rules that were applied in Westminster. The Swiss notable Étienne Dumont, who was living in Paris at the time and was the most prominent speech writer for Mirabeau, acted as a go-between. The British influence was obvious. Members of the French National Assembly started to use English expressions such as motions or Right Honourable Member. They also borrowed many rules from the British parliament. It was just a small sign of the remarkable extent to which the world of parliaments was rapidly becoming an international world.[6]

However, Samuel Romilly and Étienne Dumont were not satisfied at all. In their memoirs they both accused the French of disregarding the great British example and failing to observe any rules at all.[7] They were in favour of the debating style, sober parliamentary culture and moderate politics that dominated in Britain. That is why they thought that the French had ignored their good advice. However, it is clear that they were wrong. From the point of view of this chapter, the most interesting aspect of the matter is the difference between the adoption of British rules, on the one hand—which were largely followed, notwithstanding Romilly's and Dumont's comments—and the development of a rather different parliamentary culture, on the other. The French adopted many British parliamentary rules. Rules were copied, but the culture was not. This is almost a truism, because political cultures do not normally change that quickly, but it is still worthwhile to consider: one could introduce parliamentary rules, but in what sense did they determine or influence the new parliamentary culture? According to Dumont and Romilly, proper parliamentary politics entailed a sober exchange of arguments and (almost) disregarding the public galleries; it meant opposing views, presented in a rhetorical but also friendly and business-like manner. It meant a British parliament. The French revolutionary parliaments did not fulfil that ambition. Right from the start during the Revolution, French parliamentarians addressed the enormous public galleries. And even when these galleries had become much smaller during the Restoration, French politicians were much less part of a homogeneous debating culture than the British, whose aristocratic world provided the fertile soil for the way they debated.[8]

The difference between adoption of rules and the adoption of a culture can be observed in other cases as well. Take for instance the Dutch case, in which first the French, and afterwards the British, example was followed.

The first modern Dutch parliament was introduced in 1796, in the wake of the French Revolution.[9] It consisted at first of one chamber, and was—like its French counterpart—called the National Assembly, and it followed closely the French example, for instance by appointing its 'presidents' only for a fortnight each time. In 1814, immediately after the fall of Napoleon, a new representative assembly was invented. Something we would be inclined to call a new and largely modern parliament was set up: based on elections and a free mandate, representing the country as a whole. However, it was called Staten-Generaal, States General, in reminiscence of the closed and rather small, administrative body that consisted of representatives of the independent provinces and had existed during the Dutch Republic, with an imperative mandate and without a public audience. In 1814 the meetings were actually still closed and little real debating was going on.

In 1815 the Dutch and Belgians were joined in a common united kingdom. Following the British example of a lower and an upper house, a system of two chambers was introduced. Moreover, the proceedings became public and parliamentary debating practices were adopted again.[10] As a former part of the Habsburg Empire, the francophone Belgians had had a quite different historical experience and had lived for a longer time under French rule and, to a certain extent, took French politics as their guideline. They behaved differently in parliament. The resulting representative institution and the difference between the Dutch and the Belgians[11] demonstrate that the appeal to national traditions was not only window dressing: the national past really influenced the way the new representative assembly was set up, its culture and the way it operated. On the other hand, it appears that it was hard to escape the prominent examples of France and Britain if you wanted to set up a representative body in the nineteenth century.

## Rules and Culture

The adoption of the formal regulations of parliamentary organizations was also reflected in the development of parliamentary rules in general. It has been argued that post-1945 German parliamentary rules and regulations, or standing orders, could be traced back as far as the French and finally the British parliamentary rules of the late eighteenth century.[12] There has been a remarkable continuity in these written rules, right through almost all dramatic regime changes. This continuity irrespective of regime changes could also be observed in the French case, where none of the nineteenth-century revolutions disrupted the continuity of parliamentary staff and basic parliamentary rules.[13] It is tempting to draw the conclusion that a clear model of a parliament was thus followed and copied. However, we would do better to take this continuity of formal rules irrespective of regime rather as an indication that the adoption of formal rules does not mean that a substantive model was being copied. The rules provided the skeleton or framework but not necessarily the substance of a parliament. A lot of the rules concern the technicalities of parliaments which are only meaningful if parliaments are powerful, public and the result of elections, and seriously intend to conduct an orderly discussion. This, in turn, will happen only if these parliaments are embedded in a culture that supports them.

That is why the debate about the proliferation of parliaments at first took the form of a discussion about national characters. In the first half of the nineteenth century, the destiny of parliamentary government was closely linked to the nature of politics and society in Britain and France. These two prominent countries had important parliaments, and these parliaments were prestigious institutions. The parliamentary regulations of many countries may have originated from the British parliament, but they were introduced after the French example. This is a sign of the prominence of those two parliaments; it could be argued that the legitimacy of parliaments in general at first depended on their success. German public opinion knew more about what happened in the British and French parliaments than in their 'own' representative institutions.[14] In the first half of the nineteenth century, the word 'parliament' or 'parlement' was mainly used in connection with Britain. Even in France the word 'Chambre' was perhaps more common, although the word *parlement* was also used. The expression parliamentary government did not really exist before the 1830s, when it started to be used in Britain as well as France, and in the first decades of the nineteenth century, most representative bodies did not refer to themselves as a parliament.[15] For instance, in the Dutch States General, the word parliament was, at first, only used to denote British Parliament. This changed around the middle of the nineteenth century, when the word parliament had become more common, and liberals also started to use the word parliament in order to illustrate what type of debating politics they wanted to introduce.[16]

Internationally, the role of the Frankfurt 'Parliament' was probably crucial. Until 1848 Germans still saw 'parliament' as a foreign word, and the word was mostly used for the British or French parliaments. Germans thought that parliamentary government was an idiosyncratic institution of an idiosyncratic people, the British.[17] Even in the year 1848, the German constitutionalist Robert von Mohl still regarded parliament as an 'un-German' ('undeutsch') word, but the revolution of that year turned the word into a generally used concept.[18] According to the 1840 edition of the well-known German encyclopaedia Brockhaus, 'the great west-European countries' had a parliamentary government, a 'Parlamentarregierung'.[19] This was in the aftermath of the establishment of parliaments in a number of countries and of the liberal July Revolution in France with its flourishing parliament. In 1848, the German revolutionary movement wanted a parliament, and a democratic and national one at that. It demanded 'a German parliament' ('ein deutsches Parlament').[20] The Frankfurt 'Nationalversammlung' was this 'German parliament'. Even when this parliament turned out to be just a passing phenomenon, its supporters kept talking about parliaments and parliamentary government in general. Even though parliaments were not successful in Germany at first, for the future of the institution it helped that German authors had already made important contributions to the theory about parliaments.[21] In that way, their rather formal work was a sort of prefiguration of the conception of parliaments that began to prevail from the late nineteenth century onwards. However, before the proliferation of parliaments at the end of the century, parliamentary government first experienced a crisis in the 1850s and 1860s.

Besides Bagehot's scepticism, there were more indications in the 1850s and 1860s that parliamentary government was not seen only as something typically British, but also as something that was declining rather than progressing. In Germany, the outcome of the revolution of 1848 was often regarded as a setback for parliamentary government. In 1850–51, for instance, the German conservative Julius Stahl depicted the situation of parliaments as more dire than a temporary setback. The end of their power was near, and the days of parliamentary government were numbered! Only in Britain, he said, did this type of government have the necessary roots in society and the crucial backing of the aristocracy, which turned the peaceful transitions of power into a fencing tournament. After losing an election, the former ruling party called 'touché' and gracefully handed power over to the other party in parliament. Even in Britain, however, let alone in other countries, the advent of the masses would destroy this system—Parliamentary Government had had its day, but its era was over now.[22]

In France, the revolution of 1848 had ushered in Napoleon III's empire, and in the 1850s and 1860s there was much pessimism about the future of parliamentary government. Prominent liberal Charles de Rémusat opined in 1857 that parliamentary government was now a thing of the past, which was mainly useful to study for theoretical reasons. He wrote this in a review of the important multivolume history of the French parliamentary government by his political ally Prosper Duvergier de Hauranne, who had also lost his optimism.[23] These were the years after the failure of the Second Republic in France and after the failure of the Frankfurt Parliament in Germany.

Because parliamentary government as a model of government had lost its attraction for many people, at least temporarily, the fate of parliament as an institution also seemed uncertain. The crisis of liberalism in France and Germany carried the withering of parliaments in both countries and—in the eyes of many a commentator—seemed to spell the end of parliamentary institutions outside Britain.

## THE BEGINNING OF THE NINETEENTH CENTURY

The situation at the beginning of the nineteenth century had been quite different. Then, parliaments had been respectable elite institutions and their success should be evaluated accordingly. After the democratic experiment of the French Revolution, no country thought about adopting universal suffrage, and both the French and British parliaments feared noisy public galleries that had, they believed, had such a devastating effect during the Revolution. In the 1830s, as a reminiscence of the revolutionary troubles, Prime Minister Lord Melbourne still warned against 'the fatal effects which large galleries filled with the multitude have had upon the deliberation of public assemblies'.[24] Even though making laws was part and parcel of what they did, parliaments were not the law-making machines they would later become. They were first and foremost the centre of 'representative government' as it was then called. At the beginning of the nineteenth century, parliament was not supposed to be a faithful replica in miniature of society at large. In theory the best members, the best part of society, would gather in parliament to discuss the important questions of the day. After a clash of opinions, these superior minds would then come up with the best solutions.

In practice, the British and French parliaments were an extension of Society with a capital S. The London Society was more or less the same as 'le Monde' in Paris. This was not the whole society or the whole world, but the world that mattered socially, culturally and politically: an aristocratic or semi-aristocratic world of people who went to London for the London season of cultural events, a season that followed closely the parliamentary season.[25] The same was true for Paris; many fashionable people left Paris when parliament was not sitting.[26] Parliament was not only the centre of political, but also of cultural life in both capitals. It was the constant talk of the town; parliamentary politics and oratory were discussed at dinner parties, in the London clubs and in the Paris salons that flourished in the first half of the nineteenth century.

Aristocratic society went to parliament as if they were going to the theatre. In Paris people said around 1820: 'it is really too much of a feast for the intelligence to hear [prominent politician and orator] M. de Serre in the morning at the tribune [of the Chamber of Deputies] and [famous actor] Talma in the evening in [Racine's play] Athalie'.[27] In memoirs or letters, you will often find comments on the theatre intertwined with comments on parliaments.[28] In Paris some MPs criticized the semicircular hall of the Palais Bourbon—that is still in use—for looking too much like a theatre. The shape of this parliament stimulated a kind of theatrical oratory, delivered from the parliamentary platform, or 'tribune' as it was called in France. The critics were right in pointing out the differences between the shapes of the halls housing the British and French parliaments, between their public galleries and between the styles of oratory in the two parliaments. However, the similarities in the cultural appreciation of both parliaments predominate. Especially when the great orators would speak, the public galleries were overcrowded. Many French opinion leaders and politicians, from author Madame de Staël around 1800 to historian Hippolyte Taine in the 1860s, and from doctrinaire liberal François Guizot to conservative René de Chateaubriand, visited British Parliament as a political but surely also as a cultural attraction.[29] Conversely, it was natural that even the reactionary French Count of Artois—who was no friend of parliamentary power—told his friend the Duchess of Devonshire that he expected that she 'would like to attend our Chamber of Deputies as you like our country. You can hear and enjoy the entire show.'[30] All these people were also members of an international community with a shared culture and a shared appreciation of political oratory.

It could be objected that this is perhaps interesting or important from a cultural point of view, but that it does not concern the real business of parliament. However, that would be a narrow way of looking at things, because the prestige of the British and French parliaments of the pre-democratic era depended on their cultural meaning in a broad sense. They would not have been interesting had they been only debating chambers without real power, but, on the other hand, they would not have been popular or prestigious either, had they been closed administrative bodies. The fate of the rather unpopular closed French Senate proves the point. In the first decades of the nineteenth century, the public exposure of parliamentary proceedings was still rather new and perhaps even more important for the legitimacy of parliaments than elections. This exposure, however, was not directed at a mass audience. It was the public airing of a still largely aristocratic culture to which also commoners such as Guizot in France or prominent Tory politician George Canning in Britain wanted to belong. The reports in newspapers were important, of course, but the criterion of parliamentary achievement was what happened in the oral situation in parliament itself. This was not only important from a cultural but also a political perspective. Speeches could change votes, but, more importantly, speeches made the reputation of politicians and gave them authority. And once you had made a reputation in parliament, the doors of salons and clubs opened as well. Politics and culture were intertwined.

## The Changes at the End of the Nineteenth Century

By around 1900 many countries had adopted some sort of parliamentary government. Parliamentary government had become common. According to an influential essay by Félix Moreau, a French professor of law, *Pour le régime parlementaire*, even the Russian and Turkish autocracies would probably disappear in the near future.[31] In 1895, Gustave Le Bon, the sceptical mass psychologist, wrote that 'the parliamentary system represents the ideal of all modern civilised peoples'.[32] Parliamentary government was now seen as the most common form of government for civilized countries, even if people did not agree on its meaning or its political role. A 'parliament' had definitely become a clear thing with not only certain internal rules about debating practices, but also a certain independence guaranteed by ministerial responsibility and free elections. It had become an institution that could be observed and discussed, independently of the concrete examples in Britain and France that had given it legitimacy in the first place.

If only for its name, the foundation of the Inter-Parliamentary Union in 1889 could be regarded as a sign, that now a clear image existed of what a parliament was, formally and substantially, and as the product of an evolution of decades, if not centuries (as in the British case). The Union wanted to unite representatives from as many countries as possible. However, at first it was, for all practical purposes, a European peace movement, aiming at international arbitration, rather than a lobby group or a study group for parliamentarians. The Union did not want to interfere in the internal affairs of individual countries and initially therefore did not debate the nature of representative government. It was not until the 1920s, that the merits and problems of the parliamentary system were debated within the Union. Even then, they still did not want to interfere with domestic affairs, and they realized that parliamentary government was also a matter of national traditions, but the Union nevertheless became the focus of debates about the 'crisis of parliamentarianism'.[33]

In the meantime, parliaments had had to come to terms with democratic societies and mass audiences. The suffrage was broadened, general (male) suffrage was introduced in many countries, and the aristocratic character of the British parliament was no longer the standard. Although liberty and a vibrant civil society were still seen as preconditions for a viable parliamentary government, the regime itself was now mainly discussed in constitutional or juridical terms. Constitutional lawyers often saw themselves as the keepers of the constitution, who had to shield the constitutional and representative system against the inroads of a vulgar and intolerant democracy. In particular in France with its general male suffrage, they argued that the system was no longer in the hands of the aristocratic elite who had built it in England and knew how to play by its rules. Democracy needed to have rules of conduct and to learn to respect the law. The parliamentary system was quite flexible and could adapt to democratic circumstances, but it needed the protection of the law in order to safeguard minorities and constitutional rights. Only the law (and the lawyers) could protect individuals against arbitrary measures.[34]

Almost as a matter of course, a discussion about the nature of parliamentary government now seemed to turn into a discussion about a set of rules, a legal system, the juridical side of government. As such, parliamentary government would be debated, attacked and defended by constitutional lawyers and politicians from the late nineteenth century onwards. Even if many of these commentators did not like the Chambre des Députés of the Third Republic, this did not matter so much. The debate about the parliamentary system was no longer a debate about the unique British national character as it had been in the times of Walter Bagehot. The tacit assumption was that a parliamentary system needed (West) European cultural values, but the discussion was mostly about constitutional rules.

## CONCLUSION

It is clear that many parliaments have borrowed at least some of their rules from the British and French parliaments. Was their culture copied, too? That is not so clear. For one, the aristocratic cultural role of British and French parliaments seems to have been unique and not really copied elsewhere. The American House of Representatives perhaps came close in around 1800, when it had not developed yet into the presidential system it would later become,[35] but it was hardly a model for European countries, and there was no aristocracy in the United States. Hardly any other parliament was the centre of the aristocratic and fashionable culture of the capital in the sense the two main parliaments were. If the assumption is right, that Britain and France were special or even unique in this cultural respect, the question remains why.

To suggest an answer, we should return to the Dutch parliament. No doubt, the Dutch parliament adopted a large part of its rules and structure from the French and British parliaments. However, it kept an administrative atmosphere, its public galleries were small and often empty, parliamentary rhetoric was seldom discussed and oratory was almost unknown.[36] The legitimacy of parliaments as a modern public institution was provided by prestigious foreign examples, but the Dutch institution was, in fact, defined in legal terms. The Dutch sometimes admired the culture and rhetoric of the prestigious French, or more often, British parliaments, but even more often they regarded these features as foreign and disturbing elements that should not be copied. The Dutch did not really need them for the legitimacy of their own parliament either. The French and British aristocratic culture had shown the effectiveness of a limited form of public exposure; the Dutch adopted this limited form, but within the rules of their own bourgeois culture. The prestigious British and French aristocratic culture had provided the legitimacy of the parliamentary system. The Dutch did not need the display of that culture to establish their own parliament. They could argue that their parliament did not need the noise and theatrical show of foreign parliaments in order to properly and soberly fulfil its constitutional role. They could import an existing model and adapt it to their own needs.

With the benefit of hindsight, it could be concluded that 'parliaments' first had to become culturally prestigious public institutions in the two most important countries, France and Britain, in order to become generally available later as a formal model with basic rules and principles. In its initial phase, parliament was and perhaps had to be the centre of aristocratic culture. At the same time, both then and later, ministerial responsibility and the power and constitutional position of parliament were at stake. From the late nineteenth century onwards, the most important criteria to judge a modern and successful parliament became its capacity, on one hand, to represent the population, and, on the other, to produce laws that changed and improved society. In the meantime, in most countries the existence of a parliament in the sense of a formal institution, if not as a decisive political power, had become quite natural. At the beginning of the nineteenth century, the parliament was the powerful and prestigious centre of cultural and political life in Britain and France. Because they were the greatest powers of their time, this aspect also lent legitimacy to parliaments in general. The crisis of the middle of the nineteenth century was a sign of the transition from the situation of the beginning of the century to the changed position of parliaments at the end of it. This latter position did not preclude new crises, but the crisis of the 1930s was of a different nature. That a model existed of parliamentary government and of what constituted a parliament was no longer a question.

## NOTES

1. For example, in German (many older histories of parliamentarianism are by German historians): Kurt Kluxen, *Geschichte und Problematik des Parlamentarismus* (Frankfurt a.M.: Suhrkamp Verlag, 1983); Gerhard A. Ritter (ed.), *Gesellschaft, Parlament und Regierung* (Dusseldorf: Droste Verlag, 1974); Hans W. Kopp, *Parlamente: Geschichte, Grösse, Grenzen* (Frankfurt a.M.: Fischer Bücherei, 1966).
2. See for an overview the chapter about parliaments in Jan Romein, *The Watershed of Two Eras. Europe in 1900* (Middletown, Connecticut: Wesleyan University Press, 1978) 127–44.
3. Walter Bagehot, *The English Constitution* (originally 1872; Brighton: Sussex Academic Press, 1997) 94 and 182–3.
4. See the discussion of the idea of a political national character in general, and of Bagehot's ideas in that respect in particular, in Georgios Varouxakis, *Victorian Political Thought on France and the French* (Houndmills, Basingstoke, Hampshire; New York: Palgrave, 2002) passim. Cf. Jonathan

Parry, 'The Impact of Napoleon III on British Politics, 1851–1880' in *Transactions of the Royal Historical Society* 11 (2001) 147–75.

5. *Illustrated London News*, 7 February 1852, p. 113; *The Times*, 4 February 1852; quoted by Angus Hawkins, *Victorian Political Culture. 'Habits of Heart & Mind'* (Oxford: Oxford University Press, 2015) 29–30.

6. Georgios Varouxakis, *Victorian Political Thought on France and the French* (Basingstoke/New York: Palgrave Macmillan, 2002) 84–99 and passim; Henk te Velde, *Sprekende politiek. Redenaars en hun publiek in de parlementaire gouden eeuw* (Amsterdam: Prometheus, 2015) 47–8 (I have used some more examples from this book in this chapter); Nicolas Roussellier, 'The Political Transfer of English Parliamentary Rules in the French Assemblies (1789–1848)' in *European Review of History* 12 (2005) 239–48.

7. Samuel Romilly, *Memoirs of the Life of Sir Samuel Romilly* I (London: Murray, 1840) 101–4; Étienne Dumont, *Souvenirs sur Mirabeau et sur les deux premières assemblées législatives* (Brussels: Peeters; Leipzig: Allgemeine Niederländische Buchhandlung, 1832) 132–3. Cf. Cyprian Blamires, *The French Revolution and the Creation of Benthamism* (Basingstoke; New York: Palgrave Macmillan, 2008).

8. Te Velde, *Sprekende politiek*. Cf. the stimulating but perhaps slightly exaggerated comparison in Philip Manow, *In the King's Shadow. The Political Anatomy of Democratic Representation* (Cambridge: Polity Press, 2010).

9. Joris Oddens, *Pioniers in schaduwbeeld. Het eerste parlement van Nederland 1796–1798* (Nijmegen: Vantilt, 2012).

10. Remieg Aerts et al. (eds.), *In dit Huis. Twee eeuwen Tweede Kamer* (Amsterdam: Uitgeverij Boom, 2015).

11. Cf. Marnix Beyen and Henk te Velde, 'Passion and Reason. Modern Parliaments in the Low Countries' in Pasi Ihalainen, Cornelia Ilie and Kari Palonen (eds.), *Parliament and Parliamentarism. A Comparative History of a European Concept* (New York and Oxford: Berghahn, 2016) 81–96.

12. Bernd Mertens, 'Die europäischen Wurzeln parlamentarischer Geschäftsordnungen im Vergleich' in *Parliaments, Estates and Representation* 28 (2008) No 1, p. 87–101.

13. Delphine Gardey, *Le linge du Palais-Bourbon. Corps, matérialité et genre du politique à l'ère démocratique* (Lormont: Le Bord de l'Eau, 2015) chapter 5.

14. R. von Mohl, 'Die geschichtlichen Phasen des Repräsentativ-Systems in Deutschland' in *Zeitschrift für die gesamte Staatswissenschaft* 27 (1871) 1–69, esp. 23.

15. E.g. Klaus von Beyme, *Die parlamentarischen Regierungssysteme in Europa* (München: Piper, 1970) 33–6; short remarks also in Klaus von Beyme, *Parliamentary Democracy. Democratization, Destabilization, Reconsolidation,*

*1789–1999* (Houndmills, Basingstoke, Hampshire: Macmillan/New York: St. Martin's Press, 2000) 8. The digital sources in http://gallica.bnf.fr show that the word parlement was certainly not uncommon in France, also as another word for the modern representative assembly—not only for Ancient Regime 'parlements'.

16. Henk te Velde, 'Staten-Generaal en parlement. De welsprekendheid van de Tweede Kamer' in Aerts et al. (eds.), *In dit Huis*.
17. According to Mohl, 'Die geschichtlichen Phasen', 33.
18. Hans Boldt, 'Parlament, parlamentarische Regierung, Parlamentarismus' in Otto Brunner et al. (eds.), *Geschichtliche Grundbegriffe. Historisches Lexikon zur politisch-sozialen Sprache in Deutschland* 4 (Stuttgart: Klett-Cotta, 1978) 649–76, esp. 650–1.
19. 'Parlamentarregierung' in Friedrich Arnold Brockhaus (ed.), *Conversations-Lexikon der Gegenwart* IV (Leipzig, 1840) 40–6.
20. Examples in Werner Boldt, *Die Anfänge des deutschen Parteiwesens. Fraktionen, politische Vereine und Parteien in der Revolution 1848* (Paderborn: Verlag Ferdinand Schöningh, 1971) 99–100.
21. Heinz H. F. Eulau, 'Early Theories of Parliamentarism' in *The Canadian Journal of Economics and Political Science* 8 (1942) No 1, p. 33–55; Hans Boldt, 'Parlamentarismustheorie. Bemerkungen zu ihrer Geschichte in Deutschland' in *Der Staat* 19 (1980) No 3, p. 385–412.
22. Friedrich Julius Stahl, *Die gegenwärtigen Parteien in Staat und Kirche. Neunundzwanzig akademische Vorlesungen* (Berlin: Hertz, 1863) 160–2 (text from 1850–51).
23. Charles de Rémusat, 'Le gouvernement représentatif et la Révolution' in *Revue des Deux Mondes* (September–October 1857) 52–76; Prosper Duvergier de Hauranne, *Histoire du gouvernement parlementaire en France 1814–1848*, 10 vols (Paris: Lévy, 1857–71).
24. Quoted by Roland Quinault, 'Westminster and the Victorian constitution' in *Transactions of the Royal Historical Society* 6th series, volume 2 (1992) 79–104, esp. 96.
25. See, for example, Leonore Davidoff, *The Best Circles. Society Etiquette and the Season* (London: Croom Helm, 1973; London: Cresset Library, 1986); Hannah Greig, *The Beau Monde. Fashionable Society in Georgian London* (Oxford: Oxford University Press, 2013); Leslie Mitchel, *The Whig World 1760–1837* (New York: Hambledon Continuum, 2005).
26. See the chapter about 'Chambers and Salons' in Philip Mansel, *Paris between Empires. Monarchy and Revolution, 1814–1852* (New York: St Martin's Press, 2001).
27. Comments noted by Charles de Rémusat and quoted by Mansel, *Paris between Empires*, 105.

28. A late example (in the 1880s) from a daughter of William Gladstone is Lucy Masterman (ed.), *Mary Gladstone (Mrs. Drew): her diaries and letters* (London: Methuen, 1930).

29. See, for example, Emmanuel de Waresquiel, 'Le "moment anglais" de la Restauration. Quelques voyages outre-Manche' in Emmanuel de Waresquiel, *C'est la Révoution qui continue! La Restauration 1814–1830* (Paris: Tallandier, 2015) 323–40.

30. Quoted by Mansel, *Paris*, 106.

31. Félix Moreau, *Pour le régime parlementaire* (Paris: Thorin, 1903).

32. Gustave Le Bon, *The Crowd. A Study of the Popular Mind* (originally 1895; Mineola New York: Dover Publications, 2002) 123.

33. For example, Martin Albers, 'Between the crisis of democracy and world parliament. The development of the Inter Parliamentary Union in the 1920s' in *Journal of Global History* 7 (2012) 189–209, esp. 207; Claudia Kissling, *Die Interparlamentarische Union im Wandel, Rechtspolitische Ansätze einer repräsentativ-parlamentarischen Gestaltung der Weltpolitik* (Frankfurt: Peter Lang, 2006) esp. 118; Léopold Boissier, 'L'Union parlementaire et l'évolution du régime représentatif' in *L'Union Interparlementaire de 1889 à 1939* (Lausanne etc.: Payot, 1939) 133–45; the most comprehensive study of the history of the IPU before 1914 is Ralph Uhlig, *Die Interparlamentarische Union, 1889–1914* (Stuttgart: Steiner Verlag, 1988). Cf. Yefime Zarjevski, *The People have the Floor. A History of the Inter-Parliamentary Union* (Aldershot: Dartmouth Publishing, 1989).

34. Constitutional lawyers Félix Moreau and Léon Duguit (presided over by the conservative liberal statesman and lawyer Alexandre Ribot) at a conference of comparative law, also about the parliamentary system: *Congrès international de droit comparé à Paris 1900* (Paris: Librairie Générale de Droit et de Jurisprudence, 1905) II, 246, 274, 317 (I, 79 and passim for Ribot); Marie-Joëlle Redor, '"C'est la faute à Rousseau...". Les juristes contre les parlementaires sous la IIIe République' in *Politix* 8 (1995) No 32, p. 89–96.

35. Cf., for example, Catherine Allgor, *Parlor Politics. In Which the Ladies of Washington Help Build a City and a Government* (Charlottesville and London: University Press of Virginia, 2000).

36. Te Velde, 'Staten-Generaal en parlement. De welsprekendheid van de Tweede Kamer'; Beyen and Te Velde, 'Passion and Reason. Modern Parliaments in the Low Countries'.

# CHAPTER 3

# Parliamentary Government in Southern Europe? The Model of the Cádiz Cortes and the Ideal of the Moderate Monarchy

*Jens Späth*

The bicentenary of the proclamation of the Spanish Constitution of 1812, which represents a major achievement of the Cádiz Cortes, has sparked scholarly and public interest in the birth of the Spanish parliamentary system.[1] After almost half a century of relative neglect, research has made considerable progress by investigating the European and global dimensions of this paradigmatic constitution. Recent studies have stressed its effect on contemporary discourse and the influence it had on the rise of liberalism and democracy in Spain and other European countries as well as in Latin America in the first half of the nineteenth century. Many of these works have embedded the traditional study of political and constitutional history in a broader cultural perspective. In particular, they have led to a more nuanced understanding of the various aspects of parliamentary and constitutional culture.[2] These specific studies often refer to expanding research on conceptual history. In recent decades, this former subdiscipline of intellectual history has grown out of its mostly German and

J. Späth (✉)
Saarland University, Saarbrücken, Germany
e-mail: jens.spaeth@uni-saarland.de

© The Author(s) 2019
R. Aerts et al. (eds.), *The Ideal of Parliament in Europe since 1800*,
Palgrave Studies in Political History,
https://doi.org/10.1007/978-3-030-27705-5_3

northern European boundaries, extending its attention throughout Europe and to Spain in particular.[3]

The Cádiz Cortes are generally considered to mark Spain's entrance into modernity. They attained a symbolic and quasi-mythical status for those who pursued the idea of a liberal constitution that would combine an extraordinarily powerful parliament with a comparably weak monarchy.[4] The Cádiz Constitution had a paradigmatic impact on several countries in the Western Mediterranean: Spain, the Two Sicilies, Portugal and Sardinia. This chapter concentrates on the kingdoms of Spain and the Two Sicilies, where parliaments along the Cádiz model were convened in 1820 and tried to implement the constitutional system for three and a half years and nine months, respectively. Obviously, the very first experiences with modern representative systems in Spain and Southern Italy did not correspond in all aspects to what 'classical' parliamentary governments and reference models in Britain or France had established in the meantime.[5] In Southern Europe representative parliamentary institutions and cultures still had to be established; the alternation scheme of majority versus minority, government versus opposition did not exist yet; parliamentary discussion served to persuade rather than to give account of measures. Nonetheless, the parliament soon gained great importance as an independent forum against the executive and as a central arena for debates and decisions. Interactions with the public sphere through media, spectators in the parliament and solemn ceremonies became decisive for the self-understanding of the new institution.

This paper is based on an analysis of the official parliamentary diaries, the press and other documents of the revolutionary period.[6] It argues that the political practice of the Spanish parliament in the 'liberal Triennium', 1820–1823, and that of the Two Sicilies, 1820–1821, gave birth to institutions in these countries that usually form integral elements of parliamentary governments. However, by 1820 in these two cases, one cannot talk about a parliamentarization of the monarchy, a parliamentary government, or even a parliamentary monarchy yet. In three steps, this chapter tries to explain how Southern Europeans conceived of the ideal parliament in this period. First, it deals with the relations between the Cádiz Cortes and the Spanish nation, elucidating the context in which the Spanish Constitution of 1812 came into being. Second, it considers the transnational perception of the Cádiz Cortes by examining how Italians reacted to it. Third, it concentrates on the parliaments in Madrid and Naples by analysing the social background of the deputies, their ideals, the parliamentary culture and the relationship between constitutional theory and parliamentary practice.

## THE CÁDIZ CORTES AND THE SPANISH NATION

Modern Spanish constitutionalism and parliamentarism owed their ascent in large degree to the extraneous factor of the French invasion.[7] When King Charles IV and his son Ferdinand VII were quarrelling over the Spanish throne in 1808, Napoleon ordered his General Joaquin Murat to conquer the northern part of the Iberian Peninsula. After this goal had been reached, Napoleon asked the two Spanish Bourbons to meet him at Bayonne, where he dictated abdication statements to both of them, imposed the so-called Statute of Bayonne and put his brother Joseph on the Spanish throne as José I.[8] Soon large parts of the Spanish population began to put up resistance. By 1813 the Spanish had managed to expel the French invaders. The prospects for liberal ideas were promising, and the power vacuum that briefly prevailed opened up the opportunity to establish a new political order.[9]

In the microcosm of the occupied city of Cádiz, delegates and deputies from the free and occupied provinces flocked together to discuss the country's future. Substitutes from the occupied provinces that were occasionally represented in Cádiz were appointed to replace the missing deputies. Therefore, the number of representatives of the Spanish nation varied continually between 102 representatives at the inauguration ceremony in 1810 and 222 at the last session three years later and never came close to covering all the seats. Socially the deputies were rather well-off. About one third can be ascribed to the first estate, only 3 per cent to the nobility and two-thirds to the third estate. They referred to themselves by the traditional name of the Spanish parliament: the Cortes. Since there were enough representatives from all estates, the cities, the provinces and overseas, the Cortes could legitimately claim to represent the entire Spanish nation.[10] For the first time in Spanish history, they decided, against the will of the royalists, to meet as a single chamber that was constituted irrespective of class differences. The constituent Cortes declared that they represented the sovereign will of the Spanish nation and that the envisioned constitution was supposed to be based on the principle of separation of powers.[11] Soon three groups emerged—liberals (by far the largest group), royalists and Americans—and discussed different constitutional models.[12] On 19 March 1812, they promulgated the first proper Spanish constitutional text, which set up a constitutional monarchy, combining elements from French, American and British constitutional thought with Spanish traditions.[13] Compared to the other two contemporary European constitutional models, the Sicilian constitution of 1812 and the French *Charte constitutionnelle* of 1814, the Constitution of Cádiz was by far the most progressive, establishing with its idea of national sovereignty a monarchic constitution with the parliament clearly pre-eminent.[14]

How did this first modern Spanish parliament see itself? Most importantly, the liberals argued for national sovereignty and the primacy of the Cortes by claiming that sovereignty lay originally in the hands of the community and that this community had the right to change the constitution and to offer resistance to the king if he violated it.[15] The authors of the Constitution of 1812 believed that they had overcome the tension between monarch and people by positing the nation as a unifying body and by distributing the power between king and parliament. This model of a moderate monarchy manifested itself significantly in the classical separation of powers.[16] Notwithstanding this constitutional principle, the *Cortes* became the dominant player among the constitutional institutions because of its numerous responsibilities, which were far from limited to the legislative sphere. And since the parliament was elected by an almost universal, though indirect, male suffrage it held an extraordinarily high degree of legitimacy. After all, it gave the Spanish citizens the possibility to build the nation-state from below in which a new liberal legislative power replaced the old corporative absolutism.[17] In the medium term, the Cádiz Cortes gave birth to modern Spanish parliamentarism. The decrees on national sovereignty, separation of powers and freedom of the press became models for other European constitutions.

## THE TRANSNATIONAL DIMENSION: PERCEPTION AND TRANSFER FROM SPAIN TO ITALY

Events in Spain not only became a myth and model in the minds of people, but they also shaped the actual political reality. As a result of the export of the Spanish Constitution, many inhabitants of Southern Italy regarded the characteristics of the Cádiz text as the indisputable pillars of any legitimate constitution, namely, adherence to monarchy, Catholicism, an anti-Napoleonic outlook and national sovereignty. The written and oral discourse culminated during the years 1820–1823, when the Cádiz

Constitution was (re-)introduced in Spain, the Two Sicilies, Portugal and Sardinia. As the chapter concentrates on the first two countries, a brief look at the course of events in Spain and in the Two Sicilies up to this moment shall be useful.

Between 1814 and 1819, there was a whole series of ineffective *pronunciamientos* in Spain. The term refers to a specific type of coup d'état that originated among officers of the army, which was carried out with military means and aimed at superseding the current order with a more liberal one.[18] To explain this 'progressive' behaviour of the Spanish army, one has to bear in mind that the War of Independence against the French changed the social composition of the army considerably, ending the dominance of noble officers. While in Spain the army and parts of the middle classes were the main revolutionary force, in Italy secret societies such as the *Carbonari* took the leading role. At the same time, the *Murattiani*, the elites who had served under Napoleon's brother-in-law Murat, also became supporters of a moderate liberal constitutional monarchy. In keeping with their increasing economic influence, mercantile groups in the provinces also desired political power.[19] In Spain most of the *pronunciamientos* had the goal of re-enforcing the Constitution of 1812, while there was little discussion of other possible constitutional models. In Naples the moderate liberals were in favour of a constitution according to French or British-Sicilian models, but tactical considerations soon forced them to yield to the pressure of the *Carbonari*. The model of the Spanish constitution carried the day because it had achieved the status of a cipher and a myth in Italy with various translations and commentaries circulating. In the following years, many diplomats or Italians who had fought for Napoleon in the Spanish War of Independence, such as Cesare Balbo, spread the content of this constitution in their home countries.[20]

While modern historians disagree on how well-known the Cádiz Constitution was in Italy in the early nineteenth century,[21] we have many indications of at least considerable interest in the Spanish text: Italians characterized the Cádiz Constitution as the most democratic one[22]; the Italian translation was frequently requested in bookshops[23]; and as early as 1817, members of the secret societies sent a copy to King Ferdinand VII asking that the Spanish Constitution be introduced in the Two Sicilies.[24] A police report from July 1821 lists all the copies of constitutions printed in Naples and seized in the harbour of Livorno: among the roughly 6000 texts, the police found 457 copies of the Cádiz Constitution and 500 Spanish constitutional catechisms,[25] which shows that not only the constitutional texts but also additional materials circulated in Italy. Furthermore, there is evidence of interaction between the Spanish free-masonry and Italian secret societies: In 1817, a representative of the Salerno *Carbonari* travelled to Spain to discuss and coordinate plans for a revolution with Spanish conspirators.[26]

The renewed promulgation of the Cádiz Constitution in Spain in March 1820 caused a wave of enthusiasm for the *Carboneria*. In the following months, the myth of Spain reached its climax. Secret societies in the Mediterranean demanded the Spanish Constitution and regarded its promulgation as the highest priority of post-Napoleonic European liberalism. After the successful revolution in the Kingdom of the Two Sicilies, Spanish liberals assured the Southern Italian people of their esteem and respect: '[…] please receive the warmest congratulations for the first steps you have made on the way to liberty. They are marked by the Spanish example, and this has to be our only glory', proclaiming that Spain was well aware that the Cádiz Constitution was 'the strongest bond that will tighten the fraternal union of two free and independent nations.'[27] The Neapolitans cultivated the myth of Spain by writing hymns of praise to these heroes.[28] The promulgation of the Cádiz Constitution signified the temporary success of liberalism. Due to the freedom of press, an enormous amount of political literature was disseminated in Southern Europe.[29] More importantly free elections for a national parliament took place under peaceful conditions in Spain and in the Two Sicilies in 1820. On 9 July and 1 October 1820, the national parliaments of Spain and of the Two Sicilies convened for their constituent sessions.

## The Ideal Parliament in Practice: Madrid/Seville/Cádiz 1820–23 and Naples 1820–21

Approaching the problem of the ideal parliament in Spain and the Two Sicilies, we can raise four questions. Who were the members of parliament (MPs)? What idealized conceptions did they have of a parliament? How did they interact with the public sphere? And what can one learn about the tension between constitutional theory and parliamentary practice regarding the debates and the distribution of power? First, we will examine the electoral process, which was the same for both parliaments. The members were elected via a complex three-step procedure, which was fixed in the Cádiz Constitution and did not distinguish between active and passive citizens. All free male citizens aged 21 and older had the right to vote; for Spain this meant 30 to 51 per cent of the entire population.[30] At the first level, the parish, no restrictions based on census or socio-economic differences were imposed. The requirements for voting and for holding office rose at the second and third levels, the district and the province: whereas for both levels a minimum age of 25 years and residence within the area were required, future Cortes deputies also needed to have lived in their province for at least seven years and to have an unspecified annual income. Consequently, the overwhelming majority of deputies in Madrid and Naples consisted of well-off and educated representatives of the Third Estate.[31]

However, there were some peculiarities: while Sicily sent a high percentage of feudal noblemen to parliament (8 of 26 MPs), the number of aristocratic mainland MPs was considerably smaller (6 of 72)—thus reproducing traditional structures of Southern Italian society. About one-fifth of the members of the Spanish and of the Southern Italian national parliament were clergymen, while the number of noblemen was considerably lower still, being a bit more than 10 per cent in each case. That means that roughly two-thirds in both parliaments belonged to the Third Estate.[32] Officially, there were 172 seats in the Spanish and 98 in the Neapolitan parliament. However, after deducting all those MPs who never took their seats, the effective number of deputies was actually lower (150 and 89, respectively).[33]

The overwhelming majority of the MPs consisted of committed constitutionalists although soon a clear distinction between moderate (*moderados/Murattiani*) and radical liberals (*exaltados/Carbonari*) arose in both parliaments. Looking at the MPs' biographies, two different groups can be distinguished: in Spain the slightly older generation of the *Doceañistas* around Agustín de Argüelles was willing to compromise with the king to enhance the reform process, wanted to preserve the ideal of the moderate monarchy established in the Constitution of 1812 and was already more than happy about the renewed promulgation of the constitution in whose emergence in Cádiz they had participated.[34] The generally younger generation of the *Veinteañistas* around Rafael del Riego regarded the revolutionary process as unfinished and called for further radical political and social changes in Spanish society.

While in Spain in 1820 a few MPs had some basic experience with representative parliamentary procedures from the Cádiz Cortes, in Southern Italy everything was new for the MPs. Revolutionary experiences, however, were not completely absent in Naples: the Parthenopean Republic of 1799 determined the political thinking and action of many MPs. Since most deputies were born between 1760 and 1780, they knew both the Republic and the Napoleonic period. Nevertheless, it is wrong to consider the Neapolitan parliament exclusively as a group of old men who had already fought for the Republic in 1799 because MPs such as Tito Berni, Michelangelo Castagna or Count Luigi Dragonetti were only in their 30s.[35] It seems more plausible to characterize the protagonists of the 1820 revolution as people who had served under Napoleon and now wanted to preserve and develop these modern structures.[36]

Concerning the ideals of parliament, we might first of all state that the term 'parliament' was commonly used in 1820–1821 in the Kingdom of the Two Sicilies, while the Spanish MPs applied the traditional name 'Cortes', 'congreso' or 'representación nacional'. Regarding the representative assembly in the Two Sicilies, the commission president Matteo Galdi decided to employ the term 'parliament' because it corresponded perfectly to 'Cortes' in Italian and because it had a noble and dignified tradition in England, France and Southern Italy.[37] The Spanish references to the country's history and traditions have to be seen in the context of the liberal strategy to gain the approval of the conservatives for both the reform process and the Constitution of 1812.[38] Commemorating the medieval neo-scholastic roots of the Spanish 'constitution' they argued against their enemies' view that the Constitution of 1812 was something completely new and thus succeeded in presenting the Constitution of Cádiz not as a political and social *tabula rasa* but as a result of continuity, tradition and reform.[39]

At one point, however, the Spanish constitutional fathers oriented themselves towards France explicitly: rebuilding a national representative body according to the *Assemblée nationale*, which had been convoked by the king. By directing the theory of people's sovereignty against the Napoleonic usurper Joseph and not against the legitimate King Ferdinand VII, the liberals again convinced the conservatives to collaborate and to accept a constituent assembly.[40] While the Cádiz Cortes had had to elaborate a new constitution, the Cortes of 1820–1823 had to translate constitutional theory into political practice. Since it had to adapt an existing constitutional model to the actual situation, the role of the Neapolitan parliament was more complex. The question of whether the parliament would work as constituent or as constituted assembly had already been raised by the MP Giuseppe Poerio, indicating the consequences of the parliament's self-understanding: in the case of a constituent assembly, the decisions of the parliament would have to be announced and realized immediately, whereas in a constituted one, royal sanction would be necessary. Parliament agreed that the constituent function was covered by the oath and the decree of the king to adopt this constitution to the needs of the Two Sicilies.[41]

Many of the ideals of the Cádiz Cortes appear in the famous preliminary discourse that serves as de facto preamble to the Cádiz Constitution, saying the Cortes should represent the nation. The representative system without corporative elements was considered innovative because it guaranteed the representation of the 'general public of all Spaniards'.[42] The general elections and the unicameral Cádiz Cortes symbolized unity. Representing the Spanish nation and national unity thus lay at the heart of the concept of national sovereignty, which the Spanish had achieved after the War of Independence.[43] In order to avoid arbitrary rule, to respect the constitution and to limit royal power, the Cortes would meet annually. Further measures consisted of the biannual renewal of the MPs, fixed sessions of three months and the presence of the king only during inaugural and closing sessions. Finally, the deputies would discuss and deliberate in 'absolute liberty', and they would have complete inviolability while they were in charge.[44]

In order to fulfil their duty to represent the nation, the MPs were expected to display dignity. Adjectives such as 'noble' and 'dignified' were attributed to the institution of parliament, following the classical models of England and France.[45] Next, the MPs would act as symbols of dignity, both through their personality and through their behaviour, which included high education, good manners, a civilized, respectful way of speaking and communicating. While the MPs in Naples addressed each other usually with individual terms such as 'gentlemen', 'honourable deputies' or 'representatives', the deputies in Madrid preferred the collective term 'Cortes' or 'Congreso'.[46] The Parliament of the Two Sicilies, too, was proud of its dignified behaviour and regarded the proclamation of the 'Political Constitution of the Kingdom of the Two Sicilies' as the highlight of its effort.[47]

The dignity discourse leads to the third point: the interaction of parliament with the public sphere. The constitutional fathers in Cádiz wanted to make parliament the visible symbol of politics in the nation. This not only meant giving access to political deliberation to a huge number of people but also holding public parliamentary sessions. Publicity would guarantee the interaction, control and mobilization of parliament with and by the nation's citizens. The standing orders of the Cortes served to facilitate the functioning of the chamber and to explain the parliamentary system to the public. Part of this transparency offensive was the publication of the minutes in a proper parliamentary gazette as provided by article 24 of the standing orders.[48] To get a proper grasp of the practice of the MPs, it is necessary to examine the 'trialogic constellation of communication between parliament, media and public sphere'.[49] One has to consider both the official parliamentary sources and the extremely protean corpus of press products. To cover the information gap, the most up to date and efficient forum for political discussion was the press with its 33 newspapers and reviews in the constitutional period in Southern Italy and hundreds of equivalents in Spain.[50] Once the Neapolitan MPs had agreed to allow certain journalists to attend public sessions, press coverage blossomed.[51] Part of the press passionately endorsed the constitutional developments and came to institutionalize itself as an inherent component of the liberal system. Mirroring the split among politicians, an ideological separation arose between moderate (e.g. *El Universal* in Spain, *Il Censore* in Naples) and radical journalists (e.g. *El Zurriago* in Spain, *La Voce del Popolo* in Naples)—and, of course, conservative absolutists.

In addition to using the press, the liberal governments and parliaments tried to establish a distinct political culture. Since about two-thirds of the people in Spain and the Two Sicilies were illiterate, visual representation was of the greatest importance in convincing the masses to sustain the constitutional monarchy. There were historical manifestos, political lectures, writings of a more popular character, such as catechisms, texts in dialect (a Neapolitan peculiarity), and, at least in Spain, also illustrations circulating. In almost every case the Catholic religion served as a connection between the old and the new, surrounding the code with a sacred aura.[52] The emotional side of the liberal constitutional culture consisted not only of caricatures and pictures but also of political creeds, songs, poems and plays. Furthermore, the power of symbols manifested itself in festivities, ceremonies and monuments.[53] All these elements, together with an almost ritual admiration of the revolutionary heroes and slowly established national symbols, became part of a constitutional cultural memory, which placed the unity between the monarchy and the nation in the centre of public interest.[54]

The most visible monument of politics was the parliamentary building. It had to suit the requirements of a dignified national representation and had to be big enough to host staff, politicians, diplomats, journalists and all interested citizens. In Madrid the liberals quickly found an appropriate building: the Colegio de la Encarnación. It had already served as parliamentary building for the Cortes in 1814 after the deputies had moved from Cádiz to Madrid.[55] Given the lack of historic predecessors, the search for an appropriate parliamentary building in Naples was more difficult. While the preparatory commission held its meetings in the Palazzo di Monteoliveto, the commission decided to move to the bigger Chiesa dello Spirito Santo in Via Toledo.[56] Interestingly, both parliaments met in churches and both preferred the Westminster model for the seating order in plenary sessions with the deputies posed opposite each other.[57] The accounts of the inauguration ceremonies of the Spanish parliament in Madrid on 9 July and the parliament of the Two Sicilies in Naples on 1 October 1820 reveal many similarities (Fig. 1+2)[58]: artillery shells, light displays and theatrical shows. Both accounts named the act of taking an oath on the constitution by the monarch and by the MPs as the central event. The formula of the oath 'by the grace of God and by the Constitution of the Spanish monarchy/the monarchy of the Two Sicilies' made it clear that the constitutional monarchy was based on the nation's legitimacy. Other important features were the demonstration of respect for the monarchy, the presence of Catholic liturgical elements and solemn speeches underlining the new social contract between the king and the nation. The very fact that the king had to go to see the parliament suggested his submission to the sovereignty of the nation. Both inauguration ceremonies illustrate the fact that the goal of the festivities was to establish a parliamentary culture and to honour not only the constitution but also the institutions of the constitutional monarchy.[59]

We will now turn to the relationship between constitutional theory and parliamentary practice. Certainly, in Spain and the Two Sicilies, more people than ever before participated in the political discourse.[60] Furthermore, the amount of legislation passed by parliament is impressive, especially in the Spanish case.[61] But did this lead to a well-functioning parliamentary system? In constitutional monarchies in which the monarchs participated only reluctantly, conspired against the Cádiz Constitution despite their oath and tried everything to turn back to absolutism? Questions about the standards of rational deliberation and the efficiency of parliamentary work had already arisen among the MPs in 1820.[62] Apart from conservative absolutists who rejected the Cádiz system entirely, liberal public opinion was split into a moderate and a radical camp. The moderates espoused modifications to the constitution to give it a less progressive character. The radicals sought to implement the content of the Cádiz Constitution without any modifications and to broaden the political revolution into a social one. While the moderates were able to exercise governmental power for the duration of most of the constitutional period in Spain and the Two Sicilies, the radicals obtained or held parliamentary majorities in Madrid and Naples. This conflict between the executive and the legislative powers had a paralysing effect and partially caused the failure of the first constitutional systems in both countries.[63]

In the end, the political theory established in the Cádiz Constitution could not cope with the political praxis. Its major problem consisted in the extreme separation of powers and the lack of mediatory mechanisms between the executive and legislature. The secretaries did not possess real executive power, being only legally responsible to parliament but not politically. Thus, the six Spanish constitutional governments between 1820 and 1823 constitutionally depended on the king but for most of the time lacked parliamentary support. Only a few radical liberals like the Conde de Toreno considered the support of parliament essential for changes of government while moderate liberals around Martínez de la Rosa rejected such proposals.[64] However, the Cortes developed some strong parliamentary institutions: they succeeded with a kind of vote of no-confidence against the government led by Ramón Felíu[65]; the government obtained the character of a collective body[66]; the leading secretary became something like the chief of government; and both the government and the 'Prime Minister' were de facto politically responsible to the Cortes. All these factors favoured conventional schemes of assembly but did not facilitate any mediation between king, secretaries and parliament. The Cortes wanted a government of assembly in which the Cortes participated in all kinds of state functions.[67]

The Spanish parliament took a piecemeal approach to political issues, authoring an impressively large body of 60 decrees that were concerned with numerous policy areas. The Spanish MPs regarded it as their primary task to apply the Cádiz Constitution to real politics, which meant abolition of feudalism and inquisition and freedom of press. Their Neapolitan counterparts were faced with the task of adapting the Spanish constitution to the conditions of the Kingdom of the Two Sicilies.[68] Although the Neapolitan parliament did not devote too many sessions to this task, it took until 30 January 1821 to complete this work, which did not differ substantially from the Cádiz model.[69]

Yet the honeymoon period of constitutional liberalism à la Cádiz ended quite rapidly. At the conferences of Ljubljana, Opava and Verona, the great powers decided that Austrian forces would intervene in Italy while French troops would enter Spain in order to eliminate major threats to the order established by the Congress of Vienna. As a result, the constitutional monarchies in Southern Europe were short-lived: after parliament had moved from Madrid to Seville and then to Cádiz, the last Cortes session took place on 2 October 1823 while the parliament of the Two Sicilies convened for its last ordinary session on 21 March 1821, two days before Austrian troops occupied Naples.[70] After the Austrian and French interventions, most of the MPs were deprived of their offices, persecuted, imprisoned or forced into exile. The influence of the Cádiz Constitution began to diminish considerably, even in Spain: though it came into force for the last time in 1836, it was replaced the following year by a text that adhered closely to the Belgian model of 1831.

## Conclusion

In conclusion, many MPs and intellectuals in both countries had idealized conceptions of the nature and function of parliament, regarding it as a crucial component of a system built on the separation of powers: together with the king and the government in the executive as well as an independent judiciary, it was supposed to represent a strong legislature and to help establish an ideal form of a moderate monarchy. Taking the non-representative medieval or early modern assemblies of their home countries as models, the Spanish and Neapolitan MPs lacked direct acquaintance with parliamentary practices and had yet to acquire these abilities. In doing so, they created a particular parliamentary culture in cooperation with the public sphere through debates and ceremonies. Thus, parliament became the central arena for politics in both kingdoms. However, the Cádiz Constitution in theory and the parliaments in practice did not develop a robust parliamentary system that was able to live up to French and British standards (lacking e.g. real political parties, responsibility of government as a collective body, alternation between government and opposition). While the constitutional powers of the Cortes and of the Neapolitan Parliament were extraordinarily strong, the system of parliamentarian government was poorly developed and decisively weakened by opposing factors. Therefore, it is more accurate to talk about an assembly government with some developing parliamentary institutions rather than a parliamentary government. The myth of the Spanish War of Independence contributed significantly to the dissemination of the parliamentary system of the Cádiz Constitution, which spread to other Catholic Southern European monarchies. One cannot overemphasize the role that the Constitution of Cádiz played as an early laboratory for liberal constitutionalism and parliamentarism in the Mediterranean. The Cádiz system developed a relatively complex concept of national sovereignty in contradistinction to popular sovereignty. However, the national revolution and the general, universal male franchise were major steps towards increasing the social and political consciousness of large parts of the population and towards a realization of the parliamentary ideal of democratizing the nation.

## Notes

1. As a starting point, see the website of the Biblioteca Virtual Miguel de Cervantes: http://www.cervantesvirtual.com/portal/1812/ [8-9-2016] edited by Ignacio Fernández Sarasola. For the most coherent synthesis on the Constitution of 1812, see Joaquín Varela Suanzes-Carpegna, *La monarquía doceañista (1810–1837)* (Madrid: Marcial Pons, Ediciones de Historia, 2013).

2. See, for example, Jens Späth, *Revolution in Europa. Verfassung und Verfassungskultur in den Königreichen Spanien, beider Sizilien und Sardinien-Piemont (Italien in der Moderne*, vol. 19) (Cologne: Böhlau Verlag, 2012); Miguel Revenga Sánchez et al. (eds.), *Las huellas de la Constitución de Cádiz* (Valencia: Tirant lo Blanch, 2014); Fernando García Sanz et al. (eds.), *Cadice e oltre: Costituzione, Nazione e Libertà. La carta gaditana nel bicentenario della sua promulgazione* (Rome: Istituto per la storia del Risorgimento italiano, 2015).

3. See in general Willibald Steinmetz, Michael Freeden and Javier Fernández Sebastián (eds.), *Conceptual History in the European Space* (New York/ Oxford: Berghahn Books, 2017). For Spain see Javier Fernández Sebastián (dir.), *Diccionario político y social del mundo iberoamericano* (Madrid 2009 and 2014) 11 vols; Javier Fernández Sebastián (ed.), *Political Concepts and Time. New Approaches to Conceptual History* (Santander: Cantabria University Press//McGraw-Hill Interamericana de España, 2011); Faustino Oncina Coves (ed.), *Palabras, conceptos, ideas. Estudios sobre historia conceptual* (Barcelona: Herder Editorial, 2010).

4. See in a broader perspective José María Rosales, 'Parliamentarism in Spanish Politics in the Nineteenth and Twentieth Centuries: From Constitutional Liberalism to Democratic Parliamentarism' in Pasi Ihalainen, Cornelia Ilie and Kari Palonen (eds.), *Parliament and*

*Parliamentarism: A Comparative History of a European Concept* (New York/Oxford: Berghahn Books, 2016) 277–291.

5. For the development of the intellectual discourse in Italy from the 1840s onwards, see David Ragazzoni and Nadia Urbinati, 'Theories of Representative Government and Parliamentarism' in Ibid., 243–261.

6. For Spain see the digitalized Diario de Sesiones, Serie histórica, Legislatura 1810–1814 and 1820–1823, edited by the Congreso de los Diputados http://www.congreso.es/est_sesiones/ [8-9-2016]; for the Kingdom of the Two Sicilies see Annibale Alberti (ed.), *Atti del Parlamento delle Due Sicilie, 1820–1821* (Bologna) 1926–41.

7. See the exhibition catalogue *Ilustración y Liberalismo 1788–1814* (Madrid, 2008) especially 245–80 and 435–56.

8. For the text of the Bayonne Statute, see Peter Brandt et al. (eds.), *Quellen zur europäischen Verfassungsgeschichte im 19. Jahrhundert. Teil 1: Um 1800* (Bonn: Dietz Verlag, 2004), doc. 8.2.2 (Spanish) and 8.2.3 (German).

9. For the Spanish War of Independence, see, for example, Antonio Moliner Prada (ed.), *La Guerra de la Independencia en España (1808–1814)* (Alella: Nabla Ediciones, 2007); Joaquín Álvarez Barrientos (ed.), *La Guerra de la Independencia en la cultura española* (Madrid: Siglio XXI, 2008); Emilio La Parra (ed.), *La Guerra de la Independencia*, Ayer 86, 2012, pp. 13–139.

10. Quintí Casals Bergés, 'Proceso electoral y prosopografía de los diputados de las Cortes Extraordinarias de Cádiz (1810–1813)' in *Historia Constitucional* 13 (2012) 193–231.

11. Diario de Sesiones, Legislatura 1810–1813, Cortes de Cádiz, 24 September 1810, No. 1, p. 3.

12. Joaquín Varela Suanzes-Carpegna, 'Los modelos constitucionales en las Cortes de Cádiz' in François-Xavier Guerra (ed.), *Revoluciones hispánicas: independencias americanas y liberalismo español* (Madrid: Ediciones Complutense, 1995) 243–68.

13. Warren E. Diem, 'Las fuentes de la Constitución de Cádiz' in Warren E. Diem et al., *Estudios sobre Cortes de Cádiz* (Pamplona: Universidad de Navarra, 1967) 351–486.

14. For similarities and differences of the three constitutions, see Späth, *Revolution*, 69–104.

15. Referring to John Locke's *Two Treatises of Government*, several deputies such as Agustín de Argülles, Diario de Sesiones (DS), number (No) 207, 26 April 1811, vol. 2, p. 945, Conde de Toreno, DS, No 330, 28 August 1811, vol. 3, p. 1714, and Nicasio Gallego, DS, No 331, 29 August 1811, vol. 3, p. 1718 made this point.

16. Javier Tajadura Tejada, 'La problemática de los límites del poder de reforma constitucional en la Constitución de Cádiz: límites materiales y limitación temporal' in *Historia Constitucional* 13 (2012) 257–70.

17. María Cruz Romeo and Jesús Millán, 'Was the liberal revolution important to modern Spain? Political cultures and citizenship in Spanish history' in *Social History* (2004) 284–300.
18. Miguel Alonso Baquer, *El modelo español de pronunciamientos* (Madrid: Rialp, 1983) 9–71.
19. On the Neapolitan revolution, see Aurelio Lepre, *La rivoluzione napoletana del 1820–1821* (Rome: Editori Riuniti, 1967); Maria Sofia Corciulo, *Una rivoluzione per la Costituzione (1820–21). Gli albori del Risorgimento meridionale* (Pescara: Edizioni Scientifiche Abruzzesi, 2009).
20. Cesare Balbo, *Studii sulla guerra d'indipendenza di Spagna e di Portogallo* (Turin: Stamperia Sociale degli Artisti Tipografi, 1847).
21. Rather pessimistic: Vittorio Scotti Douglas, 'La Constitución de Cádiz y las revoluciones italianas en Turín y Nápoles de 1820 y 1821' in Alberto Gil Novales (ed.), *La revolución liberal* (Madrid: Ediciones del Orto, 2001) 257–62. More optimistic: Salvatore Candido, 'La revolución de Cádiz y el general Riego' in Ibid., 251–5.
22. Gonzalo Butrón Prida, *Nuestra sagrada causa. El modelo gaditano en la revolución piamontesa de 1821* (Cadiz: Fundación Municipal de Cultura, 2006) 54–65.
23. Santorre di Santarosa, *De la révolution piémontaise* (Paris, 1822; 3th ed.) 91.
24. Michele Manfredi, *Luigi Minichini e la Carboneria a Nola* (Florence: Le Monnier, 1932) 6.
25. Antonino De Francesco, *Rivoluzione e costituzioni. Saggi sul democratismo politico nell'Italia napoleonica 1796–1821* (Naples: Edizioni scientifiche italiane, 1996) 142–3.
26. Luigi Minichini, *Luglio 1820: cronaca di una rivoluzione*, introduzione e note di Mario Themelly (Rome: Bulzoni, 1979) XXX.
27. Biblioteca Nazionale di Napoli (BNN), Sezione Manoscritti (SM), Fogli volanti, S.Q. IV L 28, No 75, Lettera de'Carbonari di Spagna al Generale Pepe. Società patriottica degli amanti dell'ordine costituzionale, Madrid, 31 August 1820.
28. BNN, SM, Fogli volanti, S.Q. IV L 30, Versi 1820–1821, No 51, Anacreontica. Partenope riconoscente agli eroi ispani, dal cittadino Antonino Majo, Napoli I. December 1820.
29. For Spain see Jens Späth, 'Der Krieg der Federn: Pressefreiheit und Zensur in Spanien in der ersten Hälfte des 19. Jahrhunderts' in Gabriele B. Clemens (ed.), *Zensur im Vormärz: Pressefreiheit und Informationskontrolle in Europa* (Schriftenreihe der Siebenpfeiffer-Stiftung, vol. 9) (Ostfildern: Jan Thorbecke Verlag, 2013) 197–218; for the Two Sicilies see Werner Daum, *Oszillationen des Gemeingeistes: Öffentlichkeit, Buchhandel und*

*Kommunikation in der Revolution des Königreichs beider Sizilien 1820–21 (Italien in der Moderne*, vol. 12*)* (Cologne: SH-Verlag, 2005).

30. Walther L. Bernecker and Jens Späth, 'Spanien 1814–1844' in Peter Brandt et al. (eds.), *Handbuch der europäischen Verfassungsgeschichte im 19. Jahrhundert*, vol. 2: 1815–1847 (Bonn: Dietz Verlag, 2012) 740. For the Two Sicilies, a similar percentage can be assumed.

31. All Spanish deputies since 1810 can be found through the Historical Archive of the Congress: http://www.congreso.es/portal/page/portal/ Congreso/Congreso/SDocum/ArchCon/SDHistoDipu [11-9-2019]. Biographical information can be obtained in Alberto Gil Novales (ed.), *Diccionario biográfico del trienio liberal* (DBTL) (Madrid: El Museo Universal, 1991). For the Two Sicilies Alberti (ed.), *Atti*, vol. 1, pp. 104–26 offers a complete list of the deputies in Naples and short biographies.

32. For the social background of the MPs in the Kingdom of the Two Sicilies, see Daum, *Oszillationen*, 152–60 and Valeria Ferrari, 'Alle origini della rappresentanza elettiva nell'Italia preunitaria: i deputati del Parlamento napoletano del 1820–'21' in *Corciulo, Una rivoluzione*, 66–73. For the Spanish MPs see Antonio Moliner Prada, 'El juntismo en la primera mitad del siglo XIX como instrumento de socialización política' in Christian Demange et al.(eds.), *Sombras de mayo. Mitos y memorias de la Guerra de la Indepencia en España (1808–1908)* (Collection de la Casa de Velázques, vol. 99*)* (Madrid: Casa de Velázques, 2007) 65–83.

33. Werner Daum, referring to the list of MPs and short biographies in *Atti*, vol. 1, pp. 104–26, counts 86 regular MPs and 5 substitutes. Of these 91 MPs, at least 89 were always present in parliament. In the Spanish case, the distance from the colonies posed a major obstacle for many elected MPs.

34. The list of elected MPs to the first Cortes 1820–22 in the Diario de Sesiones, No 1, 26 June 1820, contains 13 names of men who had signed the Constitution of Cádiz in 1812.

35. Gentile, 'Raccolta' in *Atti*, vol. 1, p. XV.

36. Emilio Gin, *L'aquila, il giglio e il compasso, Profili di lotta politica ed associazionismo settario nelle Due Sicilie (1806–1821) (Gli uomini e il tempo 13)* (Salerno: Edizioni Paguro, 2007) especially 121–54.

37. See the debate in *Atti*, vol. 1, 25 September 1820, pp. 141–2.

38. Cf. Aymes, *La Guerra de la Independencia*, 115.

39. Fernández Sarasola, *Constitución*, part 1, pp. 6–8.

40. Klaus von Beyme, *Die parlamentarischen Regierungssysteme in Europa* (Munich: Piper Verlag, 1970) 66.

41. See *Atti*, vol. 1, Adunanza 4 October 1820, pp. 217–19.

42. Antonio Fernández García (ed.), *La Constitución de Cádiz (1812) y Discurso preliminar a la Constitución* (Madrid: Castalia, 2002) 189–270, quotation 213.

43. See José María Portillo Valdés, *Revolución de nación. Orígenes de la cultura constitucional en España, 1780–1812* (Madrid: Agencia Estatal Boletín Oficial del Estado, 2000).

44. Fernández García (ed.), *Constitución de Cádiz*, 218–220.

45. See note 37.

46. See, for example, Matteo Galdi, 'Adunanza XLII, 8 December 1820' in *Atti*, vol. 2, p. 385; Romero Alpuente, Diario de Sesiones, No 6, 10 July 1820, p. 23.

47. See the sessions of 30 and 31 January 1821 in *Atti*, vol. 3, pp. 299–356.

48. See the provisional Regolamento interno in *Atti*, vol. 1, pp. 179–202.

49. Andreas Schulz and Andreas Wirsching, 'Einleitung' in Andreas Schulz and Andreas Wirsching (eds.), *Parlamentarische Kulturen in Europa. Das Parlament als Kommunikationsraum (Beiträge zur Geschichte des Parlamentarismus und der politischen Parteien*, vol. 162; *Parlamente in Europa*, vol. 1) (Dusseldorf: Droste Verlag, 2012) 15.

50. For Spain see Juan Francisco Fuentes/Javier Fernández Sebastián, *Historia del periodismo español. Prensa, política y opinión pública en la España contemporánea* (Madrid: Síntesis, 1997) 61; Alberto Gil Novales, *Las sociedades patrióticas (1820–1823). Las libertades de expresión y de reunión en el origen de los partidos políticos*, vol. 2 (Madrid: Tecnos, 1975) 987–1047; for the Two Sicilies see Daum, *Oszillationen*, 67–87; Späth, *Revolution*, 236–53; Corciulo, *Rivoluzione*, 93–114.

51. See session of 5 October 1820 in *Atti*, vol. 1, pp. 229–30.

52. For the religious aspect, see Späth, '"La religión de la Nación española es y será perpetuamente la católica, apostólica, romana, única verdadera." Liberalismus und Religion in Südeuropa im frühen 19. Jahrhundert am Beispiel der Verfassung von Cádiz' in Thies Schulze (ed.), *Grenzüberschreitende Religion: Vergleichs- und Kulturtransferstudien zur neuzeitlichen Geschichte* (Göttingen: Vandenhoeck & Ruprecht, 2013) 68–89.

53. For the establishment of a constitutional culture in Spain and the Two Sicilies, see Späth, *Revolution*, 204–35 and 258–67.

54. See, for example, for the *Atti*, vol. 1, p. 337 and 474.

55. In Cádiz they had convened since 1810 in the Real Teatro de las Cortes, built in 1804. Today the Real Monasterio de la Encarnación hosts the Spanish Senate.

56. See *Atti*, vol 1, Prima Giunta preparativa, 22 September 1820, p. 130, and Terza Giunta preparativa, 28 September 1820, pp. 149–51.

57. Only from 1834 onwards in Madrid and from 1860 in Turin would the Spanish and Italian parliaments follow the model of the French national assembly and take their seats in a semicircle according to ideological affinities.

58. For Spain see Diario de Sesiones, 9 July 1820, pp. 15–18; for the Two Sicilies, see *Atti*, vol. 1, 1 October 1820, pp. 157–71.

59. See Nicola Calcaterra, *Importanza dei cittadini costituenti* (Naples, 1820) 14.

60. Gentile, 'Raccolta' in *Atti*, vol. 1, p. LII talks about 2422 petitions to the Neapolitan parliament before 18 March 1821.

61. Walther L. Bernecker and Jens Späth, 'Spanien 1814–1844' in Brandt et al. (eds.), *Handbuch*, vol. 2, pp. 719–79.

62. See the motion of Giovanni Maruggi in Naples on 4 November 1820 in *Atti*, vol. 1, pp. 591–2.

63. See María Cruz Romeo, *Entre el orden y la revolución. La formación de la burguesía liberal en la crisis de la monarquía absoluta (1814–1833)* (Alicante: Instituto de Cultura 'Juan Gil-Albert', 1993).

64. Diario de Sesiones, 3 March 1821, p. 44.

65. Diario de Sesiones, 15 December 1821, p. 1307.

66. Diario de Sesiones, 14 December 1821, p. 1274. Interestingly, on 19 November 1823, that is, after the collapse of the constitutional monarchy, King Ferdinand issued a royal decree which addressed the 'Council of Ministers'. From 1834 onwards this nomination became common.

67. See Joaquín Varela Suanzes-Carpegna, 'La monarquía imposible: la Constitución de Cádiz durante el Trienio' in *Anuario de Historia del Derecho Español* 66 (1996) 653–87.

68. See Späth, *Revolution*, 299–311.

69. See the official edition in the Archivio di Stato di Napoli, Archivio del Ministero della Polizia Generale, fasc. 63, 30 January 1821, Costituzione Politica del Regno delle Due Sicilie. Edizione fatta per ordine e sotto la direzione del parlamento (Naples, 1821). An easily accessible edition is included in *Atti*, vol. 3, pp. 307–52.

70. For the last session, see *Atti*, vol. 3, 21 March 1821, pp. 640–8.

# CHAPTER 4

# The Men of 1830: Remembering the National Congress in the Belgian House of Representatives, 1844–1930

*Marnix Beyen*

In a period where it has become customary to label Belgium as a 'failed state', it seems hard to believe that this same country at the end of the nineteenth and the start of the twentieth century was widely considered to be a model for others to follow. Wherever constitutional regimes were being set up—for example, in Spain, Greece, Bulgaria, Romania, Prussia, Persia and the Ottoman Empire—political elites looked towards Belgium for inspiration.[1] If indeed there existed an 'ideal Parliament', it gathered in Brussels—or so it seemed.

Many explanations have been offered for the rapid decline of the Belgian model,[2] most often giving a prominent place to the linguistic border dividing the country's population into two ethnically very distinct halves. According to an ancient, primordialist line of thought, a country straddling the frontier between the Germanic and the Latin Worlds could only be an artificial invention of foreign powers.[3] The processes of democratization that gained ground during the last decades of the nineteenth century inevitably made this cleavage highly visible and untenable.[4] Others

M. Beyen (✉)
Antwerp University, Antwerp, Belgium
e-mail: marnix.beyen@uantwerpen.be

© The Author(s) 2019
R. Aerts et al. (eds.), *The Ideal of Parliament in Europe since 1800*,
Palgrave Studies in Political History,
https://doi.org/10.1007/978-3-030-27705-5_4

have asserted, on the contrary, that the solid and long-lasting processes of nation-building taking place within the country were abruptly broken off during the First World War, as a consequence of the imperialistic politics conducted by the German occupiers keen on splitting up the country. The Second World War, in this view, delivered the fatal blow to the country, which then started to evaporate in processes of Europeanization and federalization.[5]

In an earlier contribution, I situated the germ of the Belgian breakup less in the linguistic division than in the constitutional setup of the country. Combining a central state authority with extremely liberal basic principles, I asserted, rendered the Belgian state construction vulnerable. Far from being something cherished by a large majority of the Belgians, central state authority was an object of suspicion and contest. Intermediary organizations, such as political parties, the Catholic Church, trade unions, and gradually subnational movements tried to fill the gap left open by the central state. Belgium thus offers a textbook example of what the Indian political scientist Sunil Khilnani has called 'the self-devouring capacities of modern democratic politics'.[6]

As I will try to show in this contribution, these self-devouring capacities were at work even within the very heart of the Belgian constitutional system, the House of Representatives. More specifically, I will show how they impregnated Belgian parliamentary language. I will do so by following the ways in which within nineteenth- and early twentieth-century Belgium the members of this House discursively constructed its origin and above all how this 'myth of origin' functioned within the changing parliamentary context of that period. Within the House, indeed, pride about the model function of the Belgian parliamentary system became manifest first of all in a widely shared piety towards the two hundred members of the National Congress, the constitutional body that had founded this system in the wake of the Belgian Revolution. At the same time, however, the interpretation of the heritage left by these men became one of the most emotionally charged apples of discord within Parliament. This contribution will uncover this development by following the discursive trope 'the Men of 1830' both macro- and microhistorically. Hence, my approach to parliamentary discourse can be called tropological as opposed to the genuinely linguistic one applied by scholars such as Armin Burkhardt, Cornelia Ilie or Liliana Ionescu-Ruxandoiu.[7] Whereas they tend to focus on formal linguistic features of the language used in Parliament, I concentrate on one referential aspect through which the Belgian House of Representatives imagined its own past, present and future in highly condensed way.

In order to map the trope macrohistorically, I use the heuristic possibilities offered by the digitalization of the parliamentary proceedings. The analysis properly speaking, however, is not digital, but hermeneutical and microhistorical, in the sense that it tries to interpret specific occurrences of the trope in their precise political context.[8]

## GHOSTS IN PARLIAMENT

Although the National Congress finished its constitutional work only in July 1831, its members were commonly referred to in Parliament as 'the men of 1830'. In doing so, those who saw themselves as the founders' heirs seemed to express their desire to associate the founders (and themselves) with the revolutionary events of the fall of 1830. The trope 'the Men of 1830' was sufficiently vague and polysemic to suggest at least that not only the members of National Congress, but also the revolutionaries on the streets of 1830 Belgium were included. Precisely because the Belgian independent state would not have existed without this revolution, the political representatives of the Belgian nation were extremely eager to present their activities as an attempt to bring to fruition the will expressed by the revolutionaries (who were discursively constructed into the pioneers of the Belgian nation). The ghost of 1830 was omnipresent in the nineteenth-century Belgian House of Representatives. Until the 1870s at least, it was also a material presence, since several of the members of the National Congress would be re-elected several times to the House of Representatives.

A first indication that the spirit of 1830 was pervasive in nineteenth-century Belgian parliamentary culture can be found in the sheer number of occurrences of the number '1830' in the parliamentary proceedings.[9] Between 1844 (the first year when the Proceedings were published separately) and 1880 (when the 50th anniversary of the Belgian independence was celebrated), it is safe to assume that 1830 was invoked annually at least some two hundred times (and at least twice as often during the 1850s). In the later decades, the number of occurrences decreased, but remained consistently higher than that of references to other years—and certainly of other years preceding the creation of Parliament. It is probably no coincidence that a relative peak was reached in 1893, when the first constitutional reform since 1831 was promulgated.

Obviously, these macrohistorical observations contain a certain amount of 'impurity'. Not every mention of '1830' necessarily referred to the year, and not every mention of the year necessarily refers to the revolution, let alone to the ensuing constitution. A more focused image emerges when we limit ourselves to the formula 'the men of 1830' [ *'les hommes de 1830'*]. Far from being omnipresent, it was nonetheless a recognizable trope, occurring some 50 times between 1844 and 1919[10]—with peaks in 1859 (6 occurrences), 1884 and 1913 (4 occurrences). Together with frequently occurring co-signifiers such as '(nos) ancêtres de 1830', '(nos) pères de 1830'; '(les/nos) traditions de 1830', '(l')esprit de 1830', '(membres du) Congrès National' and 'nos Constituants', references to 'the men of 1830' occupied a central place in the commemorative discourses that helped to mould the Belgian House of Representatives into a mnemonic community.

If the trope of the 'Men of 1830' was probably recognizable for all Belgian representatives throughout the nineteenth century, its discursive functions could highly vary. These functions could occur simultaneously, but at the same time contradict one another. More specifically, this trope could play at one and the same time a cohesive and a divisive role, as I will try to reveal with a microhistorical analysis of some relevant passages in their context.

## The Men of 1830 Unite

Particularly during the first decades of Belgian parliamentary history, the cohesive functions seemed to prevail. Invoking the 'Men of 1830' could tend to strengthen the corporate identity of the Members of Parliament (MPs) as a specific professional group. The prominent Brussels Liberal MP Auguste Orts (1814–80), for example, referred in 1859 to 'nos illustres devanciers dans la carrière, les hommes de 1830' (*'Our illustrious predecessors in the career, the men of 1830'*).[11] By doing so, he seemed to interpret the National Congress first and foremost as a crucial moment in the professionalization of politics. Much more frequently, however, the members of this body were framed within Belgian national history. As such, references to 'the men of 1830' served to stress the original and 'autochthonous' character of Belgium, the Belgian Constitution and the ensuing parliamentary culture. Far from being a mere application of French revolutionary ideas, these were the result of an age-old national tradition. It had been the achievement of the men of 1830 to have transformed this tradition into concrete texts, institutions and practices.

This vision was expressed as early as July 1831 by the president of the National Congress, Etienne de Gerlache (1785–1871). When addressing the members of this Constituent body after it had finished its works, he asserted:

> When you have promulgated in our current constitution so many protective measures, in reality you merely restored on its original foundations the social building that has been construed by our ancestors. At that, you added to your work what the course of the times, the experiences of other peoples and our own experiences had taught us.[12]

In statements like these, the men of 1830 incarnated continuity with a *national*, and therefore *non-partisan*, past. They were invoked in order to stress the need for unity within the parliamentary hemicycle and to revive the spirit of union which allegedly had reigned in the years leading up to the Belgian Revolution and during the first 15 years of the country's independent existence. The Catholic cabinet leader Auguste Beernaert used the trope explicitly for this reason in 1886 during a passionate discussion about the budget of the Interior and of Public Instruction. Belgium, he stressed, was at one and the same time 'profoundly liberal and profoundly religious'. That is precisely what 'our great ancestors of 1830 had understood, and by which they had been inspired'. For those who might still have doubts about it, he added that this same principle 'should never be lost from view by those who have to fulfill the difficult task to govern the country'.[13]

Beernaert made this statement only two years after the fierce 'culture war' between Catholics and Liberals on the topic of state education had ended in a landslide victory for the confessional party.[14] As a cabinet leader, he was seemingly concerned with restoring unity after this highly disruptive conflict. By stressing his piety towards 'our ancestors of 1830', he tried to convince the Liberals that their electoral defeat would not imply a return to the theocratic order of the *ancien régime*.

If the leader of the government, not surprisingly, used the reference to the Men of 1830 in a *depoliticizing* manner, within the hemicycle, on the contrary, it often functioned as a means to strengthen political claims by making them seem unavoidable. The argument was particularly prominent among advocates, on both sides of the ideological cleavage, of an extension of the suffrage. Such an extension was presented as the logical adaptation of the work of 1830 to changing circumstances. These advocates also tried to dispel the fears that the introduction of masses of new voters might instil in reticent MPs. This was in any case the strategy followed by the Catholic MP for Hasselt, Joseph Thonissen (1816–91), when in 1866 he explained why he voted in favour of lowering the electoral tax conditions. This measure was, according to him, not only an advantage but also a necessity:

> An advantage because new phalanges of voters devoted to the work of 1830 will bestow it with a new force; a necessity, because the events occurring at home and around us prove to me that, in a maybe near future, unruly movements might impose upon us larger concessions than the ones that we will vote today with our full and free will.[15]

If Thonissen's argument clearly exudes the spirit of what Brian Girvin has called preventative conservatism (conceding modest modernizations in order to prevent more radical transformations),[16] at later stages the men of 1830 were also invoked in order to plea for more radical extensions of the vote. During the discussions about the great constitutional reform of 1893, the Brussels Liberal Jean Le Poutre (1839–94) advocated the introduction of general male suffrage. 'Let us not forget, sirs', he exclaimed in this context, 'that we were at the head of the nations in 1830'. In order to retain that status, Le Poutre exhorted his fellow MPs to be worthy successors of the Constituants of 1830 and to make a constitution with 'a sufficiently big architecture to let the entire people pass beneath its porticoes without shaking its foundations'.[17]

Since the reform of 1893 only did so in a partial and ambiguous way (combining general suffrage with a system of plural votes), the demand for an unqualified form of general male suffrage continued to resonate in Parliament, but above all outside Parliament. And again, such a measure was presented as in line with the will of the members of the National Congress. This line of reasoning entered into the argumentative arsenal of the Socialist Party, which became the main mobilizing force in favour of general male suffrage. Its leading figure Emile Vandervelde exclaimed in December 1904:

> the Belgian constitution contained – because of its proclamation of the notion of popular sovereignty – the germ of the democratic reforms that

have been realized in our neighbouring countries and that we are still waiting for.[18]

Due to a succession of conservative governments, Vandervelde suggested, Belgium had lost the advanced position in which it had been placed by its founding fathers. With such a stand, Vandervelde diverged from the views of a large part of the Socialist rank and file, who believed that the proletarian impetus of the Revolution of 1830 had been 'stolen' by the bourgeoisie (and hence by the 'men of 1830'). Particularly in Flanders, this diagnosis implied a generally weak identification with the Belgian nation and sometimes even nostalgia for the Greater Dutch Kingdom of William I.[19]

Fourteen years later, the contribution of great numbers of labourers to the war effort had made Vandervelde's argument inescapable. It was adopted by the then Prime Minister, the Catholic Charles de Broqueville (1860–1940), when he urged the House to validate the constitutional reforms that had been unconstitutionally introduced by the King and his government in November 1918 during the so-called Putsch of Loppem.[20] 'We have to be today', he urged the members of the House, 'what our fathers were in 1830'. By that he implied that the MPs had to exhibit the same 'reasoned temerity' as their forefathers. Without abandoning the organic framework of the institutions created by the Men of 1830, they should be 'wisely audacious and coldly resolved' to actualize them.[21]

## THE MEN OF 1830 DIVIDE

References to the men of 1830, as we have seen, seem to have encouraged the acceptance of electoral reforms. When, on the contrary, the trope was used to strengthen political arguments in the sharpening ideological struggle between Catholics and Liberals, its effect appears to have been divisive. In these debates the use of the trope served above all to delegitimize the political claim of the opponent. This became painfully clear when one of the prominent 'men of 1830', the Catholic MP Barthélémy Dumortier (1797–1878), commented in January 1868 upon the newly formed government led by the programmatic Liberal Walthère Frère-Orban (1812–96). For Dumortier, who had been a leading figure of the Belgian Revolution in the Hainaut city of Tournai, it seemed obvious that a government had to be judged by the degree to which it was faithful to 'the dominant thought of 1830'. In order to determine what this meant precisely, he reminded his audience how 'we, the men of 1830 had lived with this great principle of liberty in everything and for all, and of respect for the right of others'. Further in his speech, he significantly added to these 'maxims of 1830' the 'age-old religion of our people'.

Not surprisingly, Dumortier found no guarantees in the government's programme that it would live up to the spirit of the founding fathers. The contrary seemed to have been true: according to him, Frère-Orban's principle was the 'supremacy of the state', which had to be at one and the same time the 'great chaplain, the great priest, the great sacristan, the great school master, the great collator of jobs'. Such a vision of the state implied the 'antithesis of liberty' and hence also the 'antithesis of the principles of 1830'.[22] A stronger rejection of the government's policy was probably unthinkable for Dumortier and for many of his fellow MPs.

This same line of reasoning would recur several times in Catholic discourse after all the original men of 1830 had disappeared from Parliament. This happened particularly in periods when Liberals were in power. The president of the Conservative Association of Brussels, Adolphe Nothomb (1817–90, who in terms of electoral politics turned out to be progressive) exclaimed in March 1881, in the midst of the 'school war':

> The liberty of conscience of the immense majority of the nation is violated: everywhere the interference and the weight of the State are present or announced, and it is incarnated in a new power that our fathers, the men of 1830, hated: the ministerial power![23]

Not surprisingly, this critique touched the Liberals in their heart. Some of them, like the already mentioned Auguste Orts, had themselves praised the men of 1830 for having juridically protected every individual citizen against 'the agents of power'.[24] Nonetheless, after the Liberal government had been dethroned in 1884 as a result of the Catholic electoral triumph, the Liberal opposition started to resist the new Catholic government's school policy by arguing that the men of 1830 had been in favour of state schooling. 'You say you are admirers of the men of 1830', the Liège MP Léonard Neujean (1840–1914) exclaimed. 'Well, I want to prove to you one more time that State education has been considered by the men of 1830 as a duty on an equal level as that of policing and justice.' And he went on to quote words that had been expressed in the National Congress by his fellow citizen Antoine Destriveau. He was eager to add that these words had been approved by the more iconic congressmen like Lebeau,

Devaux and Rogier. After which he concluded: 'Sirs, the language of these men of 1830, by which you pretend to be inspired, strongly condemns your behavior, and forms at the same time the justification of the law of 1879' [=the organic law limiting the influence of the Catholic clergy in the primary schools].

During the 1886 debate on the budget of the Interior and of Public Education which has been mentioned earlier, the *éminence grise* of the Liberal Party and former cabinet leader Walthère Frère-Orban would try to delegitimize the Catholics even more directly. He reproached the members of the Catholic party for claiming to be 'a party that draws its aspirations from the traditions of 1830', whereas in reality, 'these traditions condemn you'.[25] It was partly in response to this direct attack that Frère-Orban's successor Beernaert spoke the soothing words that I quoted above.

In the debates about social policy which became prominent during the 30 years of dominance by homogeneous Catholic governments (1884–1914), the argument continued to be used. It remained entangled, though, with the persisting struggle between confessionals and anti-confessionals. The Christian Democrat Auguste Mélot—born in 1871, more than 40 years after the Belgian Revolution—referred to the men of 1830 while pleading for the introduction of an obligatory Sunday rest.[26] In order to counteract the Liberal protestations, he counterfactually imagined what the Men of 1830 would have done had they still been around:

> if one had told them [to the Men of 1830] that in Belgium some industrial leaders inflict fines, and some others refuse to hire workers who do not accept to work on the sacred day of their cult, confronting them in this way with the alternative either to miss a job, and hence bread, or to violate what they consider a duty of conscience; if one had told to the constituants [...] that some industrial leaders, only on Sundays, advance the opening time of their factories as soon and as long as the priest advances the time of Mass, do you believe that the Men of 1830 would have answered: 'it is in order to protect this kind of abuses that we have voted article 15 of the Constitution. The freedom of the cults is the freedom to prohibit its exercise to others.'[27]

Mélot would not remain the only one to virtually reawaken the men of 1830 in the Parliament of his own time. The same strategy was followed in 1913 by Prosper Poullet (1868–1939), the Leuven Catholic who at that moment was Minister of Science and the Arts. The occasion was once more offered by discussions on school politics. While a majority was growing in favour of compulsory schooling until the age of 14, Catholics like Poullet wanted to prevent this measure from bringing back the hegemony of state schools. This implied that the subsidies for 'free' (meaning in the first place Catholic) schools should be increased, since these would otherwise be unable to guarantee education at no charge. 'If the men of 1830 would still be seated here', Poullet argued, 'they would undoubtedly speak out in favour of the organization of a system of subsidies in favour of free education.'[28]

Poullet's argument provoked an ironical reaction from the Socialist MP from Liège, Léon Troclet (1872–1946): 'You make them say many things, the men of 1830! They would be very surprised to hear you!' This reaction did not imply a rejection of the members of the National Congress and their heritage, but at first sight it did suggest that at least for a new generation of Socialist MPs, piety towards the 'ancestors in the career' no longer formed an undisputed part of parliamentary culture. Even if the Socialists at this moment still were seen as parliamentary outsiders in political life, in many ways they heralded political mores that were less steered by bourgeois or aristocratic values.[29]

In another ironical turn less than ten years later, Troclet would express the same piety towards the founders of the Belgian state as his party leader Emile Vandervelde had done in 1905. During the discussions about constitutional reforms in 1921 (involving among other things a transformation of the Senate), he expressed the hope that 'the constituants of 1921 will show themselves worthy successors of our ancestors of 1830; the constituants of 1921 will want to make of our legislative power a democratic power which is in harmony with contemporary ideas and which is susceptible to march, without shocks, on the road to progress, for the greatest good of our dear Belgium'.[30] The 'applause on the extreme left' provoked by this statement suggested that at least among the Socialist political elites the trope of the 'men of 1830' had gained acceptance due to the experience of the First World War. The Socialist leadership had supported the Belgian war effort, in exchange for which they had been able to enter into successive governments of National Unity. At the time of Troclet's statement, four Socialist ministers were part of the tripartite government led by the Christian Democrat Henry Carton de Wiart.

In this context, the Socialist MPs had become, somewhat unexpectedly, carriers of a trope whose functionality was declining among politicians of the traditional parties. If it continued to be used by members of these traditional parties, it seems to have been first and foremost in a defensive way. The same world war that had helped to integrate the Socialist party leadership into the moral and political community of the nation had radically alienated another group from it. Moreover, the same general male suffrage that had been introduced in order to reward the Socialists for their national commitment facilitated the entry into Parliament of a group of MPs that incarnated this radical alienation. Since the commitment of masses of Flemish soldiers had not been rewarded with the 'Dutchification' of Ghent University—the main pre-war request of the Flemish Movement— an important segment of the newly created Flemish Front Party quickly transformed into heirs of those who during the war had accepted the help of the German occupier in order to see radical Flemish wishes fulfilled.[31] For these 'Activists' the enemy was less the German occupier than the Belgian state. The representatives of the Front Party imported into Belgian Parliament not only these anti-Belgian sentiments—which they showed ostentatiously by refusing to speak French—but also a radical disdain for 'the men of 1830' and their heritage.

An exquisite occasion to vent these emotions was the centenary celebrations of Belgian independence in 1930. The discussions about the budget for these festivities were systematically obstructed by these Flemish Nationalist MPs, who willingly shocked the parliamentary community with overt insults aimed at the men of 1830.[32] The most radical mouthpiece of this anti-Belgian stance within Belgian Parliament was the West Flemish lawyer Jeroom Leuridan.[33] Instead of identifying with 'the men of 1830', he expressed his regrets that 'our Flemish fathers of 1830' had not opposed 'your Belgian mutineers'. This, Leuridan assured, would be different in his own day. 'We' (a pronoun in which he probably implied all Flemings rather than the Flemish Nationalists alone) will not only 'spoil your festive joy' but also 'crush the unholy work of 1830, that you want to celebrate'.[34] When the Catholic Brussels MP Corneille Fieuillien stressed during the ensuing debates that there had been many Flemings among 'the Men of 1830', another radical Flemish Nationalist, Ward Hermans, simply called him a 'Brussels zwanzer' ['zwanze' referring to an absurd form of humour deemed to be typical for Brussels].[35]

## CONCLUSION

During the first century of the existence of the Belgian Parliament, 'the men of 1830' persistently formed a crucial reference in the discourse of the Belgian Chamber of Representatives—even after those who had actually played an active role in the revolution had disappeared from the House. The quality of current parliamentary speech and practices was measured by the degree to which they corresponded to those of the founding fathers of the Belgian regime. Living up to these idealized origins of parliamentary life was a lofty mission for the Belgian representatives, but it was also a heavy burden to carry. Because they were incarnated by idealized forefathers, parliamentary ideals were the object, not only of political action, but also of piety and veneration. Not living up to these ideals, in this context, could readily be interpreted as a betrayal rather than as a simple political mistake. This situation introduced a strong emotional component into Belgian parliamentarism and rendered it exceptionally vulnerable. Throughout the nineteenth century, the memory of the 'Men of 1830' was shared by all Belgian MPs, but its potentially cohesive impact fell short of that goal and was ever less achieved. Far from healing the cleavage between confessional and anti-confessional politicians, references to the founding fathers served to widen it—and hence to strengthen party oppositions.

If both Liberals and Catholics agreed that Liberty had been the cornerstone of the building the Men of 1830 had constructed, their interpretations of this crucial notion were nearly diametrically opposed. Whereas the Liberals wanted to guarantee the 'modern' freedoms they deemed necessary for the development of the individual, Catholics aimed in the first place at protecting the freedom of 'the age-old religion of the Belgian people', and hence of the Catholic Church. That same Church was considered by the Liberals as the enemy of individual liberty, and its power had to be broken by the erection of a strong counterforce. Only a strong state—that same state against whose excessive powers the venerated Men of 1830 had fought—could perform this task. This line of reasoning enabled the Catholics to present themselves as the true champions of Liberty, and therefore as more Liberal than the Liberals themselves. Conversely, the omnipresence of the spirit of 1830 in the House of Representatives heavily mortgaged the latter's attempts at conducting a state-driven nationalization politics. Imposing one national language or one national education system could readily be interpreted as going against the will of the Men of 1830. Political strategies aimed at reaching these goals were doomed to fail.

Belgian parliamentary culture, in spite of being an object of national pride, created an enormous space where subnational communities could develop and gain political voice. Only after the First World War—and partly due to the divisive politics of the German occupier—would this space be used by a political group that had radically and openly shaken off the piety for the Men of 1830. Even if these Flemish nationalists never gained a parliamentary majority, their strategies brought the vulnerability of Belgian parliamentarism fully into the open. They would contribute to the growing recognition that the Belgian 'popular will' was not translatable into a single national representation. Subnational parliaments have emerged since the 1970s, taking away several competences from the national parliament. Transformed into a federal parliament, the latter is in constant search of democratic legitimacy. The 'ideal parliament' it had once been in the eyes of both its own members and external observers had become a distant memory. Johannes Agnoli's famous critique of the depoliticizing—and therefore anti-democratic—nature of parliamentary politics therefore does seem to apply to the *intentions* discursively expressed by Belgian MPs of the nineteenth and early twentieth century, but not to the *effects* engendered by their discourses.[36] If anything, their attempts to 'whitewash the antagonistic nature of modern society' turned out to be counterproductive.

## NOTES

1. See John Gilissen, 'La Constitution belge de 1831: ses sources, son influence' in *Res Publica* 10 (1968) 107–41. Specifically for the influence of the Belgian Constitution on those of the Persian and Ottoman empires, see Nader Sohrabi, *Revolution and Constitutionalism in the Ottoman Empire and Iran* (New York: Cambridge University Press, 2011) 41.
2. For a general overview of these debates, see Bruno De Wever and Chantal Kesteloot, 'When was the end of Belgium? Explanations from the past' in *Journal of Belgian History* 42 (2012) 218–34.
3. For some examples, see Marnix Beyen, '"En dépit de l'histoire...". Le discours sur le passé national dans quelques "professions de foi historiques" parues en Flandre pendant la seconde guerre mondiale' in *Textyles*, Hors série No 2 (1997) 85–115.
4. See Herman Van Goethem, *Belgium and the Monarchy. From National Independence to National Disintegration* (Brussels: UPA, 2010).
5. Most notably Lode Wils, *Histoire des Nations belges. Belgique, Flandre, Wallonie: Quinze siècles de passé commun* (Brussels: Espace Nord, 2005).
6. Marnix Beyen, 'Tragically Modern. Centrifugal Sub-nationalisms in Belgium, 1830–2009' in M. Huysseune (ed.) *Contemporary Centrifugal*

*Regionalism: Comparing Flanders and Northern Italy* (Brussels: KVAB, 2011) 17–28.

7. For examples of this linguistic approach, see Armin Burkhardt, 'German Parliamentary Culture from a Linguistic Point of View' and Cornelia Ilie, 'Parliamentary Discourse and Deliberative Rhetoric' both in Pasi Ihalainen, Cornelia Ilie and Kari Palonen (eds.), *Parliament and Parliamentarism. A Comparative History of A European Concept* (New York/Oxford: Berghahn, 2016) resp. 133–145 and 176–191; see also various linguistic articles in Liliana Ionescu-Ruxandoiu (in collaboration with Melania Roibu and Mihaela-Viorica Constantinescu) (ed.), *Parliamentary Discourses across Cultures. Interdisciplinary Approaches* (Newcastle: Cambridge Scholars Press, 2012).

8. In that sense, this contribution differs from my earlier article 'Het verleden vertegenwoordigd. 1830 in de Belgische parlementaire geschiedenis' in Henk de Smaele and Jo Tollebeek (eds.), *Politieke Representatie* (Leuven: Universitaire Pers, 2002) 187–204. If the general question of that article was the same, no digital version of the Proceedings of the House of Representatives was available yet at the time I did the research for it. Nowadays, they can be consulted at http://www.plenum.be.

9. Exact figures can hardly be given because of the technical problem that in the searchable text version of plenum.be '1830' is often rendered as '1850' and vice versa.

10. Here again, we have to add up the mentions *'hommes de 1830'* and *'hommes de 1850'*. This last formula being historically senseless, we can assume that it always refers to the men of 1830.

11. Proceedings of the Belgian House of Representatives, 1 April 1859, p. 846.

12. See Émile Huyttens (ed.), *Discussions du Congrès National de Belgique, 1830–1831* (Brussels, 1844) vol.3, p. 621 (text also to be found on www. unionisme.be).

13. Proceedings of the Belgian House of Representatives, 13 April 1886, p. 895.

14. On the conflict, see, for example, Els Witte, 'The battle for monasteries, cemeteries and schools. Belgium' in Christopher Clark and Wolfram Kaiser, *Culture wars. Secular-catholic conflict in nineteenth-century Europe* (Cambridge: Cambridge University Press, 2003) 102–27.

15. Proceedings of the Belgian House of Representatives, 1 May 1866, p. 664.

16. Brian Girvin, 'The Contours of the Right 1777–1914' in *The right in the twentieth century: conservatism and democracy* (London/New York, 1994) 24–58.

17. Proceedings of the Belgian House of Representatives, 9 May 1893, p. 887.

18. Proceedings of the Belgian House of Representatives, 22 December 1904, p. 425.

19. See Maarten Van Ginderachter, *Het rode vaderland. De vergeten geschiedenis van de communautaire spanningen in het Belgische socialisme voor WOI* (Tielt: Lannoo, and Ghent: Amsab, 2007).
20. See Vincent Delcorps, 'Loppem Coup' in *1914–1918-online. International Encyclopedia of the First World War*, edited by Ute Daniel, Peter Gatrell, Oliver Janz, Heather Jones, Jennifer Keene, Alan Kramer and Bill Nasson, issued by Freie Universität Berlin, Berlin 8 October 2014.
21. Proceedings of the Belgian Chamber of Representatives, 7 October 1919.
22. Proceedings of the Belgian Chamber of Representatives, 16 January 1868.
23. Proceedings of the Belgian House of Representatives, 8 March 1881, p. 677.
24. Proceedings of the Belgian House of Representatives, 1 April 1859, p. 846.
25. Proceedings of the Belgian House of Representatives, 13 April 1886, pp. 891–2.
26. With regard to these debates, see Pierre-Olivier de Broux and Florence Maertens de Noordhout, 'Repos dominical et jours fériés en Belgique. La transformation des obligations religieuses en revendication sociale' in Philippe Martin and Philippe Desmette (eds.), *Orare aut laborare? Fêtes de précepte et jours chômés du moyen âge au début du XXe siècle* (Lille: Presses du Septentrion, 2017), 215–228.
27. Proceedings of the Belgian Chamber of Representatives, 1 February 1905.
28. Proceedings of the Belgian Chamber of Representatives, 3 December 1913, p. 207.
29. See, for example, Jo Deferme, 'Van "Burgerlijke afstandelijkheid" naar "Volkse betrokkenheid". De politieke cultuur van enkele socialistische mijnwerkers in het Belgische parlement, 1894–1914' in *Brood en Rozen* 1 (2004) 11–29, and Marnix Beyen and Rik Röttger, 'En quête d'une dignité. Identités et codes de conduite des députés belges 1830–2002' in Eliane Gubin et al. (eds.), *Histoire de la Chambre des Représentants en Belgique, 1830–2002*, 337–84, more specifically 360–61.
30. Proceedings of the Belgian Chamber of Representatives, 19 July 1921, p. 2236.
31. With regard to that process, see above all Lode Wils, *Onverfranst, onverduitst? Flamenpolitik, activisme, frontbeweging* (Kapellen: De Nederlandsche Boekhandel, 2013).
32. See Marnix Beyen, 'Féconder l'avenir par le passé. La politique commémorative de l'Etat belge pendant les années jubilaires 1880, 1905 et 1930' in G. Kurgan-Van Hentenryk and V. Montens (eds.), *L'argent des arts. La politique artistique des pouvoirs publics en Belgique de 1830 à 1940* (Brussels: Éditions de l'Université Libre de Bruxelles, 2001) 80–100.
33. On Leuridan, see Marnix Beyen, 'Linguistic Syncretism as a Marker of Ethnic Purity? Jeroom Leuridan on Language Developments among

Flemish Soldiers during the First World War' in Julian Walker and Christophe Declercq (eds.), *Languages and the First World War*, vol.2: *Communicating in a Transnational War* (Houndmills, Basingstoke, Hampshire; New York: Palgrave Macmillan, 2016) 226–37.

34. Proceedings of the Belgian House of Representatives, 25 June 1930, p. 2236.

35. Ibid.

36. On Agnoli's anti-parliamentary critique, see Dirk Jörke and Marcus Llanque, 'Parliamentarism and Democracy in German Political Theory since 1848' in Ihalainen, Ilie and Palonen (eds.), *Parliament and Parliamentarism*, 262–276, esp. 273–274.

# CHAPTER 5

# New Models and Old Traditions: Debates on Parliamentarism in Hungary After the Austro-Hungarian Settlement of 1867

*András Cieger*

## Towards Modern Parliamentarism in 1848

As in other countries in Europe, it was the revolutions in 1848 that forced the political regime in Hungary to introduce institutional changes. The transition from the feudal world before 1848 to the modern bourgeois-constitutional era was like an explosion: riding on the crest of the wave of European revolutions, it took place in a matter of weeks. On 11 April 1848, King Ferdinand (1835–48) assented to the transition laws, which, among clauses, stipulated the abolition of serfdom, providing wide support for the new political regime at lower social levels, too. The Diet, the feudal assembly of estates, was replaced by a parliament based on popular representation, and the executive branch moved from Vienna to Pest. A responsible government was set up headed by Count Lajos Batthyány.

Hungary was the only country in Europe where constitutional transformation by sanctioned laws took place as early as the spring of 1848.[1] Legal

A. Cieger (✉)
Institute of History, RCH, Hungarian Academy of Sciences, Budapest, Hungary
e-mail: cieger.andras@btk.mta.hu

© The Author(s) 2019
R. Aerts et al. (eds.), *The Ideal of Parliament in Europe since 1800*,
Palgrave Studies in Political History,
https://doi.org/10.1007/978-3-030-27705-5_5

consolidation guaranteed social loyalty and, hence, stability. The first responsible Hungarian government was the only one of the governments set up as the result of the revolutions that functioned until September 1848.

The so-called April laws of 1848 were of epochal significance. Contemporaries already, slightly exaggerating, talked about 'the constitution of 1848', whereas the system was actually transformed by 31 laws, rather than a single 'charter'. The April laws continued in force, with two minor interruptions, for a century, until the written communist constitution of 1949. Thus the revolutionary achievements of 1848 were recorded in undoubtedly legal forms. To use historian István Deák's apt phrase, Hungary, alone in Europe in 1848, had a 'lawful revolution'.[2]

For Hungarian parliamentarism, the two most important laws were Acts IV and V/1848. They stipulated that parliament was to meet annually in the Hungarian capital, and the monarch could not dissolve it before the budget for the following year and the appropriation accounts of the previous year were discussed and approved. That is to say, the Hungarian parliament had the upper hand vis-à-vis the king (and his government) since it was practically impossible to dissolve. An analysis of the whole political system will conclude that what was established in Hungary in 1848 was not a constitutional monarchy (of the continental type), but a parliamentary monarchy (of the English kind). The predominance of the parliament further emphasized the special position of Hungary within the Habsburg Empire.

The most important achievement of Act V/1848 is that it based the political system on popular representation. As a result of its provisions, nearly one in every four adult males had the right to vote. Thus the proportion of the enfranchised segment of the population came close to 7% on the national average, a significant extension of voting rights. The Act prescribed property, income or educational qualifications for suffrage. Consistent with the liberal notion of rights, which eschewed taking away acquired rights, the Act allowed everyone who had earlier been voters (pauperized minor nobility, for instance) to keep their right to vote even if they failed to meet the new criteria. The law prescribed triennial elections, the ballot was public, and there was no threshold for minimum participation or validity. Constituencies had a system of absolute majority.

The April laws of 1848 adopted solutions mostly from the 1831 constitution of Belgium (such as the spheres of authority of the parliament and the functioning of the national guard). However, concerning other elements, certain points from constitutions of other countries were also possibly adapted: regarding the law on the press, it was the constitution of Bavaria that served as probable model; for the system of constituencies, that of Britain; regarding establishing the council of state, the example of France; for political law and the authority of the parliament, those of Norway (1814) and Sicily (1848); and for the accountability of ministers, the Constitution of the United States. However, Hungarian tradition, among others, served as the basis for the system of triennial, direct (without the mediation of electors) elections, with the lowest age limit (20 years) in Europe. The conservative Upper House was not reformed at that time although several possibilities were circulated.[3]

## DUAL LEGACY OF THE PAST

The fate of the Hungarian war of independence was sealed by the huge Russian army when, after a year of struggle, the new emperor, Francis Joseph (1848–1916) turned to the Tsar for help. After that, he ruled his empire with absolutist methods, and Hungary as part of the empire was in a state of war until 1854, which means that the civilian population was subject to martial law.

Finally, as the result of a long process of bargaining, the monarch and the Hungarian political elite concluded the Austro-Hungarian Settlement of 1867. Gaining acceptance for the principles of political devolution and elaborating the laws containing the details of the agreement formed a complicated political game with many players, on several levels, most of the time characterized by mutual mistrust among the negotiating parties. The writings of statesman Ferenc Deák outlining the programme, the official dialogue between the Hungarian parliament functioning again since 1865 and the monarch as well as the confidential background talks conducted in Vienna and Budapest all contributed to the conclusion of the Settlement. In a larger context, progress towards the agreement was spurred by the military defeats (battle of Solferino in 1859 and battle of Königgrätz in 1866) and international weakening of the Austrian empire, the looming state bankruptcy, and the increasing willingness to compromise of the Hungarian leading group tired of *passive resistance*.

Ferenc Deák, the decisive figure of the Settlement negotiations, built his political programme on the principle of legal continuity as against the Habsburg theory of forfeiture of rights (*Verwirkungstheorie*), founded on the belief in millennial Hungarian constitutionalism and in the power of long parliamentary traditions. In his arguments, he strongly emphasized the legacy of 1848, the legal principles and the spirit of the April laws. He also sought the possibility of a practicable compromise with Francis Joseph, who was the very embodiment of the denial of the values of 1848. For Francis Joseph's system of values did not really change during his long reign. He continued condemning the Hungarian rebellion of 1848 and had great difficulties in even moderately adapting to the functioning of parliamentarism: 'parliamentarism is not, and cannot be, an optimal institution, but is a safety valve in the sense that people feel they are represented', as he wrote in a private letter. According to one of his marginalia, he did not regard himself as a parliamentary ruler (he would always remain an unavoidable factor of the executive branch), but respected the letter of the law even if he did not always agree with its spirit.[4]

The political turn in 1867 was obvious: absolutism was replaced by bourgeois parliamentarism, while repression and autocracy gave way to legality and the rule of law. However, at the same time, the transformation of the regime was not complete, but that was a direct consequence of a long process of political bargaining, which preceded the changes. In exchange for internal autonomy (the most important elements of which were annual parliament, responsible government, free elections and civil administration) and for legal certainty, undoubted economic development and a measure of regional power status, the Hungarians reluctantly accepted to uphold, and on occasion even to widen, a few absolutist privileges of Francis Joseph (such as his exclusive right to command the army and his wide powers of appointment). They also agreed to share some of the financial burdens of the indebted Austrian empire and abandoned the idea of complete independence for Hungary.

Nevertheless, for all its reasonable political programme, the regime change of 1867 was far from having unanimous social support. It is enough to mention the great popularity of the émigré Lajos Kossuth, who questioned the morality of compromise, the peasant movements that sought to redistribute lands, the protests of some non-Magyar ethnic groups, the political association movement to completely reinstate the laws of 1848 and the resistance put up by some of the counties. Kossuth's writings indicate that he thought the principles legitimizing the Settlement were false, that what was introduced in Hungary and Austria was merely an era of pseudo-constitutionalism and that it would not bring the peoples of the empire lasting peace, but new hostilities. Kossuth regarded the Settlement of 1867 as the death of the nation.[5]

There is no doubt that by the coronation of Francis Joseph, the Hungarian liberals acknowledged a kind of continuity with the former absolutistic government. The new regime carried these two kinds of legacies simultaneously, the spirit of 1848 and the remains of absolutism. The emotional and political conflict between the programmes of '48 and those of '67 became a lasting fault line of the Hungarian party system; this antagonism would essentially determine the functioning of the parliament in Budapest during the Dual Monarchy.[6]

## The Idea of Modern Parliamentarism and the Tradition of Self-Governing

In 1867 reform fever struck nearly the entire political elite and the politically conscious public. It was the first time after hundreds of years, not counting the hectic months of 1848–49, that the political elite had the political possibility and sufficient time to transform the institutions of the state according to their own ideas. Naturally, this work of planning had long precedents: one should think of, first of all, the enlightened ideas that had been appearing in Hungary since the last third of the eighteenth century and the great debates of the Hungarian Diets during the Reform Age (1825–48) about the fundamental principles of liberalism. However, elaborating the legal and power relations binding the political institutions, and, in general, creating the modern constitutional order defining the functioning of the state and the life of society was a job for the liberal elite that came to power in 1867. A colourful political and professional discussion started on how to build a modern state. Legal periodicals and lawyers' associations were established one after another, a plethora of articles were published describing foreign political institutions and legal regulation, the translation of recent works on constitutional theory was flourishing and domestic leaflet literature was booming. There was not one Hungarian liberal politician who did not know, for instance, the famous French and American declarations of rights, constitutional texts and foreign laws regulating fundamental freedoms. The more so since Hungarian political thinking was vividly fascinated by the theoretical questions of the freedom of the individual and the community.[7]

Three main issues triggered discussions of theoretical significance concerning the political system of institutions in the years around the Settlement. (1) On the one hand, politicians set forth their opinions on parliamentarism and parliamentary government, outlining, according to their party affiliations, naturally, the structure of their preferences in the modern, bourgeois system of state. (2) On the other, many scrutinized the role of central government itself and its place in the political system. In connection with that, they discussed separately the issues of centralization, bureaucracy, and the conditions of modern (fast and efficient) governmental decision-making and execution. (3) Thirdly, many discussed the direction in which they thought social developments would take the role of society and the responsibilities of legislation in shaping the future of society.

While what pro-government contributors said was determined basically by securing the room for manoeuvre of parliament and the government, increasing the efficiency of the functioning of government and creating a new bourgeois middle class, the contributions from the opposition were characterized by efforts to create checks and balances, dwelling on the dangers of a heartless bureaucracy and extensive centralization, and demanding the broadening of social legitimation. The present paper can discuss in detail the ideas concerning parliament and parliamentary government only.[8]

### The Difficulties of Establishing Parliamentarism After 1867

The liberals who came to power in 1867 had very narrow room for manoeuvre. On the one hand, significant forces called into question the legitimacy of the new political regime; on the other, as mentioned above, many questioned the power and institutional structure of parliamentarism shaped by the Deák party. Finally, they had to take into consideration the framework of the peculiar political system created in 1867, and they regarded as a primary objective in the multinational country that Hungary was the maintenance of the supremacy of the Magyars among the other ethnic groups and the strengthening of the homogenizing-centralizing state.

As a result of the above, the practical ideas aimed at building a modern bourgeois political system could easily become the target of, or perhaps fall victim to, political skirmishes. Therefore, politicians on the side of the government had to wage a hard war to have both the Settlement regime and parliamentary government accepted. The work was not made easy by the backwardness of the legal system. The process of constitution making, which started in 1848, was interrupted with the defeat of the war of independence, and the cardinal laws passed by that time were rather incomplete and useless for practical governing. Because of the lack of time and various political compromises involved in their formulation, they contained mostly principles and failed to provide direction on important issues of detail. The anti-centre attitude, which had long been firmly embedded in Hungarian political thinking also hindered the work of governing. For hundreds of years, resisting central, usually Habsburg, government agencies, and protecting the ancient constitutionalism had been regarded as a national virtue.

The strong autonomy of the counties, which had been able to limit the absolutist imperial government for centuries (by shelving government decrees, refusing to levy taxes and such) and provided a stage for the policy of venting grievances and later for the liberal opposition, could place serious obstacles in the way of the normal functioning of autonomy on the national level (parliament). The protesting representations from the counties to the parliament after the Settlement made it clear before very long that the municipalities would not give up their ancient political rights and were not willing to function as mere units of administration in the future. They insisted on their old privileges. They saw themselves as guardians of the constitution and regarded with distaste the new parliamentary system. '[The county] *institutio* must not be sacrificed to new-fangled state doctrines' is how Sáros county made its distrust clear to the parliament.[9]

They questioned the government's right to interpret laws, to independently issue decrees or to exercise supervisory powers over county officials; indeed, some municipalities even claimed the right to give preliminary opinions on bills prepared by the government before they were placed on the table of the House of Representatives. During the first few years after the Settlement, the conflicts between the counties and the central government were not confined to theoretical debates outlining the limits of autonomy. Heves County, for example, in a resolution passed by its general court in July 1867, refused to accept the Austro-Hungarian Settlement laws and demanded the restoration of the political regime of 1848. The government was able to enforce its authority only after a lengthy conflict and by suspending the self-government of the county.

In the meantime, dissatisfied with the Settlement and forced into parliamentary minority, the opposition also discovered the counties as the chief supporting and organizational basis of its own policy. Kálmán Tisza, one of the key figures of the opposition, in a pamphlet, wished to extend the role of the counties as guardians of the constitution.[10] He suggested that if the views of the majority of representatives differed from the will of the majority of the municipal assemblies, the counties, obviously more truly representative of the will of the nation could initiate the dissolution of the parliament and call new elections. In legal conflicts between the government and the counties, 'an independent body of justices elected by the united trust of the counties, the parliament and the government' might arbitrate.

Another opposition pamphlet warned that the new political regime must not follow the French political system, where the majority was omnipotent in the government and in the legislature; instead the government should be rigorously controlled and held to account, in which process the counties should have a leading role. However, for all its merits neither should the English model be blindly followed because in England the judges and a number of administration officials obtain office by central appointment, while the counties in Hungary cannot give up their right to the administration of justice and to the election of officials. 'The disease of wanting to govern everything has deeply embedded itself into European views.' That is precisely why 'with regard to freedom, the most important thing is passing as few laws as possible and governing as little as possible', at least in the centre.[11]

The opposition's writings indicate either a textual relationship or at least familiarity with the contents of the draft constitution Kossuth had put to paper in the 1850s.[12] Kossuth, in comments on comparative systems, after the Settlement repeated his earlier views on self-government, elaborating some elements in detail, omitting others: 'the idea of French parliamentarism accepts only two elements in society: the state, the sovereign organ of which is the parliamentary majority, and the individual. [...] The individual standing alone against the immense centralized power of the state without any mediating organic institutions will also be nullified by the state.' The conflict between the centralized state inherently inclining towards absolute power and the citizens thus can easily lead to revolution or the spreading of socialist ideas, which upset bourgeois society. Kossuth advocates the British model instead:

> The French use the name parliamentary government because by that they mean that the parliament should unite all power in itself. They strive for parliamentary omnipotence. The English, on the other hand, use the term representative government because they do not want parliamentary omnipotence, but they want self-government, and they regard parliament as one very important, essential organ, but only one of the organs of self-government.[13]

At the same time, it is not possible for every country to follow in all respects the examples of either England or the United States (regarded as the home of democracy and self-government) because in the English system, for instance, judges are centrally appointed, and the American government has rather wide powers of patronage, so distributing offices has a detrimental effect on that political culture (see corruption).[14] Kossuth, therefore, thought that strong local self-government alone can maintain the freedom of the nation and of its citizens. The right to resist and to appeal protects self-governments from the absolutism of the government, while the right to elect new officials for most positions would hinder the patronage system. The legislative, executive and judicial rights of the counties would restrict state interventions to an acceptable level and, as a mediating safety valve, would also reduce social tensions. These requirements could be met by a democratized and fortified Hungarian system of self-government drawn from its glorious history.

Furthermore, Kossuth would have a constitutional court set up to guard 'the self-governmental fundamental rights of individuals, families, communities and counties', and its responsibility would be 'to review laws with a view to their constitutionality before they are published'. Thus, according to his plan, the constitutional court elected for life by the senate based on popular representation would have a veto over legislation. The parliamentary opposition also wished to have this body adjudicating conflicts between the central government and the municipalities.

It should be emphasized that the opposition wished to create more weight and room for manoeuvre for itself not only by retailoring political institutions, but also by organizing social actions, which questioned the legitimacy of those in power. They felt that the Deák party did not represent the majority of the nation because it had won the elections by cheating, by bribing the press, and, what is more, the voters had not been informed previously about the bargains around the settlement; thus they could not have authorized the compromise with Austria. Therefore, some politicians in the party demanded that the people also, not the king and the government only, should have the right to initiate the dissolution of parliament if they were not satisfied with it. The opposition also raised the desirability of introducing means of direct democracy, primarily the referendum, into the Hungarian legal and political system. In the end, however, they organized public rallies and a petition movement to oppose the Settlement and secure mass support.

It is important to emphasize that around 1867 the governing party did not have a unified standpoint either in terms of actual suggestions for solutions. The views that were published with regard to building parliamentarism, the room for manoeuvre of the central government, the new responsibilities of the counties and the role of society diverged considerably. This could also explain why the bill on settling municipalities was debated as late as in the summer of 1870.

## Debate of the Bill on Municipalities in 1870

During the debate in the House of Representatives, nearly every opposition speaker, repeating the views that they had been voicing for years, called into question and found disquieting one of the chief characteristics of parliamentary government: the absolute right of the governing majority to control the state and to pass laws that would seriously affect the future of the country. They thought the power of the central government, functioning through the will of the parliamentary majority, should be curbed, but the supervising function of the parliament itself would not provide sufficient protection against the unlawful acts it might commit. For in parliament, the will of the parliamentary majority rules, and the majority would not be interested in an impeachment process.[15] In the view of the opposition, the majority protects merely the governmental implementation of the general political principles defined by themselves (or according to less benevolent suggestions, their own self-interests) and is unable to prevent unlawful acts that coincide with their intentions. That is precisely why, on the one hand, the moves of the government should always be regarded with suspicion, and, on the other, its room for manoeuvre be made as narrow as possible.[16]

Then again, stronger guarantees are needed to protect constitutionality. The opposition believed they found these constitutional safeguards in institutions outside the parliament. They were afraid that in the framework of the newly rising parliamentarism, the legislature and the executive would be intertwined instead of maintaining the separation of the branches of power, and in that system the controlling role would be passed to the government, thanks to the parliamentary majority always obeying the government in an orderly way. So speakers from the opposition urged that an impartial state court be set up to rigorously ensure the enforcement of the constitution while they also pointed to the county as the other safeguard of the constitution.

'That is precisely why I wish that the municipalities, which have so far been bulwarks of constitutionality and liberty against the absolute power of the monarch, be henceforth bastions of the same against the parliamentary government.'[17] 'We insist on the municipal system, which has proved itself in England and Hungary for a thousand years, in Switzerland for 600 years, and has been set forth in the brightest and broadest manner in the United States since the American republic came into existence, and we can see that even in France, the homeland of centralization itself, where people are striving to extend municipal freedom as much as possible',[18] opposition members argued.

They believed it was only the counties that were able to protect effectively the rights and liberties of the individuals and smaller communities since the other means, such as the publicity of the press or the freedom of assembly, mentioned by pro-government speakers, were actually illusory and controlled by the majority. Indeed, Lajos Mocsáry described the county in his remarks as the final and immovable bulwark of national independence, which could be an important support for the central government against excessive demands from the outside (i.e. Austria), but if necessary, against the government itself should it abandon national interests.[19] Furthermore, the opposition, defending the ancient rights of the county against the 'heartless centralizing effort' of the government, rejected all proposals aimed at increasing the efficiency of public administration and making it more professional.[20]

The arguments of the opposition were answered first by Ferenc Deák. He was convinced that the counties, too, had to accept the 'epochal idea' of parliamentarism and the real political will of 1848, or else it was to be feared that the outdated, old institution, incapable of changing would inevitably perish.[21] According to Deák, the prerequisite of the desirable harmonic relationship between the central and the local levels was the comprehensive assertion of the relationship of responsibility.

Consistently building up a system of responsibility is also the precondition of effective public administration. If it is not done, the whole institution of the county in the eyes of the people could be discredited at a time when administrative tasks were growing and becoming complicated. Thus, the responsibility of legislation is to terminate the separatism of the counties by demolishing their old privileges and to connect them to the power structure outlined by the parliamentary system, designating their new place and responsibilities in the changed political environment.

I regard self-government as of great importance, I wish to maintain it at the counties, indeed, I want to extend it to villages, too, within limits prescribed by the laws, as long as it is compatible with the parliamentary system. But in my view counties are not coordinated bodies with regard to state power, but bodies that constitute the parts of all governmental systems that have been granted autonomy by the state with a view to the expedience of the government. The county has rights and powers with regard to individual citizens, has rights with regard to the government, but it cannot enforce rights with regard to the state. Counties are not federal parts of the whole state, and cannot have rights that are separate from, let alone opposite to, the state.[22]

Pointing to the resistance of some counties and the protest movements organized by the opposition, Deák called attention to the danger of the country becoming ungovernable. He emphatically warned his fellow politicians of the importance of responsible and calm politicking in parliament. He wanted a parliament capable of handling social passions, free from harmful influences of public opinion, using mostly professional arguments, and working for the happiness of the homeland together. A society, seeing and hearing politicians always questioning recently restored constitutional institutions and quarrelling with one another, could easily become disillusioned with all of political life; people could lose interest in running their own affairs or might withdraw their trust from the whole new elite, without respect to party preferences. 'Agitation can be dangerous at all times, but it would be especially dangerous in our situation. We suffered under the burden of absolute government for 19 years, and these sufferings filled the bosom of citizens with bitterness.'[23]

Many members of the governing party hastened to emphasize that central and county governments should harmoniously cooperate. On the other hand, they also pointed out that with the development of the bourgeois state system, reforming the county administration was unavoidable. Prime Minister Gyula Andrássy, while stressing the importance of the municipalities, intimated that the rigid defenders of county autonomy could choose only between the reforms and the comprehensive introduction of state public administration. The counties could not turn their backs on the demands of the age at a time when the whole political system was undergoing change. Simultaneously when limiting the political rights of the counties, it is necessary to define their new responsibilities. According to Andrássy, now that the constitutional struggles are history, the counties should rather concern themselves with the happiness of their own citizens and stimulate the self-activity of the civil society. He believed that a revival of the constitution-protecting function of the counties could be justified only in the case of a constitutional crisis: 'However, under extreme circumstances, when a government intended to remove the centre and weight of political power from this parliament where it belongs to somewhere else, then the counties shall use those rights and as before, and they will be bastions of freedom.'[24]

Minister of Education József Eötvös defined the task of legislators in three points: they would have to reconsider the relationship between the counties and the parliament and that between the counties and the government, and society should be given a voice to a larger extent in running local affairs. Therefore, he thought that the right of the counties to petition should be restricted, the constitutional room for manoeuvre of the government should be broadened (e.g. assuring the execution of decrees) and, finally, the self-government of villages ought to be strengthened and *virilism* introduced.[25] Replying to comments by the opposition, he denied that the role of the counties in protecting the constitution had ever been exclusive in the course of history, although he commended the counties for providing political publicity for liberal forces against absolutism.[26]

His fellow party member, Ágoston Trefort, argued that the need for greater state involvement derived from unfortunate characteristics of Hungarian society: 'But with us, conditions are essentially different from conditions in either England or in the United States. Here, more administration has to be done, and the central government needs more administrative officials than in England for the simple reason that although we brag of our municipal spirit and our maturity in self-government, there is little social activity with us; we demand everything from the state, that is to say, the representative of the state: the government.'[27]

It is important to emphasize, however, that establishing the state administration could not be elevated to a programme because the government party was rather divided on that issue. Indeed, even the members who accepted the principle of statism did not think it was time to introduce it.[28]

The governing party, at the same time, was unified in rejecting the proposal of the radical opposition for universal suffrage. They continued efforts to link political rights to education and property censuses. They thought the control of the country would be secure in the hands of a well-informed and independent middle class, rather than in those of unpredictable masses ruled by their passions. The rejection of the county administration based on universal suffrage was again pulled off by referring to the 1848 legislation and to the protection of the model

of parliamentarism accomplished in 1867: 'the representation of municipality cannot be laid on broader fundaments than the House of
Representatives, the representation of the country itself. We must for-
bid even the possibility of asking the question whether it is the majority
of the House of Representatives or the majority of the municipal committees that is more expressive of the circumstances of the country',
warned the justification of the bill.[29]

We have seen that the keywords used by those contributing to the debate
on the issues of public administration were essentially the same: all parties
referred to the legacy of 1848, liberal principles, society's own resources
and the examples of England, France and the United States. The difference
between the views of the government party and the opposition, however,
was insurmountable concerning the assessment of the processes in public
administration. The former regarded the narrowing of municipal autonomy as the necessary and normal result of the building of parliamentarism
initially, and later, of the growing need for state involvement, while the
latter saw in this change thinly disguised power politics and repression (e.g.
of the opposition, of the non-Magyars, of society acting upon its own initiatives). The assessments did not become any closer over time, making the
issue of public administration one of the permanent fault lines of Hungarian
politics. Throughout the period, antagonistic conceptions of autonomy
existed side by side. All these factors made it impossible to take determined
reform measures or to clearly delineate the new limits of municipal autonomy within the framework of functioning parliamentarism.

## Epilogue

According to Minister of Justice Boldizsár Horvát, recalling the birth of
the law on municipality (Act XLII/1870), the debate had been a 'confu-
sion of ideas'.[30] We would rather describe the exciting debate, often on
constitutional theory, as the beginning of a quick learning process, which
brought about a significant change in Hungarian political thinking.

By the late 1870s, the open rejection of the political regime had been
pushed into the background, and people had become accustomed to the
new institutions controlling their lives. After the fusion of the Deák party
and the largest opposition party (1875), the support of the regime
increased visibly, securing internal stability for approximately another
20 years. Most of the liberal ideas either adjusted to the compromises of
practical government or disappeared from political discourse.

However, after the Settlement, Hungarian parliamentarism, designed to follow the English model, soon veered from its ideal course of development. The rigid constitutional fault line ('48 vs '67) prevented the development of the parliamentary rotation of parties. Francis Joseph never completely accepted the principle of 'king in parliament' (see his reserved rights), while the new 'checks and balances' of government power failed to come into being in the Hungarian political system (such as constitutional court, democratized upper house or referendum).[31] And the municipalities were less and less able to fulfil their time-honoured role: during the years, they would find themselves financially completely at the mercy of the central government.

Having surveyed the legislative documents of the era, we can conclude that whereas referring to the English model remained to the end a characteristic feature of the political discourse, when it came to reforming political institutions or regulating actual legal issues, usually the Austrian (or German) legal and political models were followed. Indeed, not infrequently even the Cisleithanien example was not applied, but the peculiarities of Hungarian conditions were used as an excuse (see the declaration of fundamental human rights in Austria in 1867 or the introduction of universal suffrage there in 1907).

And the concept of citizenship would not be broadened; indeed, the policies of the government concerning nationalities excluded an increasingly wide range of people from citizenship rights.[32] Instead of state patriotism, some non-Magyar ethnic groups first responded with passivity, and by the early twentieth century their leaders had an increasingly strong desire to secede. Throughout the era the set of citizens who legitimately, for example, through their right to vote, were able to participate in shaping politics remained very small. Instead of extending the right to vote, stimulating association activities or broadening municipal autonomy, the political elite was more interested in maintaining a parochial-subject political culture.[33] Gradually, instead of extending constitutional institutions and following European norms, being locked up in national traditions became the rule.

## Notes

1. The constitutions, still in force, of the Netherlands and Denmark were passed in parliament in 1848/1849 as was the German imperial constitution (March 1849), but the latter never came into force. One constitution,

that of Prussia, was imposed on the country on 5 December 1848 (and remained in force until 1918).

2. István Deák, *The Lawful Revolution. Louis Kossuth and the Hungarians, 1848–1849* (New York: Columbia University Press, 1979). More recently, László Péter has claimed this was not correct. He believes the political regime of 1848 was rather a swerving off from the centuries-old Hungarian constitutional development and political culture: from the legislation crystallizing through lengthy parliamentary bargaining. The agreement between the king and the parliament, which came about in 1848 rapidly, under various pressures, would very probably have resulted in a conflict-ridden system even without armed struggles. See László Péter, *Hungary's Long Nineteenth Century: Constitutional and Democratic Traditions in a European Perspective. Collected Studies* (Leiden/Boston: Brill, 2012) 12.

3. András Gergely, 'Britischer Parlamentarismus oder Grundgesetz aus Belgien? Ungarns Aprilgesetze aus dem Jahre 1848' in M. Kirsch and P. Schiera (eds.), *Verfassungswandel um 1848 im europäischen Vergleich* (Schriften zur europäischen Rechts- und Verfassungsgeschichte, vol. 38.) (Berlin: Duncker und Humblot, 2001) 305–12; András Cieger and András Gergely, 'Ungarn' in Werner Daum et al. (eds.), *Handbuch der europäischen verfassungsgeschichte im 19. Jahrhundert*, vol. 3 (Bonn: Dietz, forthcoming).

4. Éva Somogyi, *Ferenc József* [Francis Joseph] (Budapest, Gondolat, 1989) 230–1.

5. The 'Cassandra Letter' of Lajos Kossuth, Paris, 22 May 1867, in Ágnes Deák, *From Habsburg Neo-Absolutism to the Compromise 1849–1867* (New York: Columbia University Press, 2008) 589–91.

6. András Gerő, *The Hungarian Parliament (1867–1918). A Mirage of Power* (New York: Columbia University Press, 1997) 5–55.

7. The most important constitutional texts and political works were translated into Hungarian in a few years after the Settlement. See, for example, *Alkotmányok gyűjteménye* [Collection of Constitutions] 2 vols (Pest, 1867); *A francia büntető törvénykönyv* [The French Penal Code] (Sopron, 1867); J.S. Mill, *A képviseleti kormány* [Considerations on Representative Government] (Pest, 1867); J.S. Mill, *A szabadságról* [On liberty] (Pest, 1867); E. Laboulaye, *Az állam és határai* [L'État et ses limites] (Kolozsvár, 1869); Reginald Palgrave, *Képek az angol alsóház történetéből és működéséből* [The House of Commons: Illustrations of its History and Practice] (Pest, 1870); J.K. Bluntschli, *A politikai pártok* [Character und Geist der politischen Parteien] (Pest, 1872).

8. András Cieger, 'Sichtweisen der Verwaltungsautonomien 1848–1918' in Jenő Gergely (ed.), *Autonomien in Ungarn 1848–2000* (Budapest: L'Harmattan, 2006) 22–77; László Katus, *Hungary in the Dual Monarchy 1867–1914* (New York: Columbia University Press, 2008) 105–52.

9. István Stipta, *Die Vertikale Gewaltentrennung. Verfassungs- und rechtsgeschichtliche Studien* (Budapest: Gondolat, 2005) 193–243.

10. Kálmán Tisza, *Parlamenti felelős kormány és megyei rendszer* [Parliamentarian responsible government and county system] (Pest, 1865).

11. Virgil Szilágyi, *A köztörvényhatósági önkormányzat biztosításáról. A szabadság híveinek* [Ensuring of the Municipal Self-government. For the Proponents of the Freedom] (Pest, 1867) 78–80.

12. 'Lajos Kossuth's Verfassungsentwurf' in Peter Brandt et al. (eds.), *Quellen zur europäischen Verfassungsgeschichte im 19. Jahrhundert: Institutionen und Rechtspraxis im gesellschaftlichen Wandel*, vol. 3. (CD-ROM) (Bonn: Dietz, 2015).

13. Lajos Kossuth, 'Angol representativ governement és franczia parlamentárius különbség' [Difference between English representative government and French parliamentary government] in Ferenc Kossuth (ed.), *Kossuth Lajos iratai* [Lajos Kossuth's Papers] vol. 7 (Budapest, 1900) 412 and 414.

14. Lajos Kossuth, 'A kormány-patronage romlasztó befolyása a nemzet jellemére' [Disruptive Influence of Governmental Patronage to the National Character] in Ibid., 402–10.

15. Kálmán Tisza's speech on 30 June 1870, *Az 1869-dik évi april 20-dikára hirdetett országgyűlés képviselőházának naplója* [Records of the House of Representatives called for 20 April 1869] vol. 9 (Pest, 1870) 36.

16. Ernő Simonyi's speech on 7 July 1870, Ibid., 234.

17. Sándor Mocsonyi's speech on 2 July 1870, Ibid., 102.

18. Ernő Simonyi's speech on 7 July 1870, Ibid., 235.

19. Lajos Mocsáry's speech on 5 July 1870, Ibid., 159.

20. Dániel Irányi's speech on 1 July 1870, Ibid., 71.

21. Ferenc Deák's speech on the recovery of taxes on 16 July 1868, in Deák Ferenc, *Válogatott politikai írások és beszédek* [Ferenc Deák's Selected Political Writings and Speeches] II. S.a.r. Deák Ágnes (Budapest: Osiris, 2001) 522.

22. Deák's speeches on the reform of justice on 1 July 1869, Ibid., 582-3.

23. Deák's speeches on the procedure of government against Heves County on 6 November 1867, Ibid., 484 and 487.

24. *Gyula Andrássy's speeches*, published by Béla Léderer, vol. 2 (Budapest, 1893) 329–30.

25. According to the act passed in 1870, the largest taxpayers would, without elections, become members of the general courts of the municipalities: this was called *virilism* at the time. By introducing virilism, the governing party wished to create a new and strong middle class, which could be the engine of bourgeois transformation. However, the opposition thought that virilism was a privilege that could help a narrow, wealthy group gain decisive influence in controlling public affairs, creating a new feudal system.

26. József Eötvös's speech on 19 July 1870, Records of the House of Representatives, vol. 10, pp. 149–53.

27. Ágoston Trefort's speech on 5 July 1870, Records of the House of Representatives, vol. 9, pp. 165–6.

28. Imre Halász, 'A közigazgatási eszmék fejlődése Magyarországban' [Development of the Ideas of Public Administration in Hungary] Part 1, *Nyugat*, 1914, vol. 13.

29. 'Indoklás a köztörvényhatóságok és a községek rendezéséről szóló törvényjavaslatokhoz' [Justification for the bill on the organisation of municipalities], *Az 1869-dik évi april hó 20-dikára hirdetett országgyűlés képviselőházának irományai*. [Documents of the House of Representatives] No 485, vol. 5 (Pest, 1870) 190.

30. Boldizsár Horvát, 'A köztörvényhatóságok rendezéséről. Kritikai visszapillantás a képviselőház vitájára' [On the organization of municipalities. Critical retrospection to the debate of the House of Representatives] *Budapesti Szemle*, vol. 46, issue 114 (1886) 440–65.

31. With regard to the above factors, according to some researchers the system of government after the Settlement was not a 'parliamentary monarchy of the western type', and, therefore, can be called at best 'pseudoparliamentarism'. See, for example, Zoltán Szente, *Kormányzás a dualizmus korában. A XIX. századi európai parlamentarizmus és Magyarország kormányformája a kiegyezés után, 1867–1918* [Governance in the dualist era. 19th-century European parliamentarism and the Hungarian form of government after the Settlement, 1867–1918] (Budapest: Atlantisz, 2011). László Péter also claims in his book that parliamentary government in the Western sense did not function in Hungary, but he also emphasizes that the parliament was the true centre of the political life of the nation, which for all its defects and peculiarities was spreading the language and spirit of Western European politicking in that bourgeois period. See László Péter, *Hungary's Long Nineteenth Century*, 213–280.

32. Capota, Crina–Vese, Vasile, 'Citizenship, Loyalty and National Identity in Austria–Hungary: the Romanian Case (1848–1918)' in Steven G. Ellis, G. Hálfdanarson and A.K. Isaacs (eds.), *Citizenship in Historical Perspective* (Pisa: Edizioni Plus Pisa Univ. Press, 2006) 127–39.

33. Gabriel A. Almond and Sidney Verba, *The Civic Culture: Political Attitudes and Democracy in Five Nations* (Princeton: Princeton University Press, 1963).

# CHAPTER 6

# Experiencing Parliamentarism: The German National Assembly of 1848

*Andreas Schulz*

When the radical German journalist Ludwig Börne arrived in Paris in mid-September 1830, he was pleased to see the Tricolour waving in the streets symbolising the victory of liberty. Like so many other activists in the constitutional movement in the German states and elsewhere in Europe, he had welcomed the July Revolution as the dawn of an age of reform which would liberate the people and create a new order. Such expectations turned out to be premature in 1830, but the liberal reform agenda remained a common claim directing the path to the European revolutions of 1848. Europe had become a closely linked space of transnational political communication, as Börne already observed back in 1830: 'Englishmen, Dutchmen, Spaniards, Portuguese, Italians, Poles, Greeks, Americans, even negroes were fighting for the liberty of the French people and thus were fighting for the liberty of all mankind', 'only', he sarcastically remarked, 'the Germans weren't'.[1]

A. Schulz (✉)
J. W. Goethe-Universität Frankfurt am Main, Frankfurt am Main, Germany

KGParl (Kommission für Geschichte des Parlamentarismus und der Politischen Parteien), Berlin, Germany
e-mail: schulz@kgparl.de

© The Author(s) 2019
R. Aerts et al. (eds.), *The Ideal of Parliament in Europe since 1800*,
Palgrave Studies in Political History,
https://doi.org/10.1007/978-3-030-27705-5_6

That verdict might have been too rough. 'The Germans' were engaged in a network of solidarity organisations supporting the Polish liberation movement in the 1830s. Parliamentary deputies in the second chambers of the German states opposed the repressive regime of the German Diet, prompting popular protest meetings. When social uprisings, constitutional and national reform movements culminated in the March Revolution of 1848, Germany was part of a turning point in European history which many experienced as the 'springtime of the peoples'. Nation-building, constitutional reform, parliamentary government and social improvements were the fundamental concerns that had caused the outbreak of the European revolutions. In Germany, constitutionalism and nation-building converged into a single movement. The Constituent National Assembly of 1848 was the first attempt at establishing a political order that would transfer the former confederation of more than 30 sovereign states into a nation state. Federal traditions were too strong to be abolished, but had to be respected, especially with regard to Prussia, where the revolutionary assembly in Berlin had replaced the United Diet (*Vereinigte Landtag*) and claimed to represent the Prussian nation. Other states of the German Federation acted similarly when citizens of the Kingdoms of Bavaria, Württemberg and Sachsen, the Grand Duchies of Hessen and Baden, and even the City-States of Hamburg and Bremen elected their own constituent national assemblies. Most of these parliaments remained of only regional relevance, while the capital cities of Vienna and Berlin were important hotspots of revolutionary and counter-revolutionary movements in Europe. But the political centre of the national revolution and the focus of public attention[2] was the National Assembly located in the impressive building of the evangelical Dome of St. Paul (*Paulskirche*), where elected deputies from all German nations had taken on the difficult challenge of creating a new political order. The members of the National Assembly in Frankfurt represented the political nation; they designed the constitution and communicated revolutionary politics. Parliamentarians exerted political power in their own right and by revolutionary legitimation.

The delegates to the constituent assembly in Frankfurt had been sent from all areas of the German Federation, including the non-German territories of the Habsburg Monarchy and Eastern Prussia. They were aware of the fact that the Assembly was not only debating the design of a constitutional political order but also the territorial shape of a powerful nation state in the heart of Central Europe. It was a tremendous challenge as the Frankfurt Parliament had to come to terms with the King of Prussia and the

Habsburg Emperor when at the same time public expectations and revolutionary movements were constantly exerting pressure on the delegates to extend revolutionary politics. Considering the situation that the parliamentarians had to arrange themselves with different political actors on the stage, the results which the National Assembly attained in the process of nation-building and constitutional reform have been assessed by historians as being remarkable.[3] The authority of the Assembly was respected, parliamentary government successfully established, and the constitutional framework that the *Paulskirche* finally adopted remained a point of reference for the restituted constitutional monarchies of the German Federation after the violent liquidation of the revolution in 1849. The experience of revolutionary parliamentarism was neither forgotten nor lost, since basic convictions and practices which the delegates performed 'on stage' were institutionalised and transformed into political culture. Some essential beliefs and customs which the delegates shared when they were reflecting on the conditions and 'rules' of parliamentary life will be discussed here.

## The 'Independent' Representative

Being part of a revolutionary assembly without any predecessors or traditions, the delegates had to conceptualise and establish parliamentary procedures. What experiences and political models could they refer to? Since many of them had been members of provincial assemblies or city councils in pre-revolutionary times, most delegates were by no means political newcomers. The bulk of the parliamentarians had served in state or council administrations, or were judges or university teachers ('political professors'[4]). About 60% of the delegates thus might be categorised as 'parliamentary functionaries' (*'Beamtenparlamentarier'*) who received a state salary or pension and had formally declared political loyalty to their government. In this respect, the social structure of the National Assembly looked very similar to the provincial parliaments of the pre-revolutionary period. The German case thus differed considerably from the French Second Republic of 1848 where the electoral provisions prohibited *'hautes fonctionnaires'* from being elected to the National Assembly. French revolutionaries suspected that *députés fonctionnaires* would be susceptible to executive control and even corruption as had obviously been the case in the *corps législatif* of the July Monarchy.[5] Considering the prohibition of double-mandating as essential to securing parliamentary sovereignty, the French Assembly incorporated it as constitutional law.

The German delegates looked back on rather different political experiences which led them to completely contrasting conclusions. In the constitutional Southwest of the German Federation, '*Beamtenparlamentarier*' were often part of the opposition against bureaucratic government and arbitrary administration. Prominent members of the state administration sat in the second chambers of provincial parliaments, where they supported and sometimes motivated the struggle for constitutional reforms. The monarchs tried to suppress inner-administrative opposition by denying its civil servants' holiday leave during parliamentary sessions. Although it seems not only contrary to the liberal theory of separation of power but also paradoxical considering the harsh criticism of 'bureaucratism' in the pre-constitutional era, the Frankfurt National Assembly relied to a large extent on the expertise of administrative elites. This explains why it voluntarily abstained from any provision that would have restricted the eligibility of civil servants.

Though the extension of manhood suffrage in 1848 had no significant effects on the social profile of the parliamentarian elite as compared to the pre-revolutionary assemblies of the German Federation, the political legitimation of the National Assembly had changed fundamentally. Whether they were elected as civil servants or 'independent' notables, the delegates knew that they represented the political nation and disposed of a democratic mandate. Liberal politicians nevertheless shared rather conservative concepts of 'society' and 'representation'. Though they recognised the existence of social cleavages, they did not appreciate the idea of a national representation dividing itself into conflicting social interests or political groups. The prominent liberal spokesman Friedrich Daniel Bassermann from Baden complained about the 'disgusting and absurd distinction between people and bourgeoisie' which political radicals made.[6] Like his political fellows in the liberal party, he conceptualised the National Assembly as a 'natural selection' of the 'middle classes', including propertied craftsmen, merchants, shopkeepers and landowners as well as the liberal professions, academicians and civil servants. It was the propertied and educated elite of male political citizens which represented the 'common interest' and thus was legitimised to speak and act in the name of the people. Neither the House of Commons, which represented a privileged landed aristocracy, nor the French Assembly's selected elite of notables and entrepreneurs nourished by the 'bourgeois monarchy' appeared to be compatible with the German liberals' harmonious concept of a 'middle-class representation'.[7]

But in fact, the ideal of a balanced representation of social interests did not mean equal representation according to the promise of universal manhood suffrage. Whereas the radical democrats straightforwardly claimed an individual right to 'one man, one vote', the liberal comprehension of democratic representation (*'Volksrepräsentation'*) meant something different. It did not particularly appreciate the political consequences of universal suffrage, which implied at least the chance that representatives of the nation were selected at random since only the mere number of votes counted. Liberals abhorred the political 'anarchy' of mass campaigning with its populist fishing for votes. In their opinion, electoral nominations should be considered carefully based on the candidate's social performance. Responsibility and credibility were qualifying characteristics that only educated and settled 'independent' men possessed. Liberal views about the right to vote came very close to those of Victorian Britain parliamentary reformers who intended to increase the number of 'respectable' voters, a term which encompassed 'a degree of economic independence' secured by 'decent wages' or smaller savings. But a far more important qualification was 'a willingness to play by existing social rules'.[8] As ordinary voters lacked information and experience, they had to be enlightened and directed politically before casting their ballot. It had to be ensured that elections could take place under circumstances that would leave their organisation to local committees and constituencies' 'managers' instead of exposing them to 'wild' and open bargaining in ballyhooed competitions. Perceptions of the British case were obviously present in the Revolution of 1848 when most countries of the German Federation opted for an indirect procedure of mandating trusties (*'Wahlmänner'*) in primary elections (*'Urwahlen'*), who would go on to a second round and have the final vote of delegating the members of parliament. Maintaining control of the elections was intended to protect the constituencies against inappropriate executive influence as well as prevent voters from being seduced by popular emotions. An open ballot or even verbal declarations of the voters were thus often preferred over an anonymous 'plebiscite' cast in the secrecy of the booth.

Historians unanimously agree that various restrictions of universal manhood suffrage were a regular practice in almost every constituency during the 1848 parliamentary elections, thus perfectly ensuring the predominance of liberal middle classes. Though revolutionaries shared a clear understanding of the inexperience of ordinary voters and guided 'their' electorate to a controlled manifestation of its political choice, the outcome of this practice was not undemocratic per se, as an average of more than 80% of male German citizens had achieved the right to vote by 1848.[9] Exceptions were made with regard to age and when material conditions prevented an individual from living without poor relief or in his own household. After all, the German National Assembly was legitimised by a fundamentally enlarged democratic mandate of the male population. The suffrage provisions of 1848 obviously tended towards democracy, but democratic elections did not necessarily encompass parliamentarisation.[10]

## PARLIAMENTARY GOVERNMENT

One major issue of the revolution of 1848 that historians have intensively investigated was the fundamental decision about parliamentary government. It has been doubted whether the National Assembly did consequently strive to claim sovereignty, as the delegates were haunted by the fear of a social revolution. Some of them, including historian Max Duncker, indeed recalled memories of the regime of terror that the '*Konventsherrschaft*' in revolutionary France had established.[11] Did the delegates mistrust parliamentarism; were they ready to arrange themselves with the authorities? Looking at the opening sessions of the Frankfurt Parliament, it becomes clear that the Assembly was more concerned with practical problems. It had to work out organisational structures and procedures which were rather quickly fixed as 'standing orders'. And when the National Assembly entered into the first political debate about establishing a provisional central executive, it treated the issue as merely a matter of formal responsibility, since someone had to be designated to represent an assembly of more than 500 members. It was during the course of a polarising debate when parliamentarians began to realise the impacts that their decision would have on power relations within the German Federation. A first step was the accreditation of delegates of the princes ('*Bevollmächtigte*') at the National Assembly. By nominating them, the German States recognised the authority of the Frankfurt Parliament. But establishing a provisional government was not merely an organisational measure, it was an act of claiming power which completely changed the constitutional framework. With this decision, the representatives of the nation presumed to govern the country.

The debate on the appointment of a national central executive that took place between 19 and 26 June in 1848 discloses fundamental beliefs that parliamentarians shared as well as conceptual divisions about parliamentary government. Friedrich Daniel Bassermann, one of the spokesmen of the liberal centre group in the Assembly, gave a fundamental statement when he said that the 'Provisional Central Power' would have to act as the executive of the 'majority of the nation'. Everyone knew that this claim implied the self-empowerment of the Assembly and thus challenged the constitutional authority of the legitimate governments of the German Federation.[12] By obliging the Provisional Central Power to execute the National Assembly's decisions, it institutionalised parliamentary government. It was the President of the Assembly himself who frankly spoke out about the revolutionary impacts of this 'bold catch' (*'kühner Griff'*): 'This system doesn't take any notice of the constitutional rights of the States of the German Federation', Heinrich von Gagern explained, 'once accepted, the National Assembly will take over Government in Germany'.[13] He also left no doubt about his own feelings, since he knew that the Assembly needed a strong central executive to express the 'national interest' regarding the threatened borders and to restrain the 'violent anarchy' spreading inside the territory of the German Federation.

Dissent existed among the deputies about the constitutional rights of the Provisional Government. Should it be entitled to act on its own, for instance, when decisions like declaring war or about maintaining law and order had to be taken, as constitutional monarchists claimed? Or should the Provisional Government strictly be bound to executing parliamentarian orders? Who would embody the Provisional Government, a board of executives or a single president, and who would nominate it? Arnold Ruge, a republican journalist, intellectual and prominent orator, pointedly marked the minority position of the parliamentarian Left when he insisted that the Provisional Government was the only legitimate executive and a plain instrument of the 'sovereignty of the people'.[14] This implied the elimination of the German Federation and the creation of a unitarian nation state. To support their claim, radical democrats referred to mass petitions of various associations and popular assemblies from southern Germany urging the Frankfurt National Assembly to close down the Federal German Diet (*'Bundestag'*) and establish a parliamentarian government. But the republican Left had to consider the strong federal state tradition which prevented a unitarian solution to the national question. The liberal historian Max Duncker ridiculed the republican concept—'a president on top and thirty princes below'—as daydreaming.[15] When the Assembly finally voted by a huge majority to nominate Archduke Johann of Habsburg as Imperial Regent ('*Reichsverweser*') of the nascent German State, it seemed as if it had opted for a constitutional monarchy. Although the peculiar title referred to the medieval tradition of the Holy Empire, executive power was invested in the cabinet ministers who were solely responsible to the National Assembly.

At first look, the presidential solution was paying tribute to the rights of the legitimate German princes. But the head of the state was destined to represent the German Nation and not a single principality or dynasty. To avoid ambitious rivalries of the German princes, the Assembly voted for a hereditary presidency of the House of Habsburg that would keep Austria closely connected with Germany. At the same time, the National Assembly insisted on its own prerogative. By establishing ministerial accountability, it obliged the Provisional Government to follow the political course that the parliamentarian majority directed. This was a concession to the parliamentary Left, which claimed full sovereignty of the parliament, a political compromise supported by a broad majority.[16] When the President of the German Diet officially recognised the authority of the Imperial Regent, the political revolution finally seemed to be accomplished. But in actuality, parliamentary sovereignty was more declaratory than fundamentally established. As the delegate of the Grand Duchy of Hessen at the Frankfurt Parliament observed, the 'language of courteoisie' which the German princes used, was destined to conceal their real convictions. They only reluctantly accepted the transfer of power which had been imposed on them by revolutionary force and thus was perceived as a 'presumptuous fraud of sovereignty'.[17]

Blinded by its own bold initiative, the Assembly ignored the fact that its constitutional framework was built on sand as long as it did not receive the acknowledgement of the German monarchs.[18] How fragile its authority really was became evident on the occasion of the war with Denmark when the Frankfurt Parliament had to accept the Treaty of Malmö, which the Prussian Monarch had concluded without its consent. Lacking the means to reverse the power structure of the German Federation completely, the National Assembly somehow had to come to terms with the German princes. But every move the parliamentarians took towards recognising the legitimacy of the sovereigns' authority was watched suspiciously by revolutionary activists. A political language had to be found which would declare political arrangements as inevitable compromises destined to preserve the achievements of the revolution.

## Languages of Consent: Politics of Compromise

The National Assembly had proven its determination to create a constitutional order based on parliamentary government. But it failed to safeguard its position against the political claims of sovereignty which the German princes still upheld. The ruling dynasties never gave up their own pretensions which they considered as legitimate. The consequence was a dual power structure producing a flagrant contradiction between a national representation of revolutionary origin and the presence of hereditary monarchies who could still rely on considerable popular devotion. Obviously, parliamentarians hoped that time would be on their side, since they were convinced that growing feelings of national unity would help build a strong common ground for constitutional reform. However, to embrace the whole country, including the German dynasties, required an integrating political discourse that would harmonise different expectations. The parliament decided to build the framework of unification on the fundamental rights of the German population because it seemed to be the least controversial issue that all political groups could subscribe to.[19]

Abolishing the repressive legislation which the German Diet had enacted and proclaiming fundamental rights of freedom were generally accepted as basic achievements of the revolution of 1848. Historians who later criticised the long and seemingly academic dispute[20] disregard the fact that parliamentarians did not perceive debating merely as time-consuming and thus potentially dangerous, but as a commitment to forge the nation together by creating a common political language. In fact, actors on the political stage had realised the revolutionary momentum of speaking not merely to a local audience or regional political body but to the nation which they represented as their elected delegates. Communication had to be redirected from the political centre to the whole country; words had to be found that could bridge the distance between representatives and people. Whenever the Assembly addressed the 'German nation' proclaiming the unity of parliament and 'people', spontaneous reactions in the gallery as well as popular consent expressed in mass petitions showed the integrating effects of this nationalising language policy.[21] But at the same time, a lack of communication may as well be observed that contributed to the revolution's failure. Whereas the Assembly was concerned about directing political messages to the public, it severely neglected to establish communication with the German courts.

It simply relied upon the political loyalty of the reform cabinets that had been designated to the state administrations of the German Federation during the March Revolution of 1848. The reports of the prince's delegates to the Frankfurt Assembly reveal how misinformed or even ignored they felt in the entourage of the new political centre.[22] Politics of compromise with the German courts were neither prepared carefully nor communicated properly, which became blatantly clear in April 1849 when the parliamentary mission of investing the Prussian King Frederick William with the crown of the German nation failed in a historical misunderstanding.[23]

The National Assembly had to face contradicting critical voices. Politics of compromise with the legitimate authorities were blamed as 'agreement policy', and arrangements between political groups in parliament denunciated as 'horse-trading' (*'Principienschacher'*). Complaints about a selling out of principles signify an idealistic misunderstanding of parliamentarism. Political 'fundamentalists' imagined parliamentary legislation as the plain result of basic convictions which they expected the prevailing majority to execute as such after controversial debating. But politicians at the parliamentarian frontline, such as Heinrich von Gagern and his fellows, experienced their policy of compromising in a rather different way. What they believed to be necessary 'transactions between conflicting parties' did not mean giving up fundamental beliefs but rather working out agreements which the parliamentary majority could accept as basic political solutions. Bargaining was thus perceived as an essential element of parliamentarism which competing political associations practised themselves in their own ranks in order to achieve a 'majority decision of the party'. Experienced politicians like Gagern, who did not hesitate to call himself a 'party-man',[24] knew very well that only internal group discipline would allow him and his followers to act successfully as a powerful force in parliament. Though a tight party regime always had to face the insubordination of single dissenters and sometimes take the risk of disappointing voters, parliamentarians in 1848 were getting accustomed to conformism and party discipline. Making political compromises which a majority of the Assembly could support would not only have significance for the public opinion but might also impress the German monarchs.[25]

A new way of talking was necessary to bridge the gap between different political groups in parliament. Republicans or radical democrats on the left, constitutional monarchists, Austrian or Prussian legitimists on the right could not be convinced to give up fundamental political positions without opening up semantic fields of 'commonness'. Parliamentarians were forced to abstain from a political game called 'all or nothing'. They had to drop some basic assumptions about parliamentarism that had guided them in the pre-revolutionary period. Many of them had been prominent orators in the second chambers of the German Federation. They had gained political reputation as speakers of the parliamentary opposition that claimed to represent the 'people'. Addressing the public from the orator tribune in pre-revolutionary Germany basically aimed at putting pressure on bureaucratic government to change its policy. The belief in the moral power of political speech was a basic experience undergone in the limited parliamentary space of constitutional monarchies.

Revolutionary parliamentarism in 1848 changed politics fundamentally because it transformed a basically *moral* pretension to speak in the name of the people into a *political* mandate to represent the sovereign. Speaking in parliament was much different since parliamentarians turned into political actors who determined the national agenda. Although political debates surely attracted a mass audience of visitors, parliamentarism in 1848 did not find its destination in a competition of orators on the stage. Impressing the public and attracting the press was a popular part of the game. The slightest accident would be immediately registered as 'hundreds of enemies' were listening, the left democrat Ludwig Bamberger remembered.[26] But what was essential for pushing political issues on the agenda was not individual talent or charisma, but rather the well-prepared performance of parliamentary groups. Even Heinrich von Gagern, who was the most famous orator in the Assembly of 1848, practised his performances in the same routinized ways British party speakers did.[27] Parliamentarians thus had to accept a loss of individual relevance, since organising majorities or directing opposition required the unanimous action of party groups in and outside of plenary debates. The romantic ideal of 'independent representatives' free of political choice quickly vanished in the machinery of working parliamentarism where political options were reduced to a minimum of alternatives. Party discipline inevitably diminished the importance of free speech and the individual gift of rhetoric. But while parliamentarians might have regretted the fading away of their ideals of deliberative parliamentarism, they at the same time experienced the growing influence and power that party commitment gave them. Oratory skills were not devaluated as such but had to be performed within the limits of time and space that the party management determined.[28]

After long and exhausting debates, delegates understood much better how limited the force of rhetoric speech actually was. It happened only rarely that someone was convinced during a plenary debate to give up his political position,[29] though this experience was sometimes ignored, especially when 'political professors' tortured the audience with speeches of extended length.[30] To cut down endless 'wild' discussions, the Assembly thus decided to rationalise deliberations by limiting the length of plenary debates. It was Arnold Ruge, a leading representative of the Left, who motivated his fellows to 'sacrifice' their individual rights of speech and motivated amendments to the requirements of an organised procedure of parliamentary debating.[31] Although the freedom of speech was in essence not touched, it became a common practice to transfer it to the rule of parliamentary groups who would designate parliamentary orators. The essential experience of the work overload that day-to-day parliamentarism produced forced the Assembly to refigure itself as an organised entity of interacting political groups which only faintly reflected the ideal of a deliberating community of individuals. The challenge of rationalising parliamentarism was delegated to a technical committee of the House, which had to propose statutory rules for regulating the plenary sessions and working procedures of the Assembly, called the '*Geschäftsordnung*' or standing orders of the House.[32]

## Recognising 'Facts' and 'Realities'

The National Assembly has been criticised for its policy of making arrangements with the monarchs and governments of the German Federation—what the liberals understood as a strategy labelled '*Vereinbarungspolitik*' later evolved into a political reproach against them, but it is a matter of fact that the Frankfurt Parliament had autonomously decided about the new political order. It had substituted the representatives of the former German Federation with loyal personalities and subordinated the 'expurgated' German Diet to the National Assembly. The German Constitution of 1849 was neither granted nor even agreed on with the German courts, but rather adopted by a parliamentary majority.[33] Even if the Prussian king had accepted the parliament's offer of establishing a hereditary monarchy with the Prince of Hohenzollern designated as 'Emperor of the Germans', his constitutional power would nonetheless have originated in a revolutionary parliamentary act—and that was exactly the reason why he denied his consent. Before the counter-revolution finally prevailed by force of violence, the National Parliament successfully obliged the German governments, including Austria and Prussia, to accept its decisions. When for the first time a parliamentary majority vote was ignored by one of the German states, which happened when Prussia signed the Treaty of Malmö, this confrontation immediately caused the demission of the Provisional Government and severely infringed on the authority of the Assembly.

Apart from its national political impacts, this serious incident obviously proved that the German nation-building was dependent on the current state of the European order, which still reflected the principles of the Congress of Vienna. The Parliament's '*großdeutsche*' ('greater German') vision of a powerful nation state that would include all Germans populating the historical territory of the former Holy German Empire was not compatible with the interests of the European powers.[34] When the National Assembly buried its imperial dreams after following controversial debates, it had concluded another very unpopular compromise which it soon labelled as 'recognising the facts'. It was a 'realistic' decision which anticipated the '*kleindeutsche*' or Prussian solution by restricting the imagined cultural borders of the nation state to the non-disputed territory inhabited by Germans.[35]

By giving up their imperial ambitions, a considerable number of liberal 'converts' like Welcker made it possible that the National Assembly would have been recognised as a part of the European concert of nation states. To insist on the imperial vision of a greater German nation obviously would have required popular consent for waging a national war.[36] The political language which the parliamentarians adopted during the heated emotional debate about the territorial borders of the German nation-state was full of moderating formulas appealing to the delegates for walking on 'solid ground'. This talk signalled the willingness to accept as 'a matter of fact' that the German question had to be solved according to the existing framework of the European order.

The recognition of seemingly given 'facts' and 'realities' guided the Assembly when it was establishing a new political order. While paying verbal tributes to popular sentiments by promising to create a new constitutional design ('*etwas ganz Neues zu schaffen*'[37]), the delegates of the people respected the international and national limits of nation-building. Restricted in their ambition of expanding the territory of the German state, they were at the same time forced to accommodate to the historical traditions of national federalism. To operate on solid ground ('*auf dem Boden der Tatsachen*') meant bargaining with the German governments and respecting patriotic particularism. Since not even the national delegates themselves would give up their particular 'nationality' as Prussians or Bavarians and loyally adhered to the legitimate dynasties,[38] the Assembly decided to leave the federal structure as well as the constitutional Monarchy, as fundamental elements of a German nation state, basically untouched. A broad liberal majority in parliament comprised convinced constitutional monarchists and federalists alike.

Prominent liberals such as Robert von Mohl, Karl Theodor Welcker, Friedrich Christoph Dahlmann, Friedrich Daniel Bassermann and Heinrich von Gagern referred to England as the model state of a parliamentary monarchy.[39] Once parliamentary government was established, it wouldn't matter at all, so Bassermann maintained, whether King George or Queen Victoria rules the country. Addressing the Left who favoured a republican state, he reminded the Assembly of the fatal outcome of the French Revolution which ended up in terror and 'military despotism'. Calling up the ghosts of the guillotine and the regime of anarchy were commonplaces the liberal political discourse needed to keep republicanism at a distance. They disregarded the vision of a '*république une et indivisible*' as a purely French experience, whereas they perceived the British version of parliamentary government as suitable for being adapted to the German tradition.[40]

Though references to England were always present, they did not motivate parliamentarians to a direct adoption of foreign practices. Some elements of British parliamentarism were of common use,[41] others, such as the custom of speaking from one's place in parliament, for example, would be viewed as peculiar and inconvenient, whereas most innovations were results of experiencing parliamentarism at home. But historical comparisons of European parliamentary cultures ('*parlamentarischer Brauch*') were repeatedly made during the debates of the Constituent Assembly. Transfers and communication of national experiences in the long run tended to converge into common standards of parliamentarism in Europe.[42] As Jonathan Sperber concludes, the revolutions of 1848 'spread from one country to the next by force of example, not by force of arms'.[43] The transfer of revolutionary experience produced similar political structures and created a common political culture with political associations, a high voting turnout and popular mass movements. Parliaments became the political centre of the nation, attracting public attention and mobilising people even in the remote countryside. Readers of newspapers were informed about what was happening in the different hubs of revolutionary events.

Although the military interventions of the constitutionalist monarchies were driving back revolutionary forces and establishing neo-absolutist governments, they could not reverse the continuing constitutional debate about a new political order of the continent. The victorious German princes in 1849 soon had to realise that restoration neither had eliminated parliamentary government from the political agenda nor dissipated the revolutionary experience of parliamentarism at all.

## NOTES

1. 'Engländer, Niederländer, Spanier, Portugiesen, Italiener, Polen, Griechen, Amerikaner, ja Neger haben für die Freiheit der Franzosen, die ja die Freiheit aller Völker ist, gekämpft, nur die Deutschen nicht': Ludwig Börne, Briefe aus Paris, Fünfter Brief, 17. September 1830, in Inge and Peter Rippmann (eds.), *Sämtliche Schriften* (Dreieich: Joseph Melzer Verlag, 1977) vol. 3, p. 23; cf. Klaus Ries (ed.), *Europa im Vormärz. Eine transnationale Spurensuche* (Ostfildern: Jan Thorbecke Verlag, 2016).
2. '[…] public attention to politics was completely absorbed by the National Assembly': Reinhard Carl Eigenbrodt, *Meine Erinnerungen aus den Jahren 1848, 1849 und 1850*, edited by Ludwig Bergsträsser (Darmstadt: Grossherzoglich Hessischer Staatsverlag, 1914) p. 96.
3. Jörg-Detlef Kühne, *Die Reichsverfassung der Paulskirche. Vorbild und Verwirklichung im späteren deutschen Rechtsleben* (Frankfurt am Main: Metzner, 1985); Dieter Hein, *Die Revolution von 1848/49* (München: Verlag C.H. Beck, 1998); cf. Heinrich Best, 'Strukturen parlamentarischer Repräsentation in den Revolutionen von 1848' in D. Dowe, H.-G. Haupt and D. Langewiesche (eds.), *Europa 1848. Revolution und Reform* (Bonn: J.H.W. Dietz Nachf., 1998) p. 636 ff.
4. Wilhelm Bleek, 'Die Politik-Professoren in der Paulskirche' in J. Kocka et al. (eds.), *Von der Arbeiterbewegung zum modernen Sozialstaat* (München: K.G. Saur Verlag, 1994); Peter Wende, 'Der "politische Professor"' in Ulrich Muhlack (ed.), *Historisierung und gesellschaftlicher Wandel in Deutschland im 19. Jahrhundert* (Berlin: Akademie Verlag, 2003); Hans-Christof Kraus, 'Zur parlamentarischen Rhetorik politischer Professoren' in J. Feuchter and J. Helmrath (eds.), *Parlamentarische Kulturen vom Mittelalter bis in die Moderne* (Düsseldorf: Droste Verlag, 2013).
5. Anna Gianna Manca, 'Die Beamten in der französischen und deutschen verfassunggebenden Versammlung von 1848' in M. Kirsch and P. Schiera (eds.), *Verfassungswandel um 1848 im europäischen Vergleich* (Berlin: Duncker & Humblot, 2001) p. 126–127; F. Julien-Laferrière, *Les députés*

*fonctionnaires sous la Monarchie de Juillet* (Paris: Presses universitaires de France, 1970).

6. [...] 'widerliche und widersinnige Unterscheidung zwischen Volk und Bourgeoisie': Manfed Botzenhart, *Deutscher Parlamentarismus in der Revolutionszeit 1848–1850* (Düsseldorf: Droste Verlag, 1977) p. 81, quoting: Friedrich Daniel Bassermann, *Denkwürdigkeiten von 1811–1855* (Frankfurt am Main, 1926) p. 25, and a speech in the Paulskirche on 16 February 1849.

7. For more on the importance of the liberal self-perception for its political concepts, see Lothar Gall, 'Liberalismus und "bürgerliche Gesellschaft"' (1975), and Lothar Gall, '"ich wünschte ein Bürger zu sein." Zum Selbstverständnis des deutschen Bürgertums im 19. Jahrhundert' (1987), reprinted in L. Gall, *Bürgertum, liberale Bewegung und Nation* (München: R. Oldenbourg Verlag, 1996) pp. 99–126 and 3–22.

8. For comparison with the British debate about enfranchising all 'respectable' Englishmen, see Eric J. Evans, *Parliamentary Reform, c. 1770–1918* (London/New York: Longman, 2000) p. 41.

9. Botzenhart, *Deutscher Parlamentarismus*, p. 157.

10. Andreas Biefang and Andreas Schulz, 'From Monarchical Constitutionalism to a Parliamentary Republic: Concepts of Parliamentarism in Germany since 1818' in P. Ihalainen, C. Ilie and K. Palonen (eds.), *Parliament and Parliamentarism. A Comparative History of a European Concept* (New York/Oxford: Berghahn Books, 2016) p. 62–81; Dirk Jörke and Marcus Llanque, 'Parliamentarism and Democracy in German Political Theory since 1848' in Ibid., p. 262–277.

11. Stenographischer Bericht über die Verhandlungen der deutschen constituirenden National-Versammlung zu Frankfurt am Main, edited by Franz Wigard, vol. 1 (Frankfurt am Main, 1848) [further on quoted: 'Minutes of the National Assembly'] 18th session, 19 June 1848, p. 384.

12. The delegate of the Grand Duchy of Hesse at the National Assembly noticed that a transfer of power was taking place: 'Embodying the nation the German National Assembly claims the exclusive right to found the federal constitution of the German State without previous consent of the German Princes or the Provisional Government'; Eigenbrodt, *Erinnerungen*, p. 100.

13. 'Dieses System nimmt keine Rücksicht auf die Rechte der deutschen Regierungen. Wird es angenommen, so hat die Nationalversammlung die Regierung über Deutschland angetreten'; Minutes of the National Assembly, 18th Session, 19 June 1848, p. 356.

14. Minutes of the National Assembly, 18th Session, 19 June 1848, p. 368; for more about the parliamentarian Left, see Christian Jansen, *Einheit, Macht und Freiheit. Die Paulskirchenlinke und die deutsche Politik in der nachrevolutionären Epoche 1849–1867* (Düsseldorf: Droste Verlag, 2000).

15. '[…] oben ein Präsident, unten 30 Fürstenthümer': Max Duncker, *Zur Geschichte der deutschen Reichsversammlung in Frankfurt* (Berlin: Duncker und Humblot, 1849) p. 51. For more on liberal and democratic concepts of a unitarian republic or a parliamentary monarchy, see Jansen, *Einheit*, p. 234.
16. Hans-Werner Hahn and Helmut Berding, *Reformen, Restauration und Revolution 1806–1848/49* (Stuttgart: Klett-Cotta Verlag, 2010), p. 570.
17. Eigenbrodt, *Erinnerungen*, p. 100 ff., quoting the delegate of the Free City of Bremen.
18. Hein, *Revolution*, p. 49.
19. Markus Lotzenburger, *Die Grundrechte in den deutschen Verfassungen des 19. Jahrhunderts* (Düsseldorf: Droste Verlag, 2015), p. 125.
20. Ernst Rudolf Huber, *Deutsche Verfassungsgeschichte*, vol. 2 (Stuttgart: Kohlhammer, 1988), p. 774–776.
21. The significance of a fundamental change of political language has been emphasized by Willibald Steinmetz, '"Sprechen ist eine Tat bei euch." Die Wörter und das Handeln in der Revolution von 1848' in Dowe et al. (eds.), *Europa 1848*, p. 1089–1139. See also Armin Burkhardt, 'German Parliamentary Discourse since 1848 from a Linguistic Point of View' in Ihalainen et al. (eds.), *Parliament and Parliamentarism*, p. 176–192.
22. The delegate of Hessen-Darmstadt, although a close friend of Heinrich von Gagern, felt like a 'mere spectator' and complained about a 'complete isolation' which separated the German governments from the National Assembly in Frankfurt; Eigenbrodt, *Erinnerungen*, pp. 304 and 271.
23. King Frederick Wilhelm's refusal to accept the crown of the German Reich which the delegation offered him in the name of the National Assembly on 3 April 1849 might not have been so predictable as historians later assumed because the signals which the Prussian monarch communicated regarding his German mission during the winter months were anything but clear; David E. Barclay, *Anarchie und guter Wille. Friedrich Wilhelm IV. und die preußische Monarchie* (Berlin: Siedler Verlag, 1995) p. 282–283; Botzenhart, *Parlamentarismus*, p. 695–696.
24. Paul Wentzcke and Wolfgang Klötzer (eds.), *Deutscher Liberalismus im Vormärz. Heinrich von Gagern: Briefe und Reden 1815–1848* (Göttingen: Musterschmidt, 1959); cf. Philipp Erbentraut, *Theorie und Soziologie der politischen Parteien im deutschen Vormärz 1815–1848* (Tübingen: Mohr Siebeck, 2016), p. 165.
25. 'We had to create a constitution by gaining moral support for our work since we lacked the bayonets to impose it by force': Duncker, *Reichsversammlung*, p. 83 ff.
26. Ludwig Bamberger, *Erinnerungen*, edited by Paul Nathan (Berlin 1899), p. 58–59.
27. Eigenbrodt, *Erinnerungen*, p. 251.

28. Veit Valentin was one of the first historians who pointed out the importance of the National Assembly of 1848 for 'experiencing' parliamentarism: V. Valentin, *Geschichte der deutschen Revolution von 1848–1849*, 2 vols. (first published Berlin 1930/31; reprint Cologne 1977) vol. 2, p. 13. 'Experience' and the 'ideas of 1848' were terms that the former '1848ers' repeatedly made reference to in their political correspondence, giving them a generational political identity: Jansen, *Einheit*, p. 25.

29. The historian Friedrich von Raumer, delegate of Berlin, described himself speaking in parliament as a 'dog barking at the moon', since political clubs decided how to vote in parliament, which made deliberations useless: Botzenhart, *Parlamentarismus*, p. 436.

30. Kraus, *Rhetorik*, p. 209.

31. Minutes of the National Assembly, vol. 1, p. 385.

32. The transformation of the 'wild' beginnings of parliamentarism into orchestrated proceedings and functional working structures is documented in the minutes which the National Assembly produced and published in 1848/49; the standing orders of the House were drafted by Robert von Mohl, who was an expert on British parliamentarism. Cf. Robert von Mohl, *Vorschläge zu einer Geschäftsordnung des verfassunggebenden Reichstags* (Heidelberg: Academische Verlagshandlung C.F. Winter, 1848) and 'Über die verschiedene Auffassung des repräsentativen Systems in England, Frankreich und Deutschland' in *Zeitschrift für die gesammte Staatswissenschaft* 3 (1846), p. 451–495.

33. Thomas Nipperdey, *Deutsche Geschichte* (München: C.H. Beck Verlag, 1984; 2nd ed.), p. 659.

34. Dieter Hein, 'Die deutsche Nation in Europa 1848/49' in K. Ries (ed.), *Europa im Vormärz* (Ostfildern: Jan Thorbecke Verlag, 2016), p. 169; Günter Wollstein, *Das 'Großdeutschland' der Paulskirche. Nationale Ziele in der bürgerlichen Revolution 1848/49* (Dusseldorf: Droste Verlag, 1977).

35. In the 1850s, the term *'Realpolitik'* served as a code word which signalled that the former revolutionaries were ready to accept the failure of their political concepts and to turn to cooperation with the Prussian monarchy to realize German nation-building in an authoritarian way; Steinmetz, 'Sprechen ist eine Tat bei euch', p. 1113–1115; Jansen, *Einheit*, pp. 30–31 and 255–265.

36. Dieter Langewiesche, *Reich–Nation–Föderation. Deutschland und Europa* (München: C.H. Beck Verlag, 2008), p. 259–277.

37. Minutes of the National Assembly, vol. 1, p. 377.

38. Conservatives as well as the Left in the Berlin National Assembly confessed loyalty to the history and tradition of the Prussian state; 'Pomeranians, Prussians, inhabitants of the Kurmark and the Altmark, Magdeburgher, a majority of the Silesians and Westphalians and also Rhinelanders want to

stay citizens of Prussia', the *Augsburger Allgemeine Zeitung* newspaper observed in 1848: Manfred Botzenhart, 'Das preußische Parlament und die deutsche Nationalversammlung im Jahre 1848' in Gerhard A. Ritter (ed.), *Regierung, Bürokratie und Parlament in Preußen und Deutschland von 1848 bis zur Gegenwart* (Düsseldorf: Droste Verlag, 1983) p. 22.

39. Hans-Christof Kraus, 'Die deutsche Rezeption und Darstellung der englischen Verfassung im neunzehnten Jahrhundert' in R. Muhs, J. Paulmann and W. Steinmetz (eds.), *Aneignung und Abwehr. Interkultureller Transfer zwischen Deutschland und Großbritannien im 19. Jahrhundert* (Bodenheim: Philo Verlagsgesellschaft, 1998), p. 89–126.

40. Cf. Friedrich Daniel Bassermann and Joseph Maria von Radowitz: Minutes of the National Assembly, 18th Session, 19 June 1848, pp. 381 and 376.

41. Heinrich von Gagern related the way of confrontational speaking directly to British parliamentarism: 'I did it in the same way in which it is daily practised by political opponents in English Parliament': Eigenbrodt, *Erinnerungen*, p. 251, note in the margin by Heinrich von Gagern.

42. Andreas Schulz and Andreas Wirsching (eds.), *Das Parlament als Kommunikationsraum* (Düsseldorf: Droste Verlag, 2012); Heinz-Gerhard Haupt and Dieter Langewiesche, 'Die Revolution in Europa 1848' in Dowe et al. (eds.), *Europa 1848*, p. 13.

43. Jonathan Sperber, *The European Revolutions, 1848–1851* (Cambridge: Cambridge University Press, 2005; 2nd ed.), p. 265.

# PART II

# Crises of Expectations

# CHAPTER 7

# Elusive Enthusiasm: Parliamentary Democracy in the Newly Founded European Nation-States After the First World War— The Case of Poland

*Stephanie Zloch*

Even today, after decades of research in the disciplines of history, political science, sociology and, more recently, cultural studies, the history of Europe in the interwar period remains difficult to grasp. Differing narratives can, at times, seem to stand diametrically opposed to one another. One narrative describes the interwar years as a long, continuous 'civil war', at times also as a mid-point in a '30-year war' dating from 1914 to 1945.[1] Another narrative places the focus on the end of the First World War as the beginning of a wave of democratization across Europe. In many countries, monarchs abdicated their thrones and new constitutions were adopted, invoking basic political rights and strengthening parliamentarism. The foundations for a universal, free, confidential, and equal right to vote

S. Zloch (✉)
Technical University Dresden, Dresden, Germany
e-mail: stephanie.zloch@tu-dresden.de

© The Author(s) 2019
R. Aerts et al. (eds.), *The Ideal of Parliament in Europe since 1800*,
Palgrave Studies in Political History,
https://doi.org/10.1007/978-3-030-27705-5_7

replaced the group voting rights of the time, as large, political, and previously marginalized groups, such as women, workers, and peasants were added to the electorate. The introduction of a parliamentary democracy in Poland after the restoration of national independence in 1918 reflected these tensions.

From the second half of the nineteenth century onwards, intellectuals, political parties, trade unions, and other organizations within societies across Europe had agitated for broad political participation and systems of representative democracy. Poles assumed a natural role in these transnational movements that came to be widely respected and was demonstrated, for example, by involvement of the Polish Socialists at the founding congress of the Second International organization in 1889 and by representatives of the women's movement around 1900. It was this spirit that Ignacy Daszyński, the first socialist prime minister of independent Poland, and brother-in-law of the national economist Zofia Daszyńska-Golińska, one of the first female doctoral students at the University of Zurich in 1891, emphasized in a speech given on 10 November 1918. He maintained that the impending elections to the Sejm, the lower house of the Polish parliament, would create the necessary preconditions for 'the first year of a free, united nation in a free, united motherland'.[2]

It may appear more surprising still that the consensus of support for parliamentary democracy extended into conservative and church circles. Both Poland's Catholic Church and its landed nobility, two highly influential groups in the country's society, approved fundamentally of democratic elections and were quick to become involved in political education by such means as producing brochures and holding talks on 'The Elections to the Sejm', 'The Duties of Citizenship', 'The Polish Provinces', 'Serving your Country', 'The Political Parties', 'The Dangers of Seditious Propaganda in Villages', and 'Your Duty to your Municipality'.[3]

In this context, parliamentary democracy initially had considerable power to mobilize Polish society. Voter turnout was high, reaching approximately 76 per cent in the 1919 elections to the Sejm that was to give the country its constitution, despite the persistent state of war on the Eastern Front and a state framework that had yet to be consolidated. For the subsequent Sejm elections in 1922, voter participation in the Prussian Partition and in former Congress Poland, the *Kresy Wschodnie*, was often above 80 per cent.[4] These elections were overshadowed by an election boycott by the Ukrainians in eastern Galicia, attempting to draw attention to their efforts towards independence. Even the eastern border region of

Poland generally seen as backwards, the *Kresy Wschodnie*, participated: The writer Zofia Nałkowska, who at the time lived near Vilnius, felt uplifted by the manner in which Lithuanian farmers and their wives, 'simple people', travelled long distances through marshy terrain in the autumn rains to give expression to their political will.[5]

Such broad popularity if not enthusiasm for parliamentary democracy was possible, because today's established notions of the task and function of a modern parliament were then quite heterogeneous. In order to analyse and contextualize these concepts more closely, a few considerations about the history of democracy and more recently emerged parliamentarism are instructive.

Firstly, an understanding of democracy and parliamentarism in their historiographical context[6] is required—hence an investigation of discourses, processes of negotiation, and practice in the concrete political and societal configurations in which they can be found. Relatedly, the more recent history of democracy and parliamentarism is more than the study of systems and institutions; it brings the 'diffuse and complicated processes of internal democratization', consequently the 'living, feeling democracy of the citizenry',[7] increasingly into view. This supports the case for the history of parliament and parliamentarism to be written with an 'integration of a history of constitution, communication, and perception' in mind.[8] Through the media, analysis of parliamentary activities can reach a politically interested public: analysis that may, for example, stand in stark contrast to the self-perception of representatives and to the professional logic of the parliamentary institution. Finally, the focus on symbols, rituals, and political socialization of representatives hones in on the ways in which meaning and tradition are created—not to be underestimated for their role in the ability of a parliamentary democracy to function.[9]

What is remarkable about the Eastern and Central European states created after the First World War is that parliamentarism had been practised in the Russian *Duma*, in the *Reichstag* of Imperial Germany, the Austrian *Reichsrat* and the Hungarian *Reichstag* of the Habsburg monarchy, and in several regional parliaments, but politicians, publicists, and historians in the newly independent states tried to avoid any symbolic continuity and attempted to build their own, national parliamentary and democratic traditions which were designed to stand in a sharp contrast to the imperial past.

In fact, the revolution in Russia in 1917 and that in Germany in November 1918 paved the way for widespread criticism of a perceived insufficiency of democratic achievements by the former empires.

Furthermore, the First World War, with broad segments of the population compelled to participate in war efforts and with the loss of legitimacy experienced by existing governing systems, was a catalyst for the implementation of new democratic concepts and institutions. The First World War thus functioned as 'the midwife of democracy'.[10] In any case, this led to the militarization and nationalization of everyday life, over time promoting a culture of violence and clashing with the culture of regulated and institutionalized conflict management and resolution.[11] Rather than one 'ideal' parliament in Poland at the time of the state's founding in 1918, there were many ideas as to what a parliament should look like and how it should function. Below, three of these ideas will be introduced in more detail and their practical implications discussed: (1) parliament as a national symbol, (2) parliament as the mirror of society, and (3) parliament as the site of political decision-making. These ideas took on a different meaning in 1926, as the coup by Józef Piłsudski and the introduction of an authoritative regime, the *Sanacja*, constituted a serious strain on parliamentarism in Poland.

## PARLIAMENT AS A NATIONAL SYMBOL

The initial enthusiasm for parliamentarism in Poland after 1918 can be traced largely to the more distant past: The Sejm was an important place of remembrance for the early modern statehood of the aristocratic republic of Poland-Lithuania.[12] Since the end of the fifteenth century, Sejm representatives from all parts of one of the largest European states, in terms of territory, had come together to vote for the king and to give political conflicts central and public stage. Poland also drafted its first written constitution at the end of the eighteenth century, which was passed by the so-called four-year Sejm on 3 May 1791. Polish politicians and historians frequently claim that Poland has been the first modern European state to create a constitution and thus was one of the pioneers of European democracy.[13] In the newly founded Polish state, the significance of this historical narrative was recognized as representatives of the Sejm constituent assembly on 29 April 1919 passed a resolution making 3 May a national holiday.

In this context, it would be nearly impossible to overestimate the symbolic importance of the new Sejm constituent assembly. At the induction ceremony on 10 February 1919, which was captured in a photograph (see Image 7.1), representatives of the parliament, the military, including well-

**Image 7.1**  Induction ceremony of the Sejm on 10 February 1919 [Narodowe Archiwum Cyfrowe, Signature: 1-A-771]

known Marshall Józef Piłsudski, and the Catholic Church were in attendance.

This staging of approval of the parliamentary system could have easily led to opposing trends in political practice, if specifically the military and the church did not see themselves as at least co-equal, if not superior, in power to parliament. Indications of such a development are to be found as early as 20 February 1919, with the Sejm's approval of the informal 'Little Constitution' (*Mała Konstytucja*): Now, by the grace of the Sejm, Józef Piłsudski was able to resume his previous position of provisional head of state. Whether or not this strengthened parliament or contributed to Piłsudski's ability to build his networks of power further remains to this day a matter of debate. A similar situation arose in the case of the Catholic Church in Poland. The constitution passed by the Sejm on 17 March 1921 declared in article 114: 'The Roman-Catholic faith, the religion of the clear majority of the nation, assumes a singular status in the state, alongside other faiths with equal rights.'[14] Here is where the debate as to the influence and activities of Catholicism in interwar Poland begins—a debate that continues to affect today's historiography.[15]

To charge parliament with national symbolism and, consequently, to define parliament itself as a national symbol was not a question of official gestures alone but clearly a need that found echo in the social mood of the time. Parliamentary speeches and proceedings dominated media coverage and political education, and members of parliament were held almost universally in high esteem. The media—politically and regionally distinct in the newly independent Polish state—did their part in contributing to the construction of parliament as a site of national unity.[16] As a result, the Sejm enjoyed positive reception even in areas where modern democratic principles had been held at arm's length for many years. An interesting example of this is provided by the position of *Ziemianka*, a newspaper of the conservative confederation of landowners. From the very opening of the Sejm constituent assembly, representatives expressed concern: 'May our merciful God, who, for us, achieved the miracle of resurrection, show mercy to those we have chosen; may he create in them pure hearts beating fervently for Poland and for justice; a clear mind, which is able to shoulder this great responsibility. We, in contrast, the women of Poland, have chosen with our votes; help with daily, devout work to provide for order, education, and prosperity in this country.'[17] It was then reported extensively how, at a federation meeting on 14 June 1919, donations were collected for a cross of dark oak with a bronze Jesus figurine. A delegation of landowners in colourful national costumes presented to the parliamentary president Trąmpczyński, before a Sejm session, this cross, furnished with the annotation that like the Sejm of the aristocratic republic, the present-day Sejm should be held under the sign of Christ.

Amidst this harmonious attempt, conveyed by the media, to construct cultural continuity between the early modern era and a state independent since 1918, we can perceive a possible source of friction: The landed nobility addressed the 'new' elite of the Sejm with the self-confidence of the 'old', politically and culturally long dominant elite and set its eyes on the goal of working towards the preservation of traditional concepts of order.[18]

Such a projection of paternalistic concepts on the Sejm was conflicting: It gave rise to the opportunity to contain the danger of an extra-parliamentary opposition by drawing the Polish political right into the consensus of support for the country's newly founded parliamentary system. On the other hand, not long into the parliament's existence, there appeared a tendency to accord preferential status to ethnic Poles and Catholics and to view the Sejm less as a forum of the democratic diversity of views and competing interests than as a national symbol possessed of inherent authority.

## PARLIAMENT AS THE MIRROR OF SOCIETY

In the context of previous experience with the parliaments of the partition powers of Prussia, Austria-Hungary, and Russia, which with their three-class or census voting systems (the German *Reichstag* being the sole exception) favoured the upper classes of society, the idea of parliament as the mirror of society had particular allure. In a henceforth independent state, with nearly three quarters of its population living in the countryside in 1918, this meant that more peasants as well as more workers were to join Parliament's representatives. At the same time, interwar Poland was an ethnically diverse state: Around one third of the population were Germans, Ukrainians, Belarusians, Jews, Lithuanians, and other so-called national minorities. The question of their representation has for some time been the focus not of Polish historical study but of international historiography. In the past few years, the largest group in Poland's population has been the object of study, namely, women—who have possessed the active and passive right to vote since 1918.

The concept of parliament as the mirror of society certainly did not mean that the goal was a static, exact distribution of representatives in accordance with the size of each and every group in the population. The people's biographies, affiliations and identities, and political alignments were too complex for this end. A look at the personnel structure of the three peasant parties Polskie Stronnictwo Ludowe (PSL)-Piast, PSL-Wyzwolenie, and PSL-Lewica, which were represented in the Sejm up until the mid-1920s, provides an informative example (Image 7.2).

On one side stood the leader of the PSL-Piast, Wincenty Witos, a farmer born in 1874 in the Galician village of Wierzchosławice, who presented himself in classic peasant fashion with vest and tie-less collar. He made himself stand out by doing so, as did Antonín Švehla in Czechoslovakia or Stjepan Radić in Croatia, who embodied the persona of the Eastern Europe political peasant leader from the first half of the twentieth century. Admittedly, Witos had entered party politics early on and procured multiple representative seats, such as in the Galician regional parliament from 1908 to 1914 and in the Austrian imperial council from 1911 to 1918. Witos was, in contrast to his external appearance, an experienced career politician and parliamentarian. On the other side stood a number of intellectuals who felt connected to the peasant parties, such as the writer Maria Dąbrowska, the social worker and educator Helena Radlińska, or the sage of Polish economic and social history at Krakow's Jagiellonian University, Franciszek Bujak, who held for a short time the position of

**Image 7.2** The Sejm fraction of the PSL-Piast in 1927, seated in the middle of the front row: Wincenty Witos [Narodowe Archiwum Cyfrowe, Signature: 1-P-123]

Minister of Farming and Agriculture. Academics, such as the economist Juliusz Poniatowski or the preparatory-school teacher Maciej Rataj, were part of party leadership. Although their involvement was often explicitly emotionally motivated, their intention was to support the rural population—outside the purview of civic life in Poland for so long—in their struggle for emancipation, and to integrate them into the nation. It was no coincidence that members of professions dedicated in some fashion to education were disproportionately represented: above all teachers, but also social scientists and journalists. Their presence in the peasant movement was well received by the peasant party members and voters.[19] The intellectuals involved in the peasant movement oscillated between a commitment to altruistic engagement for something deemed good and progressive, on the one hand, and a personal ambition to be a valued adviser and patron, on the other.

The situation of Poland's national minorities also deserves a new look. Measured against the proportion of residents who were not ethnically Polish, 31.5 per cent, as reported in Poland's first census in 1921, the ethnically non-Polish population was underrepresented in the Sejm. However, the seemingly obvious comparison of percentages followed a similar logic to the social mapping experiments—an undertaking by the peasant parties and the socialists—but did not determine the material situation but the ethnicity behind each individual vote, in this case. This approach was utilized by some later studies on elections and parliamentarism in Poland.[20] Of course, as with the oft-used parliamentary handbooks by Tadeusz Rzepecki and Witold Rzepecki in interwar Poland,[21] the risk with this approach was that an apparent confrontation between individual ethnic groups would eliminate the plurality of identity and thus any possibility for cooperation. For the first time ever, new research has focused on the parliamentary practice of the parties of national minorities, in particular on the Jewish and Ukrainian parties,[22] as well as more recently the German ones.[23]

Women were the largest group to join the electorate after 1918. Women were awarded the right to vote relatively early in Poland: later than in Australia, New Zealand, and most Nordic countries, but almost simultaneously with revolutionary Germany and the Eastern European states that emerged at the end of the Russian Empire.

As a result, women were courted intensively by all political parties.[24] Conversely, many women attempted through active participation in the elections to emphasize that women's right to vote had been rightly instituted. Chants like 'Let us be good citizens, we do not abstain from elections. By fulfilling our duties, we also obtain rights'[25] demonstrate a certain insecurity in relation to the new, civic status of women—as if the granted opportunities for participation could be withdrawn in the case of 'misconduct'. Women candidates for Sejm districts were gravely underrepresented,[26] but, in electoral practice with their organizational and passionate engagement, they proved to be an essential part of the emerging mass market of politics.

The women's right to vote had quite unexpected consequences for party politics. To the dismay of the political Left, who saw itself as the pioneer of the modern women's emancipation movement, a large proportion of women voters were sympathetic to the National Democratic project and to conservative Christian parties.[27] From the perspective of many women in the PPS, it was gullibility that led a large share of their fellow women to follow the slogans 'God', 'fatherland', 'unity', and 'fraternity' promoted by the landowner aristocracy and the Catholic priesthood.[28] The political Left's dismissal of a focus on religious and traditional values in society as merely superficial reduced its access to the lives of the many women in rural and small town regions. In contrast, conservative, Catholic, and National Democratic groups had rarely done anything to bring about women's right to vote, but as soon as it was finally granted after 1918, they approached the new regulation with clear pragmatism. Now that women possessed the right to political voice, they should use it for the good of state and nation.[29]

Parliament's function as a mirror to society meant that the elites who had played a role in imperial politics prior to 1918 maintained their position. But the elite politicians, who had been socialized during the time of partition, had little practical knowledge of parliamentary democracy to draw upon. In this sense there are marked differences between Poland and Finland, for example, where for ten years up to the parliamentary elections in 1907, after leaving the Russian Empire, the parliament, the *Eduskunta*, provided a forum for discussions of parliamentary reform as well as for Socialists and Agrarians to challenge the traditional elites.[30]

It was also true that politicians from the former Habsburg Empire had very little parliamentary experience, although, according to a dominant view long held in the historical literature, the Polish population had been politically tested longer and more intensively, due to the particular autonomy arrangements. Indeed, a stronger state-building spirit emerged in Galicia. There were only subtle differences between the monarchies of Russia, Prussia, and Austria-Hungary, which gave their citizens only restricted opportunities for civic participation and only a hesitant parliamentarization.[31] In the German *Reichstag*, Poles made up one of the 'smallest parliamentary fractions', with between only 14 and 19 representatives, and achieved few successes because of their oppositional policies.[32] It is thus rather questionable to refer to the Polish fractions in Berlin as the 'forger of future Polish politicians and parliamentarians in the reconstituted Polish state'.[33] The German parliamentary representative Trąmpczyński did go on to excel in an independent Poland as parliamentary speaker; however, in the crisis of Polish democracy of the 1920s, which culminated in a seizure of power by Józef Piłsudski and his followers, Trąmpczyński and the 'Galicians' were toothless. In fact, here the fundamental question arises as to the effects of parliamentary socialization. Discussed in the historical research of parliamentarism are the effects of collectivization, thus the integration efforts of individual parliaments, as well as the opposing role of parliament as a site of ideological, national struggle.[34]

In the case of Poland, the young parliament was shaped by the encounter and interaction of politicians who cut their political teeth in the parliaments of Prussia, Germany, Austria, or Russia with representatives of a range of ethnic groups and of sections of society, such as women or farmers, which were actively participating in politics for the first time. The historical diversity of parliamentarism, which appears here only briefly, remains to a large extent an object of future study. There is a need for studies focused more strongly on the interactions between different parliamentary groups and, given the representation of national minorities, the transnational linkages in Poland's interwar parliamentarism.

## Parliament as a Site of Political Decision-Making

Perceptions of the Polish parliament in the early days of the Second Polish Republic were characterized by tension between the momentum of political participation, the traditional order, and national ideas. In any case, the parliament to be convened was confronted with high expectations, which frequently overestimated its actual potential; for example, some anticipated parliament taking decisions on Polish territorial expansion or on protective legislation for ethnic Poles living outside the territory of the newly constituted state,[35] an expectation that ignored the necessity under international law for agreement to be reached with other states on these questions. As far as internal politics were concerned, the Sejm was primarily expected to concentrate political power and strengthen national unity.

In fact, from the first meeting of the Sejm constituent assembly in 1919 to the Piłsudski coup in 1926, Poland experienced 12 governments, which were reliant on changing parliamentary majorities or, increasingly, parliamentary minorities, thereby eluding the often euphemistic label of a supposed party-neutral 'cabinet of experts'.

Such high hopes could lead only to disappointment, which set in swiftly and accordingly.

> The Sejm elections, in accordance with the five-tiered voting system, supported the emergence of new parties that were not in expression of the

actual needs of the country but of the egotism of either individual, ambitious leaders or of social groups. Additionally, a lack of political experience also led to a lack of men of stature at the forefront of public life. In their place were trouble-makers and agitators, who sweet-talked the masses. It was no surprise that the political culture was so base. Each and every daring thought attempting to bring the whole of the national interest into view drowned in the sea of demagogy. The parties' energy was spent largely on internal conflicts between different party wings and in mending ruptured parliamentary coalitions with compromises, concessions, and semi-deals, while the smaller group often tried to tip the scales and make decisions about the most important matters facing the government, even though they were neither morally nor substantively prepared to do so.[36]

By approximately the tenth anniversary of independence, the rights of broad strata of society to political participation, pluralism, and the emergence of a political mass market were being viewed less and less frequently as positive opportunities and more and more often as a danger to the structures of the still-young state. The discourse around parliamentarism in the Second Polish Republic came increasingly to be dominated by vocabulary including 'chaos', 'demagogy', 'anarchy', 'antagonism between political parties', and 'national disunity'.[37] Historians and political scientists have frequently been critical of the 'immaturity' of Poland's parliamentary democracy during this period.[38]

The criticism levelled by the contemporary elite at the 'lack of political culture' in Poland's young democracy was, however, frequently self-contradictory, bemoaning both the population's supposed passivity and its over-politicization. It is apparent that a clear idea of elections and the parliamentary system as a structured arena of conflict, its airing, and resolution was not rooted at this time in Polish political culture. The standards by which parliamentary democracy was judged were confused by both the continued prevalence of unprocessed experiences from the pre-democratic era and the omnipresent contemporary call to national unity.

Historians' assessments of 'immature' parliamentarism and of the 'delayed' onset of parliamentarism, as discussed with great impact in the academic community with regard to the Eastern and Central European countries, including Germany and Austria, represent emphatically normative approaches to these issues. Such views are not without their legitimacy within an academic discipline committed to the promotion of and education about democracy; nevertheless, they also carry the implication that there is a 'right' time for parliamentarism and that parliamentarism can function only under specific institutional and cultural conditions. This is precisely what the early historical research called into question. In the renunciation of a normative-teleological perspective, with its focus on the successive implementation of democratic-parliamentarian institutions in linear sequence—thus extending to an imaginary point of departure in the present period of a 'fully ripened' Western democracy—the history of democracy is now conceptualized globally and fundamentally as a history of 'a perpetual attempt',[39] highlighting the repeated alternation between 'democratization and de-democratization forces'.[40] Hence, democracy and parliamentarism are not just a matter of course; they must be continually won and claimed anew.

## THE COUP OF 1926 AS A CHALLENGE
## TO THE PARLIAMENTARY SYSTEM IN POLAND

Coup d'états and counter-revolutions had become a signature of European politics in the interwar period and provided a substantial challenge to parliamentarism. That was also the case with the coup d'état led by Piłsudski in 1926 and the charismatic rule he subsequently exercised for the next decade. Of all the causes for the coup, the anti-pluralistic discourse proved to have particularly serious consequences—a discourse positioned in opposition to the parliament as a site of political decision-making. The concrete impetus for this in the spring of 1926 was the formation of another governmental coalition of the National Democrats, the Christian Democrats, and the PSL-Piast under Minister-president Wincenty Witos: Piłsudski saw the protests by military wives and the political Left against the new government as convenient pretext to bring troops loyal to him back to Warsaw on 12 May. After many days of fighting in the capital, during which PPS and unions supported Piłsudski with a general strike, the Witos government was forced to abdicate.

The coup did not lead to the dissolution of the Sejm, and elections continued to be held. Indeed, in the classroom, independent Poland continued to be proudly presented to students in the shape of dignitaries of the state, such as the provincial governor (*wojewoda*) and the *district governor (starosta)*, other government officials and teachers, and in the form of the work of the Sejm and the Senate.[41] The respect we observe here being accorded to parliamentary institutions in this authoritarian environment will surprise us only at first glance; it is the continuation of the strand of belief that saw the Polish parliament's value less in its democratic function than in its capacity to represent the nation. This made it unnecessary for the authoritarian regime in Poland to act in an extra-parliamentary manner; all it needed to do was to effectively domesticate parliament.[42]

Just as with the idea of parliament as a national symbol, the idea of parliament as the mirror of society lived on after 1926. The large and outstanding task of bringing more women into Parliament was accomplished little by little by Józef Piłsudski's party the 'Nonpartisan Block of Collaboration with Government' (BBWR, Bezpartyjny Blok Współpracy z Rządem), beginning in 1926. In doing so, the BBWR provided emancipation-oriented women's organizations with a political platform[43] and challenged the traditionally strong influence of the Catholic Church on women (Image 7.3).

Representatives of the authoritarian regime also encouraged efforts towards a 'social democracy'[44] in the years following, resulting in an organization of political life based on the corporate model. The April 1935

**Image 7.3** Women from the Sejm BBWR fraction (Nonpartisan Block of Collaboration with Government) 1930 [Narodowe Archiwum Cyfrowe, Signature: 1-A-1113-1]

constitution and the new voting regulations of the Sejm and the Senate issued on 8 July 1935 marked the first steps towards practical implementation. The introduction of a collective candidate list for every district, instead of different party lists, reduced the generality of the vote and eliminated the principle of proportional voting. A more drastic affront to democratic conventions was the change in the election of the senate. Now, one third of the senate was to be chosen by the president and two thirds of the senators chosen through a closed ballot by electoral vote.

After 1926, the parties and movements of the opposition had similar thoughts about the future of Poland's political system. What alternatives were there to an authoritarian regime? This question was met with a wide range of answers, from the strengthening of participatory elements to fascism-inspired regime models.

The Left, having since distanced itself quite significantly from its original support of Piłsudski, stood for keeping the five-tiered voting system, made its constituency aware of the still effective voting system of 1922 and its concomitant democratic principles, and encouraged real resistance to ballot rigging.[45] Even some representatives of right-wing, religious circles joined efforts to defend the voting rights of citizens,[46] collected information to document the Sanacja's violations of the constitution and standing voting regulations,[47] and completely and fundamentally criticized the authoritarian consolidation of state power.[48]

An unadulterated revival of parliamentary democracy appeared to another segment of the opposition, in its current form just as it was in the early interwar period, hardly promising in the face of the ease with which the political system had been overturned since 1926. Thoughts from the ranks of the National Democratic movement initially circled around a departure from proportional voting and the introduction of the majority vote, in order to render future parliamentary compromises and coalitions superfluous. This intention was quite practically the result of the parliamentary experience of the National Democratic movement, which emerged as the strongest power in the elections from 1919 to 1922, being ultimately unable to implement their political ideas for more than a short period of time due to unstable coalition-building. To underpin their demands following a new voting system, many National Democrats pointed to the example of France or England.[49]

Yet more perceived challenges arose from the proposed transference of the Western model to the Polish situation. In their argumentation, the National Democrats criticized the proportion of ethnically non-Polish groups in parliamentary representation. In their view, the current voting system paid too much attention to non-Polish groups, preventing the establishment of both a stable majority in the Sejm and constructive politics. Thus, a new voting system needed to be established, first and foremost, so that the ethnically Polish population could carry the responsibility of government 'as master of their own country'.[50]

Moving away from the 'Western' track allowed for attention to be turned to a 'Polish' pathway to(ward) democracy. The most important constitutive element was the constitution of 3 May 1791. One of Poland's most influential historians, Oswald Balzer, who decidedly referenced autochthone Polish and Slavic developments in his work on the constitutional history of the Middle Ages, deemed the May constitution a valuable and significant contribution, the result of Poland's own efforts: It was not a mere adoption of the Western model; rather, it was 'something that emerged from ourselves, something for which we, in the worst case, are alone responsible and which, in the best case, might bring us due credit and fame'.[51] Despite the differences in opinion on parliamentary democracy, National Democrats, as well as peasant parties and socialists, showed up for the parliamentary elections in the first years of the authoritarian regime, as an alternative to BBWR, in the hope that, despite official repression and the manipulation of election results, their political ideas would still reach the stage of the Sejm and thus be made visible to the public.

The death of Piłsudski provided new hope to the opposition, which planned to organize a boycott of the 1935 elections to the Sejm, in order to draw attention to the undemocratic regulations governing them and the disempowerment of the parliament[52] and inspire a renewal of Polish parliamentarism. This strategy, however, was to fail; the Catholic Church had set itself the goal of using the elections to ensure that the Sejm contained a significant number of its adherents, which meant it was prepared, for pragmatic reasons, if not to give its seal of approval to the authoritarianism of Polish political culture, at least to accept it.

The sections of the opposition that spoke out in support of parliamentary democracy—primarily the socialists and the farmers' movement, but also the liberal wing of the National Democracy organization—thus found themselves, in a paradoxical circumstance, forced to resort to extra-parliamentary methods. In the second half of the 1930s, public space, the 'street', became a key stage on which political conflict was enacted; processions, parades, and public rallies drew considerable attention. Supporters of parliamentarism were not only confronted with other ideas for the political mobilization of the masses, such as fascism and the left-wing 'popular front', but also frequently found themselves drawn into the political culture of the 1930s, which was characterized by the militarization of the discourse and the surrounding symbolism and behaviour, the ideal of perpetual mobilization and 'readiness for battle', and the tendency to espouse 'revolutionary' solutions to problems. In this, the contradictory climate of the interwar years in Europe reveals itself, with democracy and parliamentarism being matters of mobilization rather than established components of everyday political life.

The early excitement surrounding the parliamentarism of 1918 in a newly independent Poland did not turn into wide acceptance of parliament as an ideal. In its place, different ideas of parliamentarism existed—in some ways in competition with one another and capable of being applied to different political contexts, including even the autocratic rule of 1926.

## NOTES

1. Eric J. Hobsbawm, *Age of Extremes. The short twentieth century, 1914–1991* (London: Little, Brown Book Group, 1995; 7th ed.); Mark Mazower, *Dark Continent. Europe's twentieth century* (New York: Random House USA Inc., 2000); Harold James, *Europe Reborn. A history, 1914–2000* (Harlow: Taylor & Francis Ltd., 2003).
2. AAN, *Akta Leona Wasilewskiego*, 65, p. 10.
3. 'Ze Stowarzyszenia Ziemianek' in *Ziemianka*, 7, 1918, p. 180–3; 'Ze Zjazdu Walnego Zjednocz. Ziemianek dnia 12, 13 i 14 czerwca 1919 r.' in *Ziemianka*, 8, 1919, p. 120.
4. GUS, *Statystyka wyborów 1922*, p. XI; Tadeusz Rzepecki and Witold Rzepecki, *Sejm i Senat 1922–1927. Podręcznik dla wyborców* (Poznań: Rzepecki Karol, 1923) 478 and 482.
5. Zofia Nałkowska, 'Zameczek 6 XI 1922' in Nałkowska, *Dzienniki*, vol. 3, 1918–1929 (Warsaw: Czytelnik, 1980) 94–5.
6. John Keane, *The Life and Death of Democracy* (London: Simon and Schuster UK, 2009) XIV.
7. Paul Nolte, *Was ist Demokratie? Geschichte und Gegenwart* (Bonn: C.H. Beck, 2012) 11 and 225.
8. Andreas Schulz and Andreas Wirsching, 'Parlamentarische Kulturen in Europa–Das Parlament als Kommunikationsraum' in Andreas Schulz and Andreas Wirsching (eds.), *Parlamentarische Kulturen in Europa. Das Parlament als Kommunikationsraum* (Düsseldorf: Droste, 2012) 12.
9. Ibid.; Thomas Mergel, 'Parlamentarische Kulturen in der Moderne–Brüche und Kontonuitäten' in Jörg Feuchter and Johannes Helmrath

(eds.), *Parlamentarische Kulturen vom Mittelalter bis in die Moderne: Reden, Räume, Bilder* (Düsseldorf: Droste, 2013) 35–50; Adéla Gjuričová and Andreas Schulz, 'Über die Köpfe der Menschen hinweg? Lebenswelten von Abgeordneten in der Moderne' in Adéla Gjuričová et al. (eds.), *Lebenswelten von Abgeordneten in Europa 1860–1990* (Düsseldorf: Droste, 2014) 10.

10. Nolte, *Was ist Demokratie?*, 223; Keane, *Life and Death of Democracy*, 567.

11. Nolte, *Was ist Demokratie?*, 241.

12. Andrzej Gwiżdż, 'Sejm i Senat w latach 1918–1939' in Juliusz Bardach (ed.), *Dzieje Sejmu Polskiego* (Warsaw: Wydawnictwo Sejmowe, 1993) 147.

13. Cornelia Illie and Cezar M. Ornatowski, 'Central and Eastern European Parliamentary Rhetoric since the Nineteenth Century: The Case of Romania and Poland' in Pasi Ihalainen, Cornelia Illie and Kari Palonen (eds.), *Parliament and Parliamentarism. A Comparative History of a European Concept* (New York/Oxford: Berghahn Books, 2016) 204. Of course, such a self-confident claim often clashes with other countries' claims of democratic and parliamentary traditions, for example, in the Nordic Countries. See Uffe Jakobson and Jussi Kurunmäki, 'The Formation of Parliamentarism in the Nordic Countries from the Napoleonic Wars to the First World War' in: Ibid., 97–114.

14. Ustawa z dnia 17 marca 1921 r., 'Konstytucja Rzeczypospolitej Polskiej' in Wanda Sudnik, *Prawo polityczne Rzeczypospolitej Polskiej. Wybór źródeł* (Warsaw: Wydawnictwo Sejmowe, 2002) 60–1.

15. Stanisław Piekarski, *Wyznania religijne w Polsce* (Warsaw: M. Arct) 11–12.

16. Stefan Michalski, 'Moja droga do Klubu Sprawodawców Parlamentarnych' in Jerzy Łojek (ed.), *Moja droga do dziennikarstwa. Wspomnienia dziennikarzy polskich z okresu międzywojennego (1918–1939)* (Warsaw: Państwowe Wydawnictwo Naukowe, 1974) 225.

17. A. Grzybowska, 'Wielki dzień' in *Ziemianka*, 8, 1919, p. 51.

18. 'Złożenie krzyża w Sejmie' in *Ziemianka*, 8, 1919, pp. 142–3; 'Z walnego zgromadzenia Zjednoczonego Koła Ziemianek w Warszawie' in *Ziemianka*, 9, 1920, p. 20.

19. Gerhard Doliesen, *Die polnische Bauernpartei 'Wyzwolenie' in den Jahren 1918–1926* (Marburg: Herder-Institut, 1995) 59–63.

20. See Paweł Korzec, 'Der Block der Nationalen Minderheiten im Parlamentarismus Polens des Jahres 1922' in *Zeitschrift für Ostforschung* 24 (1975); Ludwik Hass, *Wybory warszawskie 1918–1926. Postawy polityczne mieszkańców Warszawy w świetle wyników głosowania do ciał przedstawicielskich* (Warsaw: Państwowe Wydawnictwo Naukowe, 1972).

21. Tadeusz Rzepecki, *Sejm Rzeczypospolitej Polskiej 1919 roku* (Poznań: Nakł. Wielkopolskiej Księgarni Nakładowej, 1920); Tadeusz Rzepecki and Witold Rzepecki, *Sejm i Senat 1922–1927. Podręcznik dla wyborców* (Poznań: Rzepecki Karol, 1923).

22. Szymon Rudnicki, *Żydzi w parlamencie II Rzeczypospolitej* (Warsaw: Wydawnictwo Sejmowe, 2004); Mirosław Szumiło, *Ukraińska Reprezentacja Parlamentarna w Sejmie i Senacie RP (1928–1939)* (Warsaw: Wydawnictwo Neriton, 2007).

23. Benjamin Conrad, *Loyalitäten, Identitäten und Interessen. Deutsche Parlamentarier im Lettland und Polen der Zwischenkriegszeit (1918–1935)* (Göttingen: V&R unipress, 2016).

24. Michał Śliwa, 'Udział kobiet w wyborach i ich działalność parlamentarna' in Anna Żarnowska and Andrzej Szwarc (eds.), *Równe prawa i nierówne szanse. Kobiety w Polsce międzywojennej* (Warsaw: Wydawnictwo DiG 2000) 50–1.

25. 'Wybory' in *Ziemianka*, 7, 1918, p. 197.

26. GUS, *Statystyka wyborów 1922*, p. IX.

27. Dobrochna Kałwa, 'Politische Emanzipation durch nationale Mobilisierung? Bemerkungen zur Aktivität von Frauen im polnischen nationalen Lager der Zweiten Republik' in Johanna Gehmacher, Elizabeth Harvey and Sophia Kemlein (eds.), *Zwischen Kriegen. Nationen, Nationalismen und Geschlechterverhältnisse in Mittel- und Osteuropa 1918–1939* (Osnabrück: Fibre, 2004) 51–5; Arkadiusz Kołodziejczyk, *Ruch ludowy a Kościół rzymskokatolicki w latach II Rzeczypospolitej* (Warsaw: Ludowa Spółdzielnia Wydawnicza, 2002) 124–6 and 131.

28. AAN, *PPS*, 114/IV-3, p. 1.

29. 'Z walnego zgromadzenia Zjednoczonego Koła Ziemianek w Warszawie' in *Ziemianka*, 8, 1919, pp. 1–8.

30. Pasi Ihalainen, *The Springs of Democracy. National and Transnational Debates on Constitutional Reform in the British, German, Swedish and Finnish Parliaments, 1917–1919* (Helsinki: Finnish Literature Society, 2017) 63–65.

31. Christoph Schönberger, 'Die überholte Parlamentarisierung. Einflußgewinn und fehlende Herrschaftsfähigkeit des Reichstags im sich demokratisierenden Kaiserreich' in *Historische Zeitschrift* 272 (2001); Gerhard A. Ritter, 'Die Reichstagswahlen und die Wurzeln der deutschen Demokratie im Kaiserreich' in *Historische Zeitschrift* 275 (2002).

32. Albert Kotowski, *Zwischen Staatsräson und Vaterlandsliebe. Die polnische Fraktion im deutschen Reichstag, 1871–1918* (Dusseldorf: Droste, 2007) 195.

33. Ibid, 197.

34. Gjuričová and Schulz, 'Über die Köpfe', 13.

35. 'Ze Zjazdu Walnego Zjednocz. Ziemianek dnia 12, 13 i 14 czerwca 1919 r.' in *Ziemianka*, 8, 1919, p. 135; 'Raport polityczno-informacyjny Sztabu Generalnego WP o sytuacji w Okręgach: Warszawskim, Łódzkim, Krakowskim, Kieleckim, 4. 1. 1919' in Marek Jabłonowski, Piotr Stawecki and Tadeusz Wawrzyński (eds.), *O niepodległą i granice, vol. 2: Raporty i komunikaty Naczelnych Władz Wojskowych o sytuacji wewnętrznej w Polsce 1919–1920* (Warsaw/Pułtusk: Wydział Dziennikarstwa i Nauk Politycznych UW–Wyższa Szkoła Humanistyczna, 2001) 22.

36. Tad. Bielecki, 'Demagogja bezpartyjna' in *Gazeta Warszawska*, 1 May 1928, p. 3.

37. *APW*, UW Warszawski, 46, pp. 85–6; 'Wybory' in *Polska Zbrojna*, 18 August 1922, p. 1.

38. Karl J. Newman, *Zerstörung und Selbstzerstörung der Demokratie. Europa 1918–1938* (Stuttgart: S. Hirzel, 1984; 2nd ed.) 115; Theodor Eschenburg, 'Der Zerfall der demokratischen Ordnungen zwischen dem Ersten und dem Zweiten Weltkrieg' in Eschenberg et al., *Der Weg in die Diktatur 1918 bis 1933* (Munich: Piper, 1962) 15–16: 'The democracies of southern and south-eastern Europe were improvised democracies, unprepared for intellectually and [therefore] lacking the stage of development through which traditional democracies had passed.' Jörg K. Hoensch, *Geschichte Polens* (Stuttgart: Ulmer, 1998, 3rd ed., p. 265) assessed the democratic phase of the Second Republic as an 'extreme form of parliamentarism'.

39. Nolte, *Was ist Demokratie?*, 9.

40. Agnes Laba, Maria Wojtczak, '"Aufbruch zur Demokratie?"–Aspekte einer Demokratiegeschichte Ostmitteleuropas (1918–1939)' in *Zeitschrift für Ostmitteleuropaforschung* 64 (2015) 2, p. 165.

41. *Dlaczego świętujemy dziesiątą rocznicę odzyskania Niepodległości 1918–1928?* (Warsaw: Wydawnictwo Biura Ogólnoorganizacyjnego Ministerstwa Spraw Wojskowych, 1928) 10–13 and 28.

42. Adam Próchnik, 'Przeciw fałszowaniu demokracji' in *Robotnik*, 8 May 1938, p. 4.

43. Andrzej Chojnowski, 'Aktywność kobiet w życiu politycznym' in Żarnowska and Szwarc, *Równe prawa*, 38.

44. Wojtas, A., 'Mit demokracji politycznej a demokratyzacja' in W. Wojdyło (ed.), *Wychowanie a polityka. Mity i stereotypy w polskiej myśli społecznej XX wieku* (Toruń: Wydawnictwo Uniwersytetu Mikołaja Kopernika, 2000) 26.

45. 'O wyborach' in *Wyzwolenie*, 26 October 1930, p. 4–5; R. W., 'Trzeba strzec tajności głosowania' in *Wyzwolenie*, 9 November 1930, p. 5.

46. AAN, 'Zbiór druków ulotnych', *Sign*, 103, p. 43.

47. 'Poufny Komunikat Informacyjny nr 80 (10 III 1928)' in Ministerstwo Spraw Wewnętrznych (ed.), *Komunikaty Informacyjne Komisariatu Rządu na m. st. Warszawę*, Bd. 2, H. 1 (3 stycznia 1928–26 czerwca 1928) (Warsaw: Ministerstwo Spraw Wewnętrznych i Administracji, 1992) 129.

48. Roman Rybarski, 'Ultrademokratyczna elita' in *Gazeta Warszawska*, 12 August 1928, p. 3.
49. AAN, 'Zbiór druków ulotnych', *Sign.* 73, p. 59.
50. Ibid.; Krzysztof Kawalec, *Spadkobiercy niepokornych. Dzieje polskiej myśli politycznej 1918–1939* (Wrocław: Zakład Narodowy im. Ossolińskich, 2000) 96.
51. Oswald Balzer, 'Konstytucja Trzeciego Maja' in *Warszawski Dziennik Narodowy*, 3 May 1936, p. 3.
52. Henryk Swoboda, 'Źródła apatji wyborczej' in *Robotnik*, 4 August 1935, p. 4.

# CHAPTER 8

# Closing the Expectation Gap? Crisis of Hungarian Parliamentarism in the Inter-War Period

## Kálmán Pócza

In the mid-1920s, the Inter-Parliamentary Union (IPU) recognized the widespread discontent of the electorate with the parliamentary system of government in general and, more specifically, with the institution of parliaments in many European countries. The IPU asked some internationally renowned experts to share their views on the causes and consequences of this crisis and formulated at the same time a resolution that included some proposals about how the crisis could be overcome. The Hungarian National Group of the IPU forwarded the proposals to politicians and scholars and published an edited volume with reactions from the Hungarian respondents in 1929. This chapter will present an overview of these reactions, but first we will present a narrative framework that might be applied to the Hungarian reactions to the IPU proposals (section 'Narrative Framework: The Crisis of Parliamentarism and the Expectation Gap'). Secondly, we will delineate the general political context in Hungary with

K. Pócza (✉)
Hungarian Academy of Sciences, Budapest, Hungary

Pázmány Péter Catholic University/National University of Public Service, Budapest, Hungary
e-mail: pocza.kalman@btk.ppke.hu

© The Author(s) 2019
R. Aerts et al. (eds.), *The Ideal of Parliament in Europe since 1800*,
Palgrave Studies in Political History,
https://doi.org/10.1007/978-3-030-27705-5_8

special reference to the development of Hungarian parliamentarism in the inter-war period (section 'Developments of Parliamentarism in Hungary in the Inter-War Period'). Thirdly, we will give some insights into the public discourse on the crisis of parliamentarism (section 'Developments of the Political Discourse on Parliamentarism'), and fourthly we will analyse the Hungarian reactions to the IPU proposals (section 'Hungarian Reactions to the IPU Draft Resolution from 1928').

## NARRATIVE FRAMEWORK: THE CRISIS OF PARLIAMENTARISM AND THE EXPECTATION GAP

Parliamentarism or parliamentary government has always been considered as being in perpetual crisis since it became the dominant form of government around the mid-nineteenth century.[1] The *crisis narrative* has been frequently connected with the idealization of a never existing Golden Age of parliamentarism, as expressed in the narrative also known as the 'decline of parliamentarism' or 'parliamentary decline thesis' (PDT). This view has been dominant not only among scholars of legislative studies but also in twentieth-century public discourse and continues to exercise a broad influence on the image of parliaments even today.[2] Certainly, there are differences in degree, but if one had a general and detailed overview of how European parliaments have been perceived by both scholars and the public from the late nineteenth century on, one would be confronted with a scene full of disappointment and frustration. In the absence of such a comprehensive overview, we are inclined to *assume* that public and scholarly *perceptions* of parliaments have never been very positive. Since parliaments became the focal point of political decision making, that is, after the introduction of representative and responsible government, the general impression has been that the state of parliamentarism was far from the ideal, which was posited as existing decades or even centuries earlier. The parliamentary form of government has always been in decline and has never met the expectations of both the public sphere and the academy.[3] Crisis is certainly not an ephemeral concomitance of parliamentarism but its substantive attribution—or at least parliamentarism has always been *perceived* in that way.

### *The Dominant Narrative: Parliamentary Government in Crisis*

As Gerhard Loewenberg noted as early as the 1970s, modern parliaments experienced at least three different crises beginning in the late nineteenth century. The *first crisis* emerged as political parties became the central political actors in parliaments and during the election campaigns in the late nineteenth and early twentieth centuries. The extension of voting rights meant that ever wider strata of the society would have to be reached by the politicians. But to be able to address and get the vote of the electorate, politicians and political movements needed to be more organized. The emergence of mass parties changed the nature of how parliaments worked: party discipline began to dominate the parliamentary work, which was seemingly in contradiction with the former practice of parliamentary work and with the principle of free mandate and rational discussion. *Incongruence emerged* between the demand or expectation of government by rational discussion and the realities of political life dominated by mass parties and party discipline. According to the general assessment of public opinion and scholars, parliaments performed very poorly concerning their *function of linkage* or representation (representation and articulation).[4]

The *second crisis* became apparent as the scope of the government increased and public policies became more and more complex: welfare demands of the electorate put parliaments under pressure, and they had difficulty coping with the ever expanding scope of legislation. Parliaments were deprived of both capacities and competencies (expertise) to implement public policies that could meet (or moderate) the welfare expectations of the electorate. In the 1930s parliaments in European countries found themselves under pressure from the electorate. *Incongruence emerged* between the demand (expectation) of implementing welfare measures and the real capacities and competencies of parliaments. According to the general assessment of public opinion and scholars, parliaments performed very poorly concerning their *function of welfare legislation, lawmaking* or policy making.

The *third crisis* ensued after World War II. Due to the continuously increasing scope of legislation, parliaments had to delegate ever more tasks to the executive, which, in turn, became the more dominant player on the political field. Informational asymmetry between the executive and the legislature became the normal practice, where the executive has the expertise in the policy details and the MPs' role becomes limited to supporting the governments' activity. This development led to executive domination of parliaments, which became the focal point of the third crisis of parliamentarism. *Incongruence* emerged between the principle of parliamentary sovereignty and the real dominance of the government over legislation. According to the general assessment of public opinion and scholars, parliaments performed very poorly concerning *their function of controlling* and oversight of government.[5]

Although Loewenberg presented a highly plausible narrative of the three crises of parliamentarism, we need to amend his narrative with references to the pertinent *causes* of these crises. The parliamentary decline thesis (PDT) identified the causes by referring to the *supply* side of the story, that is, to the poor performance of the parliaments and the parliamentary system. The PDT assumes implicitly an ideal situation by setting the criteria of (1) rational discussion, (2) effective (welfare) legislation and (3) parliamentary supremacy (vis-à-vis the executive) and concludes that current practices of parliaments and parliamentary government do not meet these criteria. Consequently, the real *cause* of the decline or crisis lies on the *supply side*, that is, on the inferior performance of the parliamentary system.

### The Counter-Narrative: The Expectation Gap Generated by Excessive Demands

There is, however, an ever growing literature reflecting another approach, which argues that the general *impression* of underperformance and inadequacy of parliaments and parliamentary systems is not only exaggerated but is, in fact, generated partly by the *excessive demands* on and expectations regarding the parliamentary system.[6] By taking the general functions of parliaments into account, this literature argues that the public and the academic community impose extremely high demands on parliaments concerning their representative function (government by discussion and articulation of common interest; linkage between electorate and political decision making), their legislative function (welfare regulations and ever-widening scope of policy making) and their control and oversight function (selection and removal of governments; control of government).

This literature does not deny that parliaments and their functions underwent intense *transformation* in the twentieth century but argues that the general impression of never-ending *decline* is rooted rather in unrealistic and ever growing expectations formulated by both the public and the scholarly community.[7] Idealized rational discussion, exaggerated welfare demands, an ever-widening scope of legislation and overestimated capacities and competencies of the MPs have generated false and unfulfilled expectations among the public. This *expectation gap* cannot be closed simply by trying to reform the practices of the parliamentary governments and parliaments. This gap might be closed only by trying to explain the limits of parliamentary work and by moderating the expectations towards the parliamentary system. Extreme, unrealistic and idealistic expectations will continue to generate crises that cannot be avoided or remedied by technical tinkering of the practices of parliamentarism. The fundamental thesis of this counter-narrative is that the key to crisis management lies not in *intra-parliamentary* but *in extra-parliamentary factors*. Scholars and public debate should try to *reduce unrealistic expectations* among the electorate by informing them about the real capacities and competences of the parliaments and the parliamentary system. Political education with a realistic approach to parliaments could help in decreasing the excessive demands from the electorate.[8]

This conclusion serves as the point of departure of our *historical* study of the crisis of parliamentarism in Hungary in the inter-war period. By stressing the importance of *extra-parliamentary factors* in overcoming the crisis of parliamentarism in the late 1920s, and emphasizing the role of political education, influential Hungarians of the inter-war period tried to reshape public discussion on the crisis of parliamentarism. While not denying the existence of problems, most of them were convinced that reforming how parliament worked (*intra-parliamentary factors*) might generate *only minor changes* in the performance and general perception of the Hungarian parliament. Technical adjustments in how parliaments work would not be a successful tool for overcoming the alleged crisis of parliamentarism. Consequently, they concluded that one should implement changes not (only) on the *supply* side (how parliaments work) but more on the *demand* side (what exactly will be expected from parliamentary government). And the key to this change is *political education* that gives a *realistic* picture/idea about the exact functions of parliament.

Before presenting the views of highly respected figures from Hungary's inter-war period, we need a general account of Hungarian parliamentarism of this era in order to locate those views that might be identified as manifestations of what we might call a counter-narrative of the PDT.

## Developments of Parliamentarism in Hungary in the Inter-War Period

After World War I, the Habsburg Empire broke up and Hungary became an independent state but at the same time lost two thirds of its territory and almost two thirds of its population.[9] This 'truncated Hungary' (*Csonka-Magyarország*), as it was called in the inter-war period, underwent further radical changes in its system of government. Following a rapid revolution from 28 to 31 October 1918, Charles IV, the last Habsburg Emperor, resigned and acknowledged the new system of government of Hungary in advance. This 'Declaration of Eckartsau' opened the way to the First Hungarian Republic, which was proclaimed on 16 November 1918. On the same day, the Lower Chamber of the Hungarian Parliament dissolved itself. Hungary was ruled without any legislative assemblies until 16 February 1920, and it survived even the short-lived rule of Hungarian Soviet Republic (21 March–1 August 1919)—an event with fateful consequences.

Although the First Republic replaced the Kingdom of Hungary, the exact form of government had still to be defined more accurately after the fall of the Hungarian Soviet Republic. Consequently, establishing the new system of government was a major challenge that the new National Assembly, elected by an almost entirely universal suffrage, had to face after its summoning on 16 February 1920.[10] While it was clear that parliament would play the key role in the new form of government, due to the tradition of the Hungarian Kingdom and the explicit pressures from political groups of legitimists advocating the restoration of the Kingdom (and especially the return of Charles IV), many questions regarding the structure of the Hungarian state remained unresolved.[11]

The debates over the appropriate title and constitutional powers of the new head of the state, and the relationship between the head of the state and the parliament recalled the special form of Hungarian parliamentarism of the late nineteenth century. While the self-image of the Hungarian parliament suggested that it was a full-blooded parliament, the practice showed some deficiencies. Changes in government either were completely absent between 1867 and 1918 or, if they happened, caused major constitutional crisis as in 1905–1906. Even more importantly, the dominant view among politicians and scholars interested in public law or politics was that the real form of parliamentarism presupposes a *balance* of power between the monarch and the parliament. Certainly, the determinative principle of the British form of government resembled this definition, but a major difference revealed itself in the *practice* of British parliamentarism. While the King of Hungary preserved the prerogative of confirming all legislative acts not only formally and theoretically but *in practice*, the British monarch's competences and veto power had decayed gradually, leading to an atrophy of this prerogative. However moderately Emperor Franz Joseph embraced the opportunity to veto legislative acts, this modesty and restraint did not preclude getting involved in daily politics in

Hungary.[12] Consequently, the dominant view and *practice* in Hungarian public life was that the head of the state, that is, the King of Hungary, still held veto power concerning legislative acts and the appointment of the Prime Minister. This dominant view survived not only among members of the legitimist group supporting the restoration of the Kingdom of Hungary but also among MPs of the National Assembly in 1920. Consequently, the questions regarding which competences the new head of the state should have and what would be the relationship between parliament and the head of the state were key issues of the first legislative term.

Nevertheless, power relations within the first National Assembly implied and intensified uncertainty instead of providing clear solutions in this respect. While the Social Democratic Party of Hungary (*Magyarországi Szociáldemokrata Párt, MSZDP*) boycotted the election in 1920, the two main parties which together received more than 80 per cent of the mandates were loose conglomerates based on fusions of various political movements.[13] This led to a situation where fragmentation, cleavages crossing party lines and diverging conceptions of how Hungary should be governed in the future hindered the adoption of a definitive or final solution regarding the form of government. Since reaching a final decision seemed to be almost inconceivable, MPs agreed on a *provisional* or temporary settlement.[14]

Convergence among competing ideas and parliamentary groups could be seen in their treatment of two questions: the restoration of constitutionality and establishing the interim position of the Governor. While Act I of 1920 declared the exclusive sovereignty of parliament, it established the position of Governor at the same time.[15] Although this Act provided only a weak position for the Governor and a strong parliament with full sovereignty, the idea of a *real* balance of power between the head of the state and the parliament survived in the tradition of doctrine of Holy Crown.[16] This tradition along with political developments led to the gradual extension of the competences of the Governor in the late 1920s and even more in the 1930s, to such a point that the Prime Minister had to enjoy not only the confidence of a parliamentary majority but also the Governor's trust. Consequently, the parliamentarism of the 1920s when the PM depended only on a parliamentary majority had been transformed into a specific version of parliamentarism similar to the pre-war situation in Hungary. In this specific form of parliamentarism, the PM depended on both the Governor and a parliamentary majority, and the *real* balance of power emerged between the Governor and the parliament. Certainly, it was an 'asymmetrical balance' in the sense that parliament was the dominant player, but the legislature was seriously constrained by the Governor. Moreover, some scholars argue that, by the end of the 1930s, it was the Governor who had the upper hand.[17]

## DEVELOPMENTS OF THE POLITICAL DISCOURSE ON PARLIAMENTARISM

Beyond these changes *of* Hungarian parliamentarism, the political discourse *on* the parliamentary system brought also some novelties in the 1920s. While the dominant view was that of a self-confident and proud Hungarian parliament with long-standing traditions that determined Hungarian political life and constitutional discussions, this ideal has been challenged and partly replaced by the narrative of the crisis of parliamentarism in the inter-war period. While debates *on* parliamentarism *within* the parliament have certainly more direct impact on the practice of parliamentarism, journal articles provide more thorough scrutiny and argumentation. Below, we will give an overview of the general assessments of the crisis of parliamentarism contained in journal articles published from the late 1920s to the late 1930s. We leave the analysis of parliamentary debates for another occasion.[18]

There were three types of reflections on the crisis of parliamentarism to be found in the most important journals dealing with political developments.[19] The *first group* of authors were convinced that the problems of parliamentarism originated in the emergence of mass democracies and mass parties, which dominated political and parliamentary life at least since World War I. They would have preserved the parliamentary system as it emerged in the mid-nineteenth century and were highly critical of mass parties and even more of mass democracy in general. According to these liberal-conservative authors, parliament was not a manifestation of popular but rather national sovereignty.[20] They held that democratization of the state and parliament led to the rule of passions and rages of the uneducated and pauper lower classes. While politics was not for everybody, and especially not for uneducated, lower-class people, mass parties and mass democracy could easily pave the way to dictatorship and demolition of the parliamentary system. Universal suffrage caused more problems, and representatives of this elitist-aristocratic parliamentarism would have preferred to return to the ideal and practice of nineteenth-century parliamentarism. As previously argued, this first crisis of parliamentarism was seen as a crisis of the representative function of parliaments. While the limited number of interests to be represented in the legislatures of the late nineteenth and early twentieth century facilitated rational discussion, universal suffrage and the emergence of mass parties transformed the chambers of parliaments into a jungle of interests and parliamentary elections into demagogic campaigns. Both election campaigns and discussions in parliament lost their rational character, and the cause of the crisis could therefore be found in universal suffrage. Surely, this argument had some weaknesses in Hungary where suffrage was guaranteed to approximately 30 per cent of the population and open voting was a practice in 80 per cent of the constituencies.[21] Nevertheless, the pressure of the democratization of parliaments was considered by these authors not as a solution to but as a possible escalation of the problems and crisis of parliamentarism.

In sharp contrast to this analysis and conclusion, other authors argued that the main problem was to be found in the defective democratic character of Hungarian parliamentarism. Thus democratization (manifested principally in the introduction of universal suffrage) would not escalate but help to overcome the crisis. In contrast to several Western European countries where universal suffrage had been introduced, in Hungary, following an interim regulation (1919–1920), universal suffrage had been heavily limited.[22] Authors from the left-wing and liberal political camps believed that social inequalities and injustices might be cured by the simultaneous extension of voting rights and a redistribution of wealth. They were convinced that a democratized parliament could take effective measures of redistribution. Journals connected to the social democrats (*Szocializmus*) and civic radicals (*Századunk*) argued not only for universal suffrage and the secret ballot, but also for the elimination of social injustices still prevalent in Hungarian society. Although social democrats were present in the parliament, intellectuals associated with the party criticized the parliamentary system of the inter-war period in these journals by describing it as a feudal and reactionary vestige to be abolished in order to improve the situation of the working class. The semi-legal status of the movements and intellectuals of social democrats and civic radicals was reflected in their approach to the parliamentarism of the inter-war period. Parliament was a safe space for social democrats, open debate was secured and MPs could express their views within the chambers of parliament without risking repression. In contrast to this freedom *in* the parliament, journalists of the left-wing daily press were constrained by various administrative measures of the government. Thus freedom of the press in general was more limited than freedom of expression in the parliament.[23] Authors of intellectual journals close to the left-wing-liberal parliamentary opposition were highly critical of existing parliamentary practices, but they did not have to fear repression, unlike their colleagues at the daily press. Although Social Democratic MPs published in these journals, several articles criticized the official party position of the MSZDP, which became part of the political establishment so heavily condemned in these journals.[24]

The third group of authors also recognized the crisis of parliaments and parliamentarism, but they thought that the parliamentary form of government was completely outdated. It could not be reformed either by returning to the practices of the nineteenth century or by an extension of voting rights and the inclusion of outlawed masses. A completely different form of government should replace the parliamentary form. The parliamentary form of government is inefficient and could simply not tackle the challenges modern and complex mass societies posed to this form of government. Although these authors proposed highly divergent ways for resolving the crisis, they shared also some common ground. They were unanimously anti-liberal and rejected the parliamentary form of government, in part because of the inseparable connection between liberalism and parliamentarism. They believed to some extent also in popular sovereignty not in its indirect or representative form but rather in its direct form, in which the direct linkage between the executive and the electorate is more important than the linkage between parliamentary representatives and the electorate. This new form of political system was not necessarily a democratic dictatorship since it could be also technocratic leadership or a neo-corporative form of government. They rejected the bolshevist and fascist forms of dictatorship and looked for a third way based on the authority of (a) a political leader, (b) experts or (c) corporate groups. Effective solutions could no longer be expected from parliamentary government, and challenges posed by mass societies and excessive demands might be averted only by introducing more efficient forms of government.[25] Their writings expressed a shared desire to leave the parliamentary system behind.

## HUNGARIAN REACTIONS TO THE IPU DRAFT RESOLUTION FROM 1928

### IPU Conference and Draft Resolution from 1928

As it recognized a crisis, one of the most important international bodies of parliamentarism of the inter-war period, the Inter-Parliamentary

Union, decided to make a survey of problems and give suggestions on how to resolve the crises of parliamentarism. The starting point of the investigations was the *instability* of parliamentary governments in several European countries. The IPU decided at its 23rd general conference in Ottawa/Washington (1925) to ask their members and some experts about the causes and consequences of the crises of parliamentarism. The five most important scholarly contributions were published in German and in English in 1928.[26] Based on these pieces, the Political Committee of the IPU compiled a draft resolution in May 1928, which had been discussed at the general conference in Berlin in August of the same year.

*Scholarly Contributions*

All of the authors of this small edited volume recognized the radical changes in the daily operation of parliaments, and all of them were aware of the deep impact of the political and social changes on the practice of parliamentarism. As a general observation, Harold Laski, Gaetano Mosca, Julius Bonn and Ferdinand Larnaude remarked that in the wake of World War I parliaments had to deal not only with political questions as in the nineteenth century but with an enormous number of social and economic questions. This was, of course, a consequence of the expansion of voting rights and the emergence of the masses in politics. Parliaments could no longer fulfil the function of legislating because they lacked competence and human resources. This incompetence of the MPs was connected with the growing expertise of the executive, which dominated, in turn, the parliaments by means of party discipline. On the other hand, some MPs were overly beholden to powerful enterprises and concerns, which tried to push their interests through the parliament. One way or another, MPs became voting machines, they represented only particular interests, and subsequently their reputation declined drastically. The role of parliaments was reduced to approving bills decided somewhere else in advance. This general pathography revealed by the scholars gave an almost unanimous impression not only of the phenomenon but also of the *reasons* behind the phenomenon of the crisis of parliamentarism.

Not surprisingly, it was only the Swiss scholar, Charles Borgeaud from the University Geneva, who denied that the causes of the crisis of parliamentarism lay in the mass democratization of the political systems. He was convinced that democratization was not the problem but the solution to the crisis. More direct democracy might produce a very effective instrument to overcome the problems that emerged in the inter-war period. But Borgeaud was in this respect an exception. It is also interesting that while all but one scholar agreed on the phenomenon and the causes of the crisis, they differed radically regarding their *recommendations* on how to overcome the crisis.

*IPU Draft Resolution*
Despite this divergence among the scholars concerning their recommendations on how to remedy the weaknesses of parliamentarism, the IPU formulated a draft resolution. They published a set of proposals, which was an incoherent mixture of ideas suggested by the scholars. The IPU put the following suggestions on the table:

1. To provide stability of governments, the IPU suggested that governments be elected for fixed terms as in Switzerland and in the USA and/or introduce a majoritarian electoral system, which could prevent the fragmentation of the parliamentary party system.
2. MPs should be able to remain independent from any powerful lobby organizations.
3. MPs' competence should be improved by providing administrative and expert assistants to them.
4. To make the connection between politics and the electorate more vital, they suggested establishing an impartial information system for the electorate. They also called for an official shadow cabinet along with the institution of referendum and the institution of public hearings.
5. To provide relief to parliaments, some competences should be transferred to local or functional autonomous organs.
6. The quality of parliamentary debates should be improved by introducing new standing orders.

In an introduction to the booklet that included the Hungarian reflections on these suggestions of the IPU, Albert Berzeviczy noted that these proposals did not provide a coherent action plan. They were highly abstract and even divergent in their directions. Nonetheless, they circulated among Hungarian MPs and professors of law and politics, as well as among some highly respected political actors. In the next section, we will examine their reflections on the suggestions of the IPU.

## Hungarian Reactions to the IPU Resolution

Although only one Hungarian MP (Viktor Haraga) attended the first conference of the Inter-Parliamentary Union, Hungary was recognized as a founding member of the Inter-Parliamentary Union in 1889. It was originally established as a meeting for individual MPs, while national groups were formed later. The Hungarian National Group was founded in 1895 with 131 members, and, apart from the interim regime of the Hungarian Soviet Republic, the Hungarian group of MPs attended the meetings of the IPU regularly until 1948. The reputation of the Hungarian group emerged very early, and efforts to organize the IPU meeting in Budapest in 1896, a year of grandiose celebrations of the anniversary of the establishment of the Hungarian principality in 896, succeeded.[27] Although members of the Hungarian National Group were not provided with official appointment by the Hungarian parliament, nor were they obliged to present a report on the IPU meetings and their activities were not necessarily on the agenda of the parliamentary work, it was a prestigious body of MPs even if sometimes domestic debates caused turbulence within the Hungarian group.[28]

Since members of the Hungarian National Group as well as other respondents to the IPU questionnaire were either MPs or engaged adherents of elitist or more democratic forms of parliamentarism, reactions to the proposals of the IPU reflected either the first or the second groups of intellectuals' views on the crisis analysed above. Consequently, it is hardly surprising that the Hungarian contributors were not delighted at IPU's proposals.

As a general impression, Albert Berzeviczy, President of the Hungarian Academy of Sciences for more than 30 years (1905–1936), Member of the Upper House of the Hungarian Parliament, and last but not least President of the Hungarian Group of the Inter-Parliamentary Union, declared in the foreword of the edited volume of the Hungarian reactions that the draft resolution of the IPU contained few elements that could improve the situation.[29] He remarked that in large and complex organizations like the IPU, it was hard to reach consensus regarding the proposals. Also, he added that the recommendations failed because of their generality and lack of sensibility towards local circumstances. Almost all Hungarian contributors to the volume agreed that local solutions were needed instead of universal answers. Berzeviczy, like many other contributors, agreed that the fundamental reason behind the crises lay in the introduction of universal suffrage, but he admitted that there was no way back. Ferenc Albrecht argued also that with the introduction of universal suffrage, parties of highly divergent world views got into the parliament. Debates and political life in general thus became polarized, which in turn diminished the authority of parliaments and MPs. He concluded that the question of universal suffrage should be reconsidered.[30]

*The PDT Narrative*

Certainly, there were some contributions that fit the *crisis narrative* and the PDT: László Buza, professor of law at the University of Szeged, argued that party interests had replaced the principle of fair criticism of the government and sober parliamentary discussion of government proposals. Party interests dominated the plenum of the legislative body, which was originally a place of calm and rational discussions about the general interests of the nation. Buza agreed also with some of the IPU's suggestions, which would, if implemented, restore the original atmosphere and function mechanisms of parliaments.

Béla Földes, former minister and professor emeritus, referred also to the problem of party dominance, which had replaced the expertise and the rational discussion of the MPs. According to his proposal, highly important policy questions should be debated not in plenary sessions but only in standing committees where MPs with expertise in the specific field should rationally debate. After the debate by experts in the committee, the plenum should not be allowed to open a new debate on details. Földes suggested that the bill should be either adopted or rejected by the plenum in total. This would prevent non-expert MPs from altering the bill approved by expert MPs in the committee.[31] Gyula Moór, professor of the Pázmány Péter University Budapest, identified the core problem of parliamentarism as the decline of parliamentary and general morals as well as the lack of expertise. By accepting some suggestions of the IPU (expert hearings, new standing orders, lobbying regulations), he also seemed to confirm the PDT and the crisis narrative. Gusztáv Gratz, a prominent historian and MP, referred to the expansion of policy issues to be regulated by legislation. This expansion required that MPs become experts on various policy fields in order to be able to fulfil their roles as the most important decision makers of the country. Like Földes, Gratz proposed the transformation of the parliamentary committee system and the abolition of plenary debates on policy issues that require expertise. Gratz could even imagine that the introduction of public hearings could lead to an improvement in the quality of legislation.[32] All contributions fit into the PDT model and presented proposals for technical, *intra-parliamentary* changes.

### The Counter-Narrative

It is striking, however, that beyond these contributions reflecting the PDT narrative, the volume included several other pieces that fit the counter-narrative: while the authors in line with the PDT and crisis narrative opted mainly for supporting one or another technical suggestion of the IPU, several other respondents were clearly sceptical concerning the suggested *intra-parliamentary* solutions proposed by the IPU Committee.

It is salient that several authors stressed the *extra-parliamentary* factor of *political education*, which was, in their view, the decisive factor in overcoming the crisis of parliamentarism. Ferenc Albrecht, Member of the Board of the Hungarian Association for Foreign Affairs, argued that crisis cannot be overcome by technical improvement of parliamentary processes as suggested by the IPU. The most pressing problem was, rather, how to restore the authority of the parliaments. As he put it: 'The draft resolution of the Inter-Parliamentary Union tries to overcome the crises of parliamentarism by means of new parliamentary regulations. We are, however, convinced that this crisis might be surmounted only by extra-parliamentary expedients and practices. Proposals included in the draft resolution of the IPU might be useful only as secondary means.' Thus, he concluded, political education must be the first step to overcome the crisis of parliamentarism.

Also, Vilmos Haendel, Professor of Politics at the University of Debrecen, remarked that institutional and technical changes of parliamentary practices may generate only moderate effects regarding the trust in parliaments. According to his analysis, it was not the parliamentary institution but the mentality of the political actors that had to be changed. Nevertheless, moral and professional improvement of the parliamentary elite depended to great extent on the quality of public spirit. Thus, the first step should be the political education of the masses.[33]

Another professor of public law, József Kun, explicitly rejected the proposals of the IPU as overly mechanical solutions. Instead, political life (and not the institutional mechanism) should be renewed in order to overcome the present crisis. Kun referred to the *two-party system* as a *condition sine qua non* of a well-functioning parliamentarism which was a *topoi* of Hungarian legal scholarship before World War I.[34]

To go a step even further, Gyula Lakatos, MP of the governing Unity Party (*Egységes Párt, EP*) at that time, laid out the changes he saw in the proper functions of parliaments in the inter-war period. In his response to the survey of the IPU, he explained that while parliaments of the pre-war period had to deal only with political issues, legislatures of the twentieth century had to struggle with economic and social issues, which are so complex that parliaments' capacities are heavily challenged by them.[35] He argued that the most important function of parliaments was no longer producing legislation. The institution of parliament was overwhelmed concerning its legislative function. It no longer had the ability to pass the best bills. Lakatos concluded that the most important functions of parliaments were (1) the selection of leaders, election of governments, granting the support of a parliamentary majority needed for stable government and (2) providing linkage between the electorate and the government.[36] Although this extremely modern approach to the functions of parliament seems to be an isolated opinion, the general impression of most contributors was that extra-parliamentary factors (like political education) might be the key in overcoming the crisis, and intra-parliamentary factors (like institutional/technical renewal) might be at best additional expedients.

Albert Berzeviczy, President of the Hungarian National Group of the IPU, stressed two points in his introductory remarks to the edited volume. As noted above, he pointed out that the most grievous problems of parliamentarism are direct consequences of the introduction of universal suffrage and its implications (mass parties and instable governments), and that one should not be averse to reconsidering the case against universal suffrage. Although a serious intention of limiting universal suffrage seems to loom behind this utterance, the genre of an introductory remark did not allow for explicit and lengthy argumentations on this topic. Berzeviczy brought up, however, another neglected issue that has not been mentioned in any contribution. The emergence of the mass parties, and especially the socialist parties, led to the awakening of hopes and expectations that might be never fulfilled. He argued explicitly against the socialist and social democratic parties:

> Based on their principles, programmes and the expectations they induced in their adherents, these parties should implement reforms which would convulse our present social and economic order. Sober leaders of these parties would refrain from doing this, they cannot forebear, however, to induce other expectations they will not be able or simply do not want to fulfil.

This polemical passage is clearly directed against the left-wing political camp. The President of the Hungarian Academy of Sciences with his liberal-conservative background does not conceal his antipathy towards political ideas generating excessive hopes and expectations.

## CONCLUSION

Certainly, Berzeviczy's liberal-conservative approach to parliament and parliamentarism originated in the idea of the nineteenth-century parliament and parliamentarism with a limited scope of legislation and a limited number of interests to be regulated, but what is more interesting even from the perspective of the twenty-first century is the disposition of limiting expectations towards the parliament. Since historical developments prevent us from acting and thinking exactly as our ancestors acted and thought and since historical developments change radically the circumstances we are living in, in fact, it is not the substance but rather the form of our thinking that could have some resemblance to that of previous historical periods and political situations. Reducing expectations and having a realistic idea of what parliaments can and cannot achieve is certainly an excellent starting point for a reevaluation of the ever-lasting crisis of parliamentarism and the parliamentary decline thesis. Beyond many other lessons, this is what we can learn from a historical analysis of Hungarian parliamentarism of the inter-war period.

## NOTES

1. David Judge, 'A Crisis of Parliament' in David Richards et al. (eds.), *Institutional Crisis in 21st-Century Britain* (Basingstoke: Palgrave Macmillan, 2014) 81.
2. Matthew Flinders and Alexandra Kelso, 'Mind the Gap: Political Analysis, Public Expectations and the Parliamentary Decline Thesis' in *British Journal of Politics and International Relations,* vol. 13 (2011) No 2, 249.
3. To a highly useful overview, see Marie-Luise Recker and Andreas Schulz (eds.), *Parlamentarismuskritik und Antiparlamentarismus in Europa* (Dusseldorf: Droste Verlag, 2018).
4. On various functions of parliaments from the perspective of political science: Ami Kreppel, 'Typologies and Classifications' in Shane Martin, Thomas Saalfeld and Kaare W. Strøm (eds.), *The Oxford Handbook of Legislative Studies* (Oxford: Oxford University Press, 2014) 85; Werner J. Patzelt, 'Parlamente und ihre Funktionen' in Werner J. Patzelt (ed.), *Parlamente und ihre Funktionen. Institutionelle Mechanismen und institutionelles Lernen im Vergleich* (Wiesbaden: Westdeutscher Verlag, 2003) 13.

From the perspective of history of ideas: Pasi Ihalainen, Cornelia Ilie and Kari Palonen, 'Introduction: Parliament as a Conceptual Nexus' in Pasi Ihalainen, Cornelia Ilie and Kari Palonen (eds.), *Parliament and Parliamentarism. A Comparative History of a European Concept* (New York/Oxford: Berghahn, 2016) 6.

5. Gerhard Loewenberg, 'The Role of Parliaments in Modern Political Systems' in Gerhard Loewenberg (ed.), *Modern Parliaments: Change or Decline* (New York: Aldine, 1971) 5–13.

6. For early reflections on the phenomenon of expectation gap, see Harold Laski, *Reflections on the Constitution* (Manchester: Manchester University Press, 1951); Herbert Morrison, *Government and Parliament* (Oxford: Oxford University Press, 1954); Ivor Jennings, *Parliament* (Cambridge: Cambridge University Press, 1957); Bernard Crick, *The Reform of Parliament* (London: Weidenfeld & Nicolson, 1964). Most recently: Gerry Stoker, *Why Politics Matters? Making Democracy Work* (Basingstoke: Palgrave Macmillan, 2006); Colin Hay, *Why We Hate Politics?* (Cambridge: Polity Press, 2007); Matthew Flinders, *Defending Politics. Why Democracy Matters in the Twenty-First Century* (Oxford: Oxford University Press, 2012).

7. Flinders and Kelso, 'Mind the Gap', 251.

8. Ibid., 264.

9. For the following summary of political developments, see Romsics Ignác, *Hungary in the Twentieth Century* (Budapest: Osiris Kiadó, 2010).

10. Boros Zsuzsanna and Szabó Dániel, *Parlamentarizmus Magyarországon 1867–1944* [Parliamentarism in Hungary 1867–1944] (Budapest: Eötvös Kiadó, 2014) 159.

11. On legitimist groups see Békés Márton, 'A legitimisták és a legitimizmus' [The legitimists and the legitimism] in Romsics Ignác (ed.), *A magyar jobboldali hagyomány* [The Hungarian Right-Wing Tradition] (Budapest: Osiris Kiadó, 2009) 214.

12. On the differences between Hungarian and British parliamentarism of the late nineteenth century, see Pócza Kálmán, 'Distrust in Government. A Comparative Historical Analysis' in Kontler László and Mark Somos (eds.), *Trust and Happiness in the History of European Political Thought* (Leiden: Brill, 2018) 236–256.

13. Gergely Jenő, 'Titkos választás és ellenforradalom–1920' [Secret elections and counter-revolution–1920] in Földes György–Hubai László (eds.), *Parlamenti választások Magyarországon 1920–1998* [Parliamentary Elections in Hungary 1920–1998] (Budapest: Napvilág Kiadó, 1999) 75.

14. On this provisional constitutional settlement, see Schweitzer Gábor and Szabó István (eds.), *A közjogi provizórium (1920–1944) időszakának alkotmányos berendezkedése I.* [Constitutional settlement and provisional constitutional arrangement 1920–1944] (Budapest: Pázmány Press, 2016).

15. Olasz Lajos, 'A kormányzói jogkör' [Constitutional Powers of the Governor] in Romsics Ignác (ed.), *A magyar jobboldali hagyomány* [The Hungarian Right-Wing Tradition] (Budapest: Osiris Kiadó, 2009) 102.

16. The doctrine of the Holy Crown refers to a simple idea of Hungarian public law: sovereignty belongs neither to the King nor to the people of Hungary, but to the Holy Crown. This idea excludes both the absolute sovereignty of the King of Hungary and the people since the absolute sovereign is only the Holy Crown. This is the final source of legitimacy for the kings and the state. The doctrine of the Holy Crown refers to the Crown of the first Christian king of Hungary, which was sent by the pope to the inauguration of King Stephen I (1000–38). This crown has been lost, but the crown known today as the Holy Crown dates back certainly to the twelfth century according to historians. This holy object had a highly adventurous 'life'. Nevertheless it has been preserved and transmitted through centuries. From the thirteenth century on, the inauguration and coronation of Hungarian kings was valid and accepted by Hungarian nobles only if the Archbishop of Esztergom put that very crown on the head of the new king. Péter László, 'The Holy Crown of Hungary, Visible and Invisible' in Péter László, *Hungary's Long Nineteenth Century. Constitutional and Democratic Traditions in a European Perspective* (Leiden: Brill, 2012) 15.

17. Püski Levente, *A Horthy-korszak parlamentje* [Parliament in the Horthy era] (Budapest: Országgyűlés Hivatala, 2015) 325.

18. Leading theoretical journals with a special focus on political developments included *Társadalomtudomány* [Social Science], *Századunk* [Our Century], *Magyar Szemle* [Hungarian Review] and *Szocializmus* [Socialism].

19. Boros Zsuzsanna, 'Parlamentarizmus a két világháború közötti Magyarországon' [Parliamentarism in Hungary in the Inter-War Period] in Boros Zsuzsanna, *Parlamenti viták a Horthy korban* [Parliamentary debates in the Horthy era] (Budapest: Rejtjel Kiadó, 2006) 47.

20. Boros, 'Parlamentarizmus', 50.

21. Püski, *A Horthy-korszak parlamentje*, 21. Only two elections were held on the basis of universal suffrage, in 1920 and in 1939.

22. Erényi Tibor, 'Többpárti választások és parlamentarizmus Magyarországon 1920–1947' [Multi-party elections and parliamentarism in Hungary 1920–1947] in Földes György and Hubai László (eds.), *Parlamenti választások Magyarországon 1920–1998* [Parliamentary Elections in Hungary 1920–1998] (Budapest: Napvilág Kiadó, 1999) 259.

23. Sipos Balázs, 'Sajtó, sajtópolitika és nyilvánosság a Horthy-korszakban' [Press, press regulation and public sphere in the Horthy-era] in *Korunk* vol. 23 (2012) No 11, p. 76.

24. Boros, 'Parlamentarizmus', 51.

25. Ibid., 53.

26. Inter-Parliamentary Union (ed.), *The Development of the Representative System of Our Times: Five Answers to an Inquiry Instituted by the Inter-Parliamentary Union* (Lausanne/Geneva: Libr. Payot, 1928). And in German: Interparlamentarische Union (ed.), *Die gegenwärtige Entwicklung des repräsentativen Systems. Fünf Antworten auf eine Rundfrage der Interparlamentarischen Union* (Berlin: Carl Heymanns Verlag, 1928).

27. Arday Lajos and Katona Tamás, *110 év. Az Interparlamentáris Unió Magyar Nemzeti Csoportjának története* [110 Years. History of the Hungarian National Group of the Inter-Parliamentary Union] (Budapest: Magyar Országgyűlés, 2006) 29.

28. Püski, *A Horthy-korszak parlamentje*, 244.

29. Berzeviczy Albert, 'Bevezetés' [Introduction] in Radisics Elemér (ed.), *Válságban van-e a parlamentarizmus?* [Is Parliamentarism in Crisis?] (Budapest: Gergely R. Könyvkereskedése, 1930) 8.

30. Albrecht, in Radisics (ed.), *Válságban van-e a parlamentarizmus?*, 17.

31. Földes, in Radisics (ed.), *Válságban van-e a parlamentarizmus?*, 26.

32. Gratz, in Radisics (ed.), *Válságban van-e a parlamentarizmus?*, 31.

33. Haendel, in Radisics (ed.), *Válságban van-e a parlamentarizmus?*, 43.

34. Kun, in Radisics (ed.), *Válságban van-e a parlamentarizmus?*, 46.

35. Lakatos, in Radisics (ed.), *Válságban van-e a parlamentarizmus?*, 50.

36. Ibid., 51.

# CHAPTER 9

# 'A Bad Parliamentarism': Normative Expectations and Criticism of Parliamentarism in the Weimar Reichstag

## Thomas Raithel

Parliamentarism in the Weimar Republic was under strong political pressure during the short period of its existence, to which it ultimately succumbed bit by bit from 1930 onwards. Even if it has been correctly emphasized in recent scholarship that Weimar parliamentarism should not be viewed exclusively from the perspective of the crisis and the failure,[1] and that in the 1920s there were some indications of positive developments,[2] in the end this observation cannot be denied. It was not only 'external' factors that contributed to the fateful downfall of parliamentarism, that is, above all the volume and the dimensions of foreign and domestic policy challenges, but also 'internal' problems of parliamentary practice and the underlying ideas regarding the parliamentary system of government. This chapter will limit itself to central aspects of this last-named topic area: the normative basic notions of the role of parliament within the political system and the frequently related criticism of Weimar parliamentarism.

T. Raithel (✉)
Ludwig Maximilian University, Munich, Germany

Leibniz Institute for Contemporary History, Munich, Germany
e-mail: raithel@ifz-muenchen.de

© The Author(s) 2019
R. Aerts et al. (eds.), *The Ideal of Parliament in Europe since 1800*,
Palgrave Studies in Political History,
https://doi.org/10.1007/978-3-030-27705-5_9

159

In spite of recent studies on Weimar parliamentarism,[3] the specific state of research concerning the conceptions, perception and criticism of parliamentarism in the Weimar period is—with some exceptions—still rather underdeveloped.[4] Therefore, this contribution will focus on one perspective and one kind of source: the statements made by parliamentarians in the Reichstag plenum.[5] It is thus first and foremost a question of the parliamentary discourse of those men—the female deputies barely expressed themselves on this topic[6]—who operated at the centre of the parliamentary system. I will examine several discussions during the early and late phases of the Republic, especially the large and in its exhaustiveness unique debate on parliamentarism that took place in the Reichstag on 28 February and 1 March 1929.[7] The parliamentary voices will be placed in the context of the general discussion of parliamentarism during the Weimar period, to the extent that the state of research allows.

The analysis proceeds in three steps:

- First of all, the fundamental criticism of parliamentarism within the radical political forces, notably the Communists and the National Socialists will be singled out.
- Second, the normative conceptions of parliamentarism and the critical topoi that dominated within the non-extremist political spectrum of the Reichstag will be portrayed in more detail.
- After a brief summary, in a third step a few comments follow on the question regarding to what extent this criticism contributed to an erosion of the parliamentary system.

## PARLIAMENTARISM AND THE RADICAL POLITICAL FORCES

The Communists and the National Socialists not only rejected the parliamentary regime but also parliamentarism in general and scorned the institution of parliament, even though they used their own parliamentary presence, which had become a relevant factor since the Reichstag elections of May 1924, as a political weapon against the system. Therefore, in this political spectrum, normative conceptions of parliamentarism simply did not exist. Instead, there was a radical and fundamental criticism of parliamentarism.

As an example, I will cite Adolf Hitler, who initially stated in *Mein Kampf*, that in his youth, he overcame 'a certain admiration for the English parliament'.[8] Faced with the conditions in the Wiener Reichsrat, he claimed to have realized that parliamentarism in Austria possessed not only a 'misshapen form' but that 'parliament as such' was a 'calamity'.[9] A decisive factor for Hitler was that the principle of parliamentary majority presented a stark contradiction to his 'Führer idea'. This understanding basically constituted National Socialist anti-parliamentarism during the Weimar period. Thus, on 1 March 1929, Joseph Goebbels observed smugly in the Reichstag 'that what we witnessed here yesterday and today was the swansong of the parliamentary system in its entirety'. He continued by stressing the core element of National Socialist criticism of parliamentarism, 'that namely the parliamentary-democratic system in and of itself is wrong, and that one cannot rule a nation in liberty with this system, much less free an enslaved nation'.[10]

The rejection of parliamentarism on the part of the extreme left was just as vigorous. Among the Communists, anarchists and far-left socialists, parliamentary democracy was regarded as a formal facade for bourgeois class rule determined by the power of capital.[11] 'This parliament and this democracy', according to the KPD[12] deputy Peter Maslowski in March 1929, was 'nothing more than a route [...] to the dictatorship of finance capital'.[13] Nonetheless, the KPD used the Reichstag as a propaganda forum for its own ends. As the most senior member of the Reichstag (*Alterspräsidentin*), Clara Zetkin openly stated in August 1932 that 'parliament can be exploited within certain limits for the struggle of the workers'.[14]

It should be noted that ideas of council democracy, which had been set against the model of parliamentary democracy during the early period of the Weimar Republic above all by left-wing Social Democrat circles within the USPD,[15] had ultimately remained only a brief episode. At the latest with the 'reunification' of the SPD[16] and USPD in autumn 1922, the parliamentary system of government had become—with a very few exceptions—the general orientation of German Social Democracy in its entirety.[17]

## Normative Conceptions of Parliamentarism
## and Criticism of Weimar Parliamentarism Within
## the Non-extremist Political Spectrum

Roughly stated, one might say that among the other political forces, opinions about the conveniences of a parliamentary regime or rather its suitability for German conditions considerably differed. Nonetheless, parliamentarism as such and the institution of parliament had undoubtedly a, greater or smaller, distinctive significance for their political thinking. Here, it is therefore possible to distinguish normative conceptions—even though they often remain rather diffuse. With a view to the topic of the current collection of essays (*The Ideal of Parliament*), however, it needs to be noted that it is possible only in a very limited way to talk of 'ideals' of the parliament or of parliamentarism for . Even its supporters, who were forced most of the time onto the defensive, showed very little enthusiasm for parliamentarism.

This already manifested itself in the period of system change in 1918/1919, that is, in the phase of the 'last minute' parliamentarisation of the German Empire during the course of the 'October reform' of 1918 until the announcement of the new Reich constitution in August 1919.[18] The inevitable transition to a parliamentary system, which was also supported by the bourgeois centre, was tarnished by the distrust of a strong parliament present within the liberal-conservative spectrum and shared by most specialists in constitutional law.[19] This led to the establishment of significant, though at the time by no means fully developed, presidential constitutional components.[20] In accordance with the terminology of Robert Redslob, the influential Alsatian expert on constitutional law, a parliamentary government 'in its true form' was to be created by means of such a system of equilibrium.[21] This construction was later accurately described in historical scholarship as the 'presidential-dictatorial reserve constitution'.[22]

It would go beyond the scope of this chapter—and it would also be rather difficult—to attempt to run through the various positions of the political parties apropos parliamentarism. I will therefore limit myself to some basic aspects that became apparent in the political discourse of the Weimar parliamentarians. A certain methodological problem is that normative conceptions of parliamentarism first and foremost emerged in the critical discourse about its Weimar manifestation. This is the reason why the image of parliamentarism seems more concrete in the centre-right spectrum than among the Social Democrats and also parts of the Left-Liberals (DDP[23]) and the Catholic Centre Party (Deutsche Zentrumspartei), which actually had a more positive relationship to Weimar parliamentarism.

Criticism of parliamentarism in the Weimar Republic stemmed from many sources: of fundamental significance were the high expectations towards politics in the face of immense challenges—expectations that were almost impossible to fulfil; I will only mention the multiple burdens resulting from the defeat in World War I. To this, almost permanent functional problems of Weimar parliamentarism can be added, especially concerning the formation of the cabinet and the parliamentary backing of the government. Here, the generally long duration of crises of government formation[24] can be cited as well as the short life expectancy of only eight months that a Weimar national government was granted on average[25]—periods in which the political capacity of the coalition government to act was repeatedly restricted by internal tensions. Dissatisfaction therefore grew over the years in view of the interminable government crisis, which repeatedly resulted from the problems of building steady coalitions and parliamentary majorities.

On 28 February and 1 March 1929, for example, the Reichstag discussed possibilities for stabilizing governmental conditions. This had been preceded by a phase of political paralysis lasting for over half a year, during which there had been an informal grand coalition acting as a 'cabinet of personalities', but it had not yet been possible to conclude a formal coalition of SPD, DDP, Centre Party and DVP.[26,27] In this situation, the parliamentary party of the DVP had submitted at the end of 1928 a motion for altering the Weimar constitution that envisaged a modification of Article 54.[28] This article was the core of the Weimar parliamentary system. It reads: 'The Reich Chancellor and the Reich Ministers require for the exercise of their office the confidence of the Reichstag. Any one of them must resign if the Reichstag withdraws its confidence by formal resolution.' The most important suggestion of the DVP was now to link the withdrawal of confidence to a two-thirds majority, a measure which would make the parliamentary overthrow of an appointed government extremely difficult.

In the parliamentary discussion about this proposal, two different fundamental conceptions about the role of parliament appeared: while the Social Democratic speaker Otto Landsberg highlighted the necessity of a stabilizing coalition policy,[29] the deputies of the two liberal parties—DDP and DVP—and also the conservatives of the DNVP[30] expressed, with different intensity, their ideal of a weaker parliament. Their aim was to release the government—completely or partly—from direct dependency on the Reichstag and from its party conflicts. The DVP attempted, as mentioned above, to weaken Article 54, as it were. The DNVP went further and wanted to completely abolish the binding of the government to parliament, which had been in place since 1918/1919[31]—a demand that had already been made in the political and constitutional discussion during the middle phase of the Republic.[32]

Contrary to the view dominating later historical research, the Reichstag appeared to most liberal and conservative speakers of the Weimar Republic as too powerful. The fact that, under the conditions of a parliamentary system, the Reichstag had since 1918/1919 become a central political authority and that the government was now directly dependent on this authority caused some uneasiness in the centre-right spectrum of the Weimar parties. Furthermore, the negative term 'parliamentary absolutism' or 'absolute parliamentarism', which had already influenced the constitution-drafting process in 1918/1919 and contributed to the strong position of the Reich President, was still heard in the late 1920s.[33] This is remarkable because during the crisis years 1922 to 1924, a further expansion of the power of the Reich President had taken place. The term 'parliamentary absolutism' reflected a disapproving vision of the parliamentary system that originated with conservative French criticism of the very different political conditions in the Third Republic and had been introduced into German discourse above all by Robert Redslob.

In particular, the influence of coalition factions on the government was viewed negatively from the early days of the Republic onwards. The idea that factions should have little or no influence on the forming of the government was especially widespread among the liberal and conservative groupings. This attitude reflected the permanent suspicion that the parliamentary parties were dominated by 'party egoism and party fanaticism'.[34] In this context, the parliamentarians often made reference to the wording of the Weimar Constitution, which states in Article 53: 'The Reich Chancellor and, on his recommendation, the Reich Ministers, are appointed and dismissed by the Reich President.'[35]

In general, however, the vast majority of the parliamentarians elided the fact that in a party-based parliamentary system, the participation of the coalition factions in the formation of the government is, in practice, indispensable, if a structurally extremely weak position on the part of the new cabinet is to be avoided. The Social Democrats and individual deputies from the left wing of the DDP were the only ones to defend, now and then, this basic element of a modern parliamentary system—which, in a state like Germany, where political parties had a very strong influence on political life, had assumed considerable significance. Rudolf Breitscheid (SPD), for example, clearly differentiated in November 1922 between the system of the Weimar Republic and that of the German Empire, and he pointed out that now in Germany it was 'impossible, considering the history and the structure of the parliament, to form a cabinet at one's own will and independently of factions'.[36] A similar appraisal was made by the DDP parliamentarian Anton Erkelenz in December 1922 in a newspaper article following the difficult formation of the Cuno government, which was for the first time in the Weimar Republic strongly determined by the Reich President. Erkelenz criticized the 'pale theory that says that governments are to be formed without any consultation of the parliamentary parties'.[37]

A cutting back of parliamentary competences in the area of legislation was also met with broad liberal-conservative sympathy within the Reichstag. This had already been shown by the developments of the years 1922 and 1923, a period when inflation caused economic, societal and political crises.[38] At this time, under President Friedrich Ebert, the temporary but far-reaching suspension of the legislative competences of the Reichstag took place in two different ways:

On the one hand, the Reichstag tolerated the legislative broadening of the famous Article 48 of the Weimar constitution concerning presidential authority in a state of emergency. The possibility foreseen by paragraph 2 that the President meet 'the necessary measures for the reestablishment of public safety and order if public safety and order are considerably disturbed or endangered in the German Reich' was now used for the establishment of the government's intensive legislative activity supported by the President. The right of parliament contained in paragraph 3 to suspend the decrees issued remained unused.

On the other hand, parliament gave extensive legislative powers to the government through broadly defined enabling acts. Here, above all the extensive empowerments for the Stresemann and Marx governments from August and December 1923 should be cited, which placed de facto full legislative discretionary powers at the disposal of the executive. Whilst the Social Democrat parliamentary party agreed only under strong internal pressure, in the bourgeois centre, the parliamentary agreement to an empowering law—as Chancellor Wilhelm Marx emphasized to the

Reichstag in December 1923—was regarded as an expression of 'patriotism' and a 'sense of duty of the people's representatives' in view of the 'distress of people and Reich'.[39] Prelate Ludwig Kaas from the Catholic Centre Party even extolled the empowerment as an 'exertion of genuine parliamentary spirit'.[40]

It is evident that criticism of Weimar parliamentarism resulted not only from actual functional problems of the parliamentary system, but also from the deep gulf between the outlined normative conceptions of parliamentarism and the daily parliamentary reality. Aside from the acute government crises, the latter was generally regarded very critically, for example, when the governing parties sought to exert significant influence on the formation of government and government activity. As already indicated, from today's point of view, this is a completely normal and appropriate occurrence in a parliamentary system based on parties. In this sense, the intense crisis discourse of the Weimar period also frequently appears as an expression of an understanding of parliamentarism that—frankly—was inadequate for the new era that had begun in 1918/1919. This contradiction between parliamentary daily life in the Weimar Republic and the dominant concepts of norms was, in my view, responsible for the fundamental acerbity of liberal-conservative criticism of German parliamentarism.

I will give three examples: in December 1921, Ludwig Haas of the DDP attacked the Social Democratic parliamentary party because the SPD had demanded the repeal of an exceptional decree: 'Now, it is no longer the government that rules, but it is you [...] and if the parliaments rule and take the potential of governance from the government, then it is a bad parliamentarism (*böser Parlamentarismus*).'[41] In November 1928, the representative of the DVP Franz Brüninghaus made a comment on the possibility for a new Reichstag majority to abrogate decisions of the preceding Reichstag, and he stated that 'in this way parliamentarism' was 'reversed into its opposite'.[42] Similarly, Ludwig Haas documented in March 1929 the influence of the parliamentary parties on the formation of governments: 'This is a household of parliamentary parties, and that is the paradox of a real parliamentary system.'[43] Expressions like these did not constitute an explicit rejection of the parliamentary system. However, they suggested that this system did not work at all in Germany. The DNVP deputy Walther Graef spoke in March 1929 with regard to Germany of a 'travesty of parliamentarism [...] such as we have not seen in any other country in the world'.[44]

At this point, it would appear sensible to briefly sketch some contexts of the outlined normative perceptions: first of all, the ongoing orientation, especially in the liberal and conservative political factions, towards the parliamentary situation in the constitutional monarchy of the German Empire must be mentioned. A fundamental assumption within the constitutional and public discussion in the German Empire and the Weimar Republic was that the Reichstag should be a mirror, representing the whole of society as accurately as possible.[45] Among other things, the Wilhelmine view of German constitutional doctrine continued to be in effect, which recognized the monarch as the 'only state organ with a free will and pillar of state authority' and which conceded to parliament merely a representative function.[46] Last but not least, this view had also affected the strictly representative Weimar electoral law. In the framework of this conceptual horizon, it was also difficult in the Weimar period to grant the Reichstag central political functions. This was coupled with a strong contempt for parliamentary 'talking' as opposed to governmental 'action'.[47] Residual views from the German Empire continued to pose government and parliament as dualistic opponents, even in a parliamentary system. The close connection between government and parliamentary governmental majority, characteristic of the new system, was therefore generally met with incomprehension.

Furthermore, among large parts of the liberal-conservative spectrum, there was a deeply rooted and—considering the political commitment to one's own party almost schizophrenic—mistrust of a pluralistic party system, and there was also a strong belief in non-party expert knowledge and in a kind of public welfare that would transcend party lines. In liberal and conservative circles, an 'ideology of non-partisanship'[48] still prevailed that was connected with a fierce criticism of supposed 'Parteiismus' (self-referentiality of the parties).[49] A 'holistic'—that is, integrated-cohesive and precisely not pluralistic—understanding of the nation had intensified as a result of World War I, along with the broad and vague longing for a very differently understood 'people's community'.[50]

In the characterization of German parliamentarism as the opposite of a 'genuine parliamentary system', quoted above, it becomes clear that this ideal-typical frame of reference still existed at the end of the 1920s. The exact meaning of this admittedly remained unclear: at any rate, a system with a weaker parliament and one that was balanced out by other bodies. The statements of the liberal-conservative parliamentarians reflected overall a dominant normative concept of parliamentarism, which could be characterized in broad strokes as follows: even if there was a formal responsibility of the government to parliament and thus a parliamentary system, the influence of parliament and especially the parliamentary parties on the formation of government executed by the president and on the work of government was to remain limited. Should it be necessary, the parliament should also be prepared to temporarily surrender its legislative competences to the government. While the bourgeois centre clung to the principle of a representative people's assembly, the delegates of the DNVP occasionally revealed that their ideal of a parliament was an advising, professional 'parliament of the productive estates'—in the words of Oskar Hergt in November 1928.[51]

In the search for parliamentary reference points or even models, comparative glancing beyond German borders was frequently evident among the parliamentary deputies. The approach of Weimar deputies comparing the parliamentarism of other Western states, especially Great Britain and France, with the German case definitely reinforced the discontent with their own condition. The British two-party system seemed vastly superior to the German multi-party system; for this reason, Great Britain was the only country to be protected from the global international 'crisis of parliamentarism', according to the DVP parliamentarian Siegfried von Kardorff in June 1929.[52] The parliamentary circumstances in the French Third Republic—often only vaguely perceived—were in fact not a model with regard to stability, but they certainly contrasted with the party-based German parliamentarism because of their more individualistic character and the relatively weak position of political parties and parliamentary factions.[53] As the deputy of the German Nationals Walther Graef claimed in March 1929, this made it 'much easier for France to control this system than for us, where the ideological and also the economic differences are so profound that it […] has been and will always remain extremely difficult to pursue coalition politics'.[54]

Moderate voices directed against the sharp parliamentary criticism of parliamentarism came above all from the ranks of the Centre Party, the DDP and the SPD. However, this advocacy generally remained relatively defensive. Thus, the Centre Party deputy Johannes Bell warned in March 1929 that in the case of the criticism of the parliamentary system—which was, in his opinion, not completely unjustified—one should not 'throw the baby out with the bathwater'.[55] As the remarks by Rudolf Breitscheid and Anton Erkelenz already indicated, concepts of parliamentarism manifested themselves furthermore within the SPD and also on the left wing of the DDP that could be reconciled with parliamentary conditions in the Weimar Republic. Such voices were admittedly largely lost in the relentless chorus of criticism of parliamentarism.

## CONCLUSION: THE EROSION OF THE PARLIAMENTARY SYSTEM

This chapter has shown that the mismatch between the widespread ideas about a parliament's tasks and parliamentary reality was a serious 'internal' problem of Weimar parliamentarism. This problem can be blamed not only on the permanent instability of the governments but also on the gulf between the normative expectations of a relatively contained parliament and parliamentary reality, in which the coalition factions regarded themselves as governmental factions and strove for a correspondingly high degree of influence over the formation and activity of governments. This gulf promoted above all a repeated and extremely severe criticism of existing parliamentary conditions.

The immediate 'impact' of internal parliamentary criticism on the societal and constitutional crisis discussions is difficult to assess in detail. In general, however, we can assume that the parliamentary debates, which were for the most part reproduced at length in the daily newspapers, had some influence on the public discussions. Conversely, the discrediting of German parliamentarism by parliamentarians was reinforced by allusions to its (assumed) perception among the German population: for example, the delegate of the DNVP Ernst Oberfohren spoke in March 1929 about a 'permanent crisis of parliamentarism, which among large parts of the German nation only causes revulsion and contempt'.[56]

It seems to me that the overall very critical view of German parliamentarism that dominated within the Weimar Reichstag provided impulses for the erosion of the parliamentary system in three respects:

First of all, it encouraged debates on a revision of the constitution, which aimed ultimately at restricting or removing the parliamentary regime. Such discussions were also held among the public and by specialists in constitutional law.[57]

Second, the outlined normative conceptions and the linked criticism of parliamentarism worked in favour of a partial devolution of legislative authority to the government. The latter occurred not only in 1930 with the transition to the presidential regime, but in a paradigmatic way already in the years from 1922 to 1924, as a result of the inflation crisis. The instruments of non-parliamentary legislation created at the time were henceforth at the disposal of the opponents of the parliamentary system. From 1930, they were used first for the presidential reorganization of the Weimar state and in 1933 for the removal of Weimar democracy and the establishment of the National Socialist dictatorship.

Third, I would like to point to a factor that goes beyond the scope of this chapter: the severe criticism of parliamentarism—which can be observed not only in large parts of published opinion and in the field of constitutional theory, but, as we have seen, also within the Reichstag—certainly contributed to the decline in reputation that parliamentarism suffered in the public eye. Since during the Weimar period no public opinion analyses on this topic were carried out, this connection cannot be unequivocally proven. However, it seems just as plausible as the more far-reaching assumption that the loss of prestige on the part of the parliamentary system became a decisive factor in the ever poorer results achieved in the Reichstag elections by those parties loyal to the system.

## Notes

1. The classic work on this subject is Karl Dietrich Bracher, *Die Auflösung der Weimarer Republik. Eine Studie zum Problem des Machtverfalls in der Demokratie* (Stuttgart/Düsseldorf: Ring Verlag, 1955; 1st ed.). I would like to thank Dr Alex J. Kay and Dr Eva Oberloskamp for assisting me with the translation of this contribution into English.

2. See especially Thomas Mergel, *Parlamentarische Kultur in der Weimarer Republik. Politische Kommunikation, symbolische Politik und Öffentlichkeit im Reichstag* (Düsseldorf: Droste Verlag, 2005) in particular with regard to the 'integrative dynamic of the Reichstag' (Ibid., p. 473). In spite of an overall more critical perspective, I have also acknowledged some positive indications of parliamentary development. See, for example, on the integration of the USPD and the DVP in the circle of potential government parties Thomas Raithel, *Das schwierige Spiel des Parlamentarismus. Deutscher Reichstag und französische Chambre des Députés in den Inflationskrisen der 1920er Jahre* (Munich: Oldenbourg Verlag, 2005) 115–20.

3. Alongside the works cited in note 2, the following should be mentioned: Heiko Bollmeyer, *Der steinige Weg zur Demokratie. Die Weimarer Nationalversammlung zwischen Kaiserreich und Republik* (Frankfurt am Main/New York: Campus-Verlag, 2007); Nicolas Patin, *La catastrophe*

*allemande (1914–1945). 1674 destins parlementaires* (Paris: Fayard, 2014). More recent works on individual aspects will be cited in this chapter's notes.

4. On the development of German concepts of parliamentarism, see the overview in Andreas Biefang and Andreas Schulz, 'From Monarchical Constitutionalism to a Parliamentary Republic: Concepts of Parliamentarism in Germany since 1818', in Pasi Ihalainen, Cornelia Ilie and Kari Palonen (eds.), *Parliament and Parliamentarism. A Comparative History of a European Concept* (New York-Oxford: Berghahn, 2016) 62–80. Particularly lacking are larger studies with a broad perspective and adequate consideration of tendencies in the bourgeois centre that were critical of parliamentarism in the Weimar period. For a concise account of various tendencies of right- and left-wing anti-parliamentarism, see Wolfgang Durner, *Antiparlamentarismus in Deutschland* (Würzburg: Verlag Königshausen & Neumann, 1997) 92–127. A short overview with source texts can be found in Hartmut Wasser, *Parlamentarismuskritik vom Kaiserreich zur Bundesrepublik. Analyse und Dokumentation* (Stuttgart/Bad Cannstatt: Frommann-Holzboog Verlag, 1974) 65–107. Important points regarding the stance of the political right were already made in Kurt Sontheimer, *Antidemokratisches Denken in der Weimarer Republik. Die politischen Ideen des deutschen Nationalismus zwischen 1918 und 1933* (Munich: Nymphenburger, 1968) 147–65. From more recent research, see above all the references in Mergel, *Parlamentarische Kultur*, 399–408, as well as Ibid., 'Führer, Volksgemeinschaft und Maschine. Politische Erwartungsstrukturen in der Weimarer Republik und dem Nationalsozialismus 1918–1936' in Wolfgang Hardtwig (ed.), *Politische Kulturgeschichte der Zwischenkriegszeit 1918–1939* (Göttingen: Vandenhoeck & Ruprecht, 2005) 91–127. On criticism of parties and parliament in leading press organs of a broadly understood centre ranging from the SPD to the DVP, see Jörn Retterath, *'Was ist das Volk?' Volks- und Gemeinschaftskonzepte der politischen Mitte 1917–1924* (Munich: Oldenbourg Verlag, 2016). On criticism of parliament in Weimar constitutional theory, to which over time democratic constitutional teaching also showed itself to be susceptible, see Kathrin Groh, *Demokratische Staatsrechtslehrer in der Weimarer Republik. Von der konstitutionellen Staatslehre zur Theorie des modernen demokratischen Verfassungsstaats* (Tübingen: Mohr Siebeck, 2010) esp. 583–5, and Dirk Jörke and Marcus Llanque, 'Parliamentarism and Democracy in German Political Theory since 1848' in Ihalainen et al. (eds.), *Parliament and Parliamentarism*, 262–276. On criticism of parliament in contemporary historical scholarship, see Bernd Faulenbach, *Ideologie des deutschen Weges. Die deutsche Geschichte in der Historiographie zwischen Kaiserreich und*

*Nationalsozialismus* (Munich: C.H. Beck Verlag, 1980) 257–67. On the understanding of parliamentarism on the part of Reichstag deputies, see Patin, *La catastrophe allemande*, 130–5, as well as Raithel, *Das schwierige Spiel*, esp. 68–100.

5. *Verhandlungen des Reichstags*, Vol. 352, 357, 361, 423, 424, 425, 433 and 454 (Berlin 1921, 1922, 1928, 1929 and 1932). The stenographical reports and appendices are available online at http://www.reichstagspro-tokolle.de/rtbiiiauf.html [last accessed on 15 March 2017]. For fundamental biographical information on the quoted Reichstag deputies, see the 'Datenbank der deutschen Parlamentsabgeordneten' on the basis of the parliamentary almanacs and the Reichstag handbooks at http://www.reichstag-abgeordnetendatenbank.de/ [last accessed on: 15 March 2017] as well as M.d.R., *Die Reichstagsabgeordneten der Weimarer Republik in der Zeit des Nationalsozialismus. Politische Verfolgung, Emigration und Ausbürgerung 1933–1945*, ed. by Martin Schumacher (Düsseldorf: Droste Verlag, 1994). Due to a lack of space, I have refrained from citing specific biographical works.

6. With the exception of a comment by Clara Zetkin), women did not contribute to the discussions on parliamentarism studied in this chapter. The proportion of female deputies never surpassed 10% in the Weimar National Assembly or in the Reichstag. See Gabriele Bremme, *Die politische Rolle der Frau in Deutschland. Eine Untersuchung über den Einfluß der Frauen bei Wahlen und ihre Teilnahme in Partei und Parlament* (Göttingen: Vandenhoeck & Ruprecht, 1956) 121–5.

7. On the political contexts of this session, see below.

8. Hitler, *Mein Kampf. Eine kritische Edition*, ed. by Christian Hartmann et al. (Munich: Institut für Zeitgeschichte, 2016) vol. I, p. 261: 'Nicht wenig trug dazu bei, daß mir als jungem Menschen infolge meines vielen Zeitungslesens […] eine gewisse Bewunderung für das englische Parlament eingeimpft worden war […].' On the anti-parliamentarism of Hitler and the NSDAP, see Ibid., p. 261, note 73; Martin Döring, *'Parlamentarischer Arm der Bewegung'. Die Nationalsozialisten im Reichstag der Weimarer Republik* (Düsseldorf: Droste Verlag, 2001) 30–6.

9. Hitler, *Mein Kampf*, vol. 1, p. 265.

10. *Verhandlungen des Reichstags*, vol. 424, p. 1388. An example of the exploitation of the forum of the Reichstag in the political struggle of the National Socialists is provided by Alex J. Kay, 'Death Threat in the Reichstag, June 13, 1929: Nazi Parliamentary Practice and the Fate of Ernst Heilmann', in *German Studies Review* 35.1 (2012) 19–32.

11. See Riccardo Bavaj, *Von links gegen Weimar. Linkes antiparlamentarisches Denken in der Weimarer Republik* (Bonn: Verlag J.H.W. Dietz Nachf., 2005) esp. 488–9; Durner, *Antiparlamentarismus*, 118–27.

12. Kommunistische Partei Deutschlands (Communist Party of Germany).
13. *Verhandlungen des Reichstags*, vol. 424, p. 1381 (1 March 1929).
14. *Verhandlungen des Reichstags*, vol. 454, p. 2 (30 August 1932).
15. Unabhängige Sozialdemokratische Partei Deutschlands (Independent Social Democratic Party of Germany).
16. Sozialdemokratische Partei Deutschlands (Social Democratic Party of Germany).
17. See Durner, *Antiparlamentarismus*, 121–2.
18. On the positions of the parties in the context of the consultations on the constitution, see Bollmeyer, *Der steinige Weg*, 255–373.
19. See the summary in Gusy, *Weimarer Reichsverfassung*, 64–5.
20. See the overview in Ibid., 98–115.
21. Robert Redslob, *Die parlamentarische Regierung in ihrer wahren und unechten Form. Eine vergleichende Studie über die Verfassungen von England, Belgien, Ungarn, Schweden und Frankreich* (Tübingen: J.C.B. Mohr [P. Siebeck], 1918). On Redslob see Horst Möller, 'Parlamentarismus-Diskussion in der Weimarer Republik. Die Frage des "besonderen" Weges zum parlamentarischen Regierungssystem' in Manfred Funke et al. (eds.), *Demokratie und Diktatur. Geist und Gestalt politischer Herrschaft in Deutschland und Europa* (Düsseldorf: Droste Verlag, 1987) 140–57, here 146–7; Christoph Schönberger, *Das Parlament im Anstaltsstaat. Zur Theorie parlamentarischer Repräsentation in der Staatsrechtslehre des Kaiserreichs (1871–1918)* (Frankfurt am Main: Klostermann, 1997) 384–404.
22. Karl Dietrich Bracher, 'Demokratie und Machtvakuum: zum Problem des Parteienstaats in der Auflösung der Weimarer Republik' in Karl Dietrich Erdmann and Hagen Schulze (eds.), *Weimar. Selbstpreisgabe einer Demokratie. Eine Bilanz heute* (Düsseldorf: Droste Verlag, 1980) 109–34 and 117.
23. Deutsche Demokratische Partei (German Democratic Party).
24. This was the difference between the Weimar Republic and the French Third Republic, for example, which also had a high level of instability of governments, but where, however, a generally very rapid formation of a new government took place following the overthrow of a cabinet. See Raithel, *Das schwierige Spiel*, 102–5 and 525–6.
25. The 20 Weimar national governments had a total period in office of approximately 159.5 months (my own calculation).
26. Deutsche Volkspartei (German People's Party).
27. The 'cabinet of personalities' had been formed on 29 June 1928 following difficult negotiations. A formal coalition was not achieved until 13 April 1929. This government—the last parliamentarily formed and supported

cabinet of the Weimar Republic—failed less than a year later, on 27 March 1930.

28. *Verhandlungen des Reichstags*, vol. 433, Printed Matter No 704, 'Entwurf eines Gesetzes zur Abänderung der Verfassung des Deutschen Reiches vom 11. August 1919' (14 December 1928).
29. *Verhandlungen des Reichstags*, vol. 424, p. 1371 (1 March 1929).
30. Deutschnationale Volkspartei (German National People's Party).
31. *Verhandlungen des Reichstags*, vol. 424, p. 1365 (Walther Graef). The stance within the DNVP towards parliamentary democracy had by no means been uniform. Principal rejection stood alongside pragmatic acceptance of existing circumstances. See Maik Ohnezeit, *Zwischen 'schärfster Opposition' und dem 'Willen zur Macht'. Die Deutschnationale Volkspartei (DNVP) in der Weimarer Republik 1918–1928* (Düsseldorf: Droste Verlag, 2011). The DNVP—like the DVP—had rejected the Weimar constitution in 1919 in the National Assembly, but nonetheless constructively contributed beforehand to consultations on the constitution. See Christian F. Trippe, *Konservative Verfassungspolitik 1918–1923. Die DNVP als Opposition in Reich und Ländern* (Düsseldorf: Droste Verlag, 1995). The thesis advocated by Mergel, *Parlamentarische Kultur*, 323–1, of a temporary 'silent republicanisation' of the DNVP is in my view not tenable. Along these lines also Ohnezeit, *Zwischen 'schärfster Opposition'*, 453–4.
32. See, for example, Gusy, *Weimarer Reichsverfassung*, 399.
33. See, for example, Oskar Hergt (DNVP) on 27 November 1928, *Verhandlungen des Reichstags*, vol. 423, p. 493.
34. As expressed, for example, by the DVP deputy Albert Zapf on 28 February 1929 during the explanation of the aforementioned motion; *Verhandlungen des Reichstags*, vol. 424, p. 1340.
35. An example for a reference to this article is given by Haas for the DDP in *Verhandlungen des Reichstags*, vol. 424, p. 1383 (1 March 1929).
36. *Verhandlungen des Reichstags*, vol. 357, p. 9109.
37. Anton Erkelenz, 'Von Wirth zu Cuno' in *Die Hilfe*, 1 December 1922, 459–60, here 460. It should be noted that Erkelenz left the DDP in 1930 and switched to the SPD.
38. Detailed on this: Raithel, *Das schwierige Spiel*, 171–341.
39. *Verhandlungen des Reichstags*, vol. 361, p. 12297 (4 December 1923).
40. Ibid., p. 12301 (5 December 1923).
41. *Verhandlungen des Reichstags*, vol. 352, pp. 5284–5285 (16 December 1921).
42. *Verhandlungen des Reichstags*, vol. 423, p. 354.
43. *Verhandlungen des Reichstags*, vol. 424, p. 1383 (1 March 1929).
44. Ibid., p. 1364.

45. See Mergel, *Parlamentarische Kultur*, 362–7; Raithel, *Das schwierige Spiel*, 35.
46. See Schönberger, *Das Parlament im Anstaltsstaat*, 406–7. On its continued effect, also within democratic Weimar constitutional doctrine, see Ibid., 7 and 409–10.
47. In general on the tradition and the continued effect of this topos in Germany, see Jörg Kilian, 'Das alte Lied vom Reden und Handeln. Zur Rezeption parlamentarischer Kommunikationsprozesse in der parlamentarisch-demokratischen Öffentlichkeit der Bundesrepublik' in *Zeitschrift für Parlamentsfragen* 27 (1996) 503–18.
48. See Rainer Hering, '"Parteien vergehen, aber das deutsche Volk muß weiterleben". Die Ideologie der Überparteilichkeit als wichtiges Element der politischen Kultur im Kaiserreich und in der Weimarer Republik' in Walter Schmitz and Clemens Vollnhals (eds.), *Völkische Bewegung–Konservative Revolution–Nationalsozialismus. Aspekte einer politisierten Kultur* (Dresden: Thelem, 2005) 33–43.
49. See Mergel, *Parlamentarische Kultur*, 401–2. Especially on the liberal criticism of parties, see Stefan Grüner, 'Zwischen Einheitssehnsucht und pluralistischer Massendemokratie. Zum Parteien- und Demokratieverständnis im deutschen und französischen Liberalismus der Zwischenkriegszeit' in Horst Möller and Manfred Kittel (eds.), *Demokratie in Deutschland und Frankreich. 1918–1933/40. Beiträge zu einem historischen Vergleich* (Munich: Oldenbourg Verlag, 2002) 219–49, here 226–34.
50. For further references to the now rich research, see Retterath, *'Was ist das Volk?'*, 272–327.
51. *Verhandlungen des Reichstags*, vol. 423, p. 492 (27 November 1928). On constitutional demands for the introduction of a parliament of estates, see Gusy, *Weimarer Reichsverfassung*, 452–3.
52. See, for example, Siegfried von Kardorff (DVP), *Verhandlungen des Reichstags*, vol. 425, p. 2155 (7 June 1929).
53. Thus, Rudolf Breitscheid (SPD), who was knowledgeable when it came to French parliamentarism, criticized on 14 November 1922 the German orientation towards the procedures of government formation in France, *Verhandlungen des Reichstags*, vol. 357, p. 9109.
54. *Verhandlungen des Reichstags*, vol. 424, p. 1363 (1 March 1929).
55. Ibid., p. 1373.
56. *Verhandlungen des Reichstags*, vol. 424, p. 1420 (14 March 1929).
57. The fact that experts in constitutional law who had originally been sympathetic towards parliamentary democracy were also involved in this development is shown by Groh, *Demokratische Staatsrechtslehre*. See, in summary, Ibid. 584–5.

# PART III

# Resilience of Parliamentary Ideals

# CHAPTER 10

# Trial and Error: Post-War Democracies and the Restoration of Parliamentarism— Italy, Austria, Germany

*Marie-Luise Recker*

The aftermath of the First World War seemed to be the high tide of parliamentarism: all European states west of the Soviet Union adopted constitutions based on the principles of parliamentary democracy and universal suffrage. By the eve of the Second World War, this had changed dramatically: only in the west and in the north of the continent had parliamentarism survived, whereas, in the centre, the south and the east of Europe autocratic, dictatorial or Fascist regimes had been established.[1] The Second World War aggravated this picture even more: all countries under German occupation which up to this time had preserved democratic rules now switched over to dictatorial regimes or had no government whatsoever but suffered direct German rule.

So, in the aftermath of the Second World War, the European states[2] faced decisions: Was parliamentary democracy, which seemed to have failed so visibly in the past, still the ideal to adopt in their new constitutions? Should fundamental changes be made in the role, the combination and the influence of the different players in the constitutional order so that

M.-L. Recker (✉)
Goethe University, Frankfurt, Germany
e-mail: mlrecker@t-online.de

© The Author(s) 2019
R. Aerts et al. (eds.), *The Ideal of Parliament in Europe since 1800*,
Palgrave Studies in Political History,
https://doi.org/10.1007/978-3-030-27705-5_10

it would be balanced better in the future? Or should the task of the day be to agree upon a new, a different constitutional order? In those countries which revived after Nazi occupation like France, Belgium, the Netherlands, Denmark, Norway and even in Czechoslovakia, the return to parliamentary democracy was not questioned, since the restoration of the former constitution—at least with regard to its principal regulations—could be seen as wiping out the dark days of occupation and Nazi rule.

The countries which had the most obvious reasons to think twice about their new constitutions and about the ways to make them safe for a more stable and viable democracy were Italy, Germany and Austria, those countries which had produced Fascist or National Socialist regimes first and where the post-First World War constitutional order had been too weak to prevent their leaders from taking over political power and disbanding the political system. How did these three states approach the problem of making a new constitution? Did the four Allied Powers and their occupational forces influence the work of their constitutional assemblies or play a decisive role using other means? How much were the new political parties in the three countries disposed to go back to their former government system? To what extent did they feel it necessary to take precautions against descending again into malfunction and malpractice? Were they disposed to look to foreign countries as models and guides? What were, in their view, the fundamental traits of an ideal constitution? These are the questions this chapter will address.

## ITALY

The most complex case is the Italian one, since it took nearly five years from the erosion of the Fascist regime to the passage of a constitutional law which installed a parliamentary democracy.[3] When King Vittorio Emanuele III dismissed Mussolini in July 1943, he did this according to the existing political order. Nevertheless, this act shifted the gravitational centre of the political forces towards the monarchy and the army. But both institutions soon lost much of their newly gained reputation when in September 1943 they agreed upon a unilateral armistice and, as a result, German forces occupied most of the country, disarmed the Italian army and took its members prisoner. The precipitated and shameful escape of the King and the new Prime Minister, Badoglio, from Rome to Brindisi completely undermined any authority and respect which they still claimed. Even had the monarchy survived its alliance with Fascism during

Mussolini's reign, its moral and political failure after the dismissal of the Duce deprived it of all loyalty and appreciation even among many liberal and conservative quarters of its subjects. So, the attempt by Vittorio Emanuele III to alleviate the situation by his retirement and by the appointment of his son, Umberto II, as regent did not help to save the monarchy.[4] In a plebiscite held in June 1946, a majority of the electorate, though a narrow one (54.3%), voted for the installation of a republic in post-war Italy. Whereas in the south of the country, the monarchy still enjoyed much sympathy, in the north and the central parts the political preferences tended towards a republican order and carried the day. In these elections, women, too, were given a vote for the first time so that the principle of universal suffrage was implemented in Italy at last.

Fascism was not a political option for the future. Mussolini's disgraceful politics of subordination to Hitler's whims and German military strategy had undermined his authority even before his dismissal in 1943, and the extent to which he submitted himself and his new *Repubblica Sociale Italiana* to the German ally and to its political, economic and military demands discredited him definitively in the eyes of his former followers. A resurrection of Fascism in post-war Italy was not a probable option, and pro-Fascist parties were to play only a fringe role in these days.

The political vacuum which the dismissal of Mussolini and the King's loss of authority had produced was filled more and more by other forces,[5] especially by the *Resistenza*, the partisan movement, where socialist and communist groups employed the strongest divisions. In these circles, ideas of direct democracy, of Soviet power or other Jacobin ideas initially had quite a few adherents, since such forms of grass-roots activities seemed to be in a better position to destroy the remains of Fascism than was the liberal democracy of the old type. In particular, the idea that ad hoc bodies like the Liberation Committees which had taken the lead in the purge of Fascism might play a decisive role in a future constitutional order was advanced here and there.

For the creation of a new political order, it was quite decisive that the Communists, gathered under the banner of the *Partito Communista Italiano* (PCI) under the leadership of Palmiro Togliatti, rejected all these proposals and became unequivocal adherents of a parliamentary democracy of the Western type. In Togliatti's view—and in accordance with Stalin's directives concerning the strategic course of all communist parties in the West European countries—the future of post-war Italy should not be based on the support of a single class, the workers, but was to be determined by the whole nation.[6] Since the Italian bourgeoisie had betrayed the aims of the nineteenth-century movement for national unity, the *Risorgimento*, had destroyed the liberal political order and had given birth to Fascism, now after the end of Fascism it was the task of the communist movement to complete the *Risorgimento* so that Italy would be able to build up socialism through democratic means. The establishment of a parliamentary democracy was seen as a first step in this direction of creating the traditional communist utopia as it would help to foster a far-reaching democratization of Italian society. Then, in a second step, the creation of a socialist society (and a PCI-headed government) would follow, though not by revolutionary violence as in the October Revolution, but within the constitutional order of a representative democracy and accompanied by a broad social consensus. Socialism, so to speak, was to be attained the 'Italian way' without the use of political violence. These at first sight quite astonishing ideas regarding the future of the Italian political system showed the influence of Antonio Gramsci, whose *Lettere* and *Quaderni del Carcere* had had a decisive impact on Communist intellectuals.[7] So, deputies of the PCI were to be among the most influential fathers of the new Constitutional Law.

This preference of the mighty PCI for a parliamentary democracy influenced also the various socialist and social democratic groups. Even when in their ranks advocates of direct democracy or of other grass-roots conceptions still stuck to their convictions, the great majority switched over to the constitutional strategy of their Communist fellow party with which they intended to cooperate closely for the common weal of the Italian society.

For the broad acceptance of the Constitutional Law, it was quite decisive that on the other side of the political spectrum the re-emerging liberal and Catholic parties, too, opted for a Western-style representative democracy. For them as well, the common experience of the *Resistenza* as the Italian people's movement for liberation and national unity shaped their vision of the future constitutional order. Now, after the Second World War, a 'second' *Risorgimento* had to give birth to a renewed national state in which the masses, excluded from the 'first', the nineteenth-century, *Risorgimento* and from the political order that had ensued, were to be fully integrated and in which they should enjoy all liberal rights of democratic participation. The *Democrazia Christiana* (DC), the most influential political party in this sphere, under the leadership of Alcide de Gasperi left the authoritarian roots of its predecessor, the *Partito Popolare Italiano*, behind and turned to the values of freedom, democracy, individual rights and social welfare. This made the DC as well as the PCI and the Socialists a strong pillar of the new political order.

On the day of the referendum on the question of monarchy or republican order, 2 June 1946, elections for a Constitutional Assembly, too, took place. The results were a great disappointment for the PCI (18.9%) and the Socialists (20.7%), whereas the DC became the strongest political force (35.2%).[8] The two political camps counterbalanced each other. But this situation did not produce gridlock; on the contrary, the parties in question had many constitutional concepts in common and in general were disposed to cooperate in central political questions. Contentious points could be (and were) postponed into the future when—as both sides hoped—the election results would enable them to have their way in the question concerned.

At first sight, the new Italian constitution[9] resembled to a great degree the liberal constitution of the mid-nineteenth century; the most conspicuous and radical change was the abolition of the monarchy in favour of a republican order. But looking into details produces a slightly different picture. In general, the new constitution reflected the idea of rejecting the concept of a big state and a powerful executive; instead it emphasized the role of the legislative bodies as true representatives of the electorate. So, the position of the new President of the Republic was restricted to more or less ceremonial duties. In particular, he lost the old freedom of the King to choose the Prime Minister; instead, this power went to Parliament or, to be more exact, to the deputies of the parliamentary groups on which the Government relied. This was the main step for the introduction of a modern parliamentary democracy where the government is supported by a majority of the House and the controlling function has switched over to the opposition parties. The new Prime Minister, as well, was modelled as a weak head of government: he was only primus inter pares in his cabinet and could not dismiss his ministers or state secretaries. On the other hand, both Houses of Parliament, the *Camera dei Deputati* and the *Senato*, got much influence. They had to give a vote of confidence to the new Prime Minister before he was sworn in and could dismiss him and his ministers by a vote of no-confidence. They were the central legislative body and had to pass all bills jointly. This *bicameralismo perfetto* was seen as a means to guarantee optimal and well-balanced decisions, but it tended also towards gridlock and delays.

Both the Chamber of Deputies and Senate were elected on the principle of proportional representation, with no thresholds to impede fringe parties from taking seats there. The Communist and the Socialist deputies in the Constitutional Assembly favoured this idea of mirroring the electoral vote in the composition of the legislative bodies, and they also had insisted on giving comparatively more power to the two Houses of Parliament at the expense of the Prime Minister and his cabinet. This was a pattern they promoted in all constituent assemblies in Europe in these days.

Italy was defined as a democratic and antifascist republic based on citizen rights. These rights, including special social rights, were guaranteed as unalterable regulations which a Constitutional Court, created in 1956, had to observe. A highly controversial point was the affirmation of the Lateran Treaties of 1929 concerning the role of the Catholic Church; as the DC made the inclusion of this article in the new constitution a precondition for its consent to it. The PCI finally accepted this stipulation through gritted teeth whereas Socialists and Liberals rejected it. In return, the DC gave in to the demands of the left-wing parties on social questions. The regulations concerning the future regionalization of Italy were also important innovations though they were realized only slowly and incompletely. On 22 December 1947, the new Constitutional Law passed the Assembly with an overall majority and came into force on 1 January 1948.

Even though the different players in the constitutional order were rebalanced to a certain extent and some new elements were included in the new constitution, its resemblance to the former nineteenth-century liberal constitution is quite remarkable. The Italian Constitutional Assembly did not make great efforts to discuss far-reaching new ideas but was determined to improve the old constitutional order. The new constitutional order rested on two beliefs, shared across the political spectrum. First, it deleted Fascism from the history of twentieth-century Italy. There were no serious efforts to get to the bottom of the reasons—be they political, economic or social—for the rapid rise of Fascism, but all members of the Constitutional Assembly were convinced that with the victory over Fascism and the (actual and future) pre-eminence of the 'progressive' political forces in post-war Italy, this danger had disappeared forever. Fascism was seen as the incarnation of all ills and wrongdoings of Italian history and character, representing the 'false Italy', whereas Mussolini's sudden fall had brought forward the 'real Italy' again, starting with the 'first' *Risorgimento* in the nineteenth century and triumphing now in the 'second' *Risorgimento* of the mid-1940s. Fascism was an error, an impasse, an intrusion into the development of Italy which now had been corrected by the mutual efforts of all ranks of the Italian people.

Secondly, in the eyes of the founding fathers of the new Italian republic, this concept of 'first' and 'second' *Risorgimento* banished all thoughts that it was not only or in the first instance the *Resistenza* which had overthrown Fascism, but that the essential forces had been the Anglo-American soldiers and their military strength. Instead, the adherents of the new constitution expelled this truth from their deliberations and put the emphasis on their own efforts and on their own victory over the evil enemy. They seem not even to have been open to good advice from the Allied powers. It is difficult to decide how much the Military Government in Rome put limits on the constitutional choices of the new political parties or whether they interfered openly or secretly in the work of the Constitutional Assembly; given what we know at this point,[10] it looks as if such interference was not an important factor. On the other hand, with the emerging Cold War the European countries under Allied control in general tended to look to the constitutional order of 'their' hegemon and to adapt its model even without much pressure or persuasion. This tendency also favoured a return in 1945 to the former liberal system.

## Austria

Austria took more or less the same decision.[11] When the Red Army reached Vienna on 13 April 1945, the Soviet Military Commissioner immediately tried to form a provisional government for Austria including the three licensed political parties: the Communists (KPÖ), the Social Democrats (SPÖ) and the Catholic Austrian People's Party (ÖVP). This new government formed on 27 April 1945 under the leadership of Karl Renner was immediately recognized by the Soviets as the legitimate voice of the Austrian people notwithstanding the fact that for the moment its authority was limited to the parts of Austria occupied by the Red Army. Renner who had been the first chancellor of Austria's First Republic in 1919/20 saw his overall task as re-establishing the independence and territorial integrity of the Austrian state and shaking off Allied control as soon as possible. To this end he tried to proclaim immediately the restoration of the Republic of Austria and to build up new administrative authorities. 'We can't wait until the others dictate their concepts to us'[12] was how one of his cabinet colleagues characterized the general position towards the occupation forces.

The proclamation on the creation of a new and independent Austrian Republic on 27 April 1945, the day of the installation of the provisional government, was not a contested issue since the Allies had already agreed upon this step in their Moscow Declaration in November 1943. More controversial was the re-enactment of the former constitution of 1920 as provisional constitution for the new state. For Renner, one of the main tasks of his government was to agree upon a new constitution as a basis for its political activities which would be in effect until a newly elected Constitutional Assembly could pass a new one. So, he favoured the return to the constitution of the First Republic in the version of 7 December 1929, in his words the last democratic and non-fascist constitution of the Austrian Republic.[13]

When this was discussed in the Cabinet Council, most participants agreed on this decision though one of its members, Johann Koplenig (KPÖ), doubted that the provisional government could do this on its own authority and characterized this step as an anti-democratic activity. But Renner had no intention of permitting the KPÖ to push for a broad discussion on the new constitution, since this would have opened a dangerous debate on the political development of the First Republic, a taboo topic for both SPÖ and ÖVP. Instead, the resurrection of the former constitution could kill these discussions for the moment. And the Chancellor got his way. As he outlined, for him and his fellow Social Democrats, the first option had been to go back to the constitution of 1920, 'but we do not feel entitled to cancel the results of a democratic development of fourteen years'.[14] They were, however, willing to accept the re-enactment of the constitutional order of 1929 which had been in force until parliament had been paralysed and an authoritarian government had taken over. And Koplenig gave in. So, on 13 May 1945, a fortnight after its installation, the government decreed that the Austrian Federal Constitution of 1 October 1920 in the version of 7 December 1929 would come into effect again. According to the regulations in this constitution, national elections were held in November 1945, a new government under Chancellor Leopold Figl (ÖVP) was formed and the former Chancellor Karl Renner was elected the first Federal President of the resurrected republic. The intention of convoking a Constitutional Assembly in order to elaborate a new constitution was never taken up again.

What does this speedy, perhaps even precipitate, return to the constitution of the First Republic tell us about the self-image and the self-comprehension of the Second Republic? In the first instance, it was a reassertion of the territorial integrity of Austria[15] according to the boundaries at the time of its creation as a national state. In the eyes of Renner and his fellow politicians, during the First Republic the striving for *Anschluss* had impeded the consolidation of the newly formed democratic Austria and had given it a somewhat provisional status. This was to be ruled out now. But they were not only eager to take precautions against a new *Anschluss*, they also wanted to oppose all claims of Austria's neighbours—Hungary, Czechoslovakia, Yugoslavia—for territorial detachments. This was not an idle consideration since such claims concerning parts of Carinthia or Lower Austria were discussed in these days. And last but not least, a return to the constitution of the First Republic would ward off any future allotment of Austria among the four victor states or any other idea of redrawing the boundaries in Central Europe. In this sense, the return to the constitution of 1920 can be seen as an assertion of national integrity and of the feeling of being an independent nation.

In addition, this decision symbolized the ultimate break with its German neighbour and with the NS regime. There was no serious discussion of the reasons for democratic Austria's descending into civil war and authoritarian rule even before coming under the German yoke. Instead, the *Anschluss* and German rule after 1938 were seen as acts of invasion and occupation, as an intrusion from outside into the national development of the First Republic. We can find the image of Austria as the innocent victim to Nazi aggression here for the first time. If Austria was a victim and not a perpetrator or at least a beneficiary of Nazi rule, it was legitimate and obvious to return to the preceding constitutional regime.

Finally, the re-implementation of the constitution of the First Republic built a bridge from the coalition governments of the early 1920s to those of the Second Republic. These 1920s coalition governments included the strongest political parties, the Social Democrats and the Christian Socialists, and stood for the consolidation of the newly born First Republic which would eventually be brought down by anti-parliamentary forces in the 1930s. Going back in 1945 to the cooperation of the pro-democratic political forces was an attempt to heal and to overcome this fateful descent into street fighting and civil war. This Great Coalition of Social Democrats and Austrian People's Party, first with, then without the Communists, was to characterize the Second Republic for decades. It symbolized the close cooperation of the leading political parties overcoming class barriers or other social or ideological divisions for the benefit of the re-established democratic order. If the early 1920s were regarded as the most hopeful and vital time of democratic Austria, then it was consistent that after 1945 all political forces consented to restoring the constitution of these earlier days. And the cooperation of the two strongest political parties was to protect and safeguard this reborn national state.

## GERMANY

West Germany went the same way that Austria and Italy had gone before. Antifascist Committees, formed directly after the collapse of the National Socialist regime and consisting mostly of members of the labour movement, were only a transitory phenomenon. No forms of direct democracy or Soviet organizations had any adherents among the re-emerging political parties or the Allied powers and were soon forbidden by the Military Governments. Instead, the political parties were to become the central actors in the political field and the creators of new constitutions. Their concepts were to determine these documents still to be elaborated.

Debates on the future constitutional order started immediately after the war in the *Länder* of the western occupation zones.[16] On this level, the overall model implemented was a liberal representative democracy as it had existed in some of these *Länder* during the Weimar Republic. Even when there were differences in details of the respective constitutions, the general preference for this pattern is undeniable.

This was true again for the members of the Parliamentary Council which, on 1 September 1948, had gathered in the city of Bonn in order to discuss a new constitution for the future West German State.[17] They, too, looked back to Germany's constitutional traditions from the *Paulskirche* deliberations in 1848/49 via the constitutional charters of Imperial Germany in 1866 and 1871 towards the Weimar constitution in 1919. In particular, the Weimar constitution was the reference point[18] in their deliberations on the future Basic Law. Here, the Westminster model stood in high esteem. The American government system was not considered as appropriate for imitation. Certainly, there were some members in the Parliamentary Council who voted for a presidential system in analogy to the one across the Atlantic Ocean, but the great majority of their colleagues argued that this would be a too far-reaching rupture with German traditions of parliamentarism.

So, without longer discussion, the general features of the Westminster model were agreed upon as principles of the new *Grundgesetz*: the rule of law, the division of power, the sovereignty of parliament and governing through parliament. But these were principles which had characterized earlier German constitutions from the *Paulskirche* version to the Weimar constitution. Other foreign models were mentioned only sporadically. This is amazing since some members of the Parliamentary Council had come to know the political life in their countries of exile quite well—in Great Britain, Sweden, Switzerland—but they hardly ever referred to specific regulations of the constitutional order there during their work on the Basic Law.[19] Instead, the new constitution was a document written with an eye to the perceived weaknesses of the Weimar constitution. The overriding aim of the founders of the *Grundgesetz* was to improve this constitutional law of 1919, to expel from it those regulations which in their view had upset the balance of power, had impeded government stability, had undermined the role of parliament and had split up the party system.

The measures they took can be summarized briefly.[20] They minimized the position of the Federal President who, from now on, more or less had only ceremonial functions, who—as in the Italian case—no longer had the right to choose the future chancellor and who could not base his authority on a popular vote but was elected by the legislative body. Instead, they strengthened the position of the Federal Chancellor who, at the beginning of the legislative period, had to be elected by the *Bundestag* and whom parliament could no longer depose by a vote of no-confidence without designating his successor. In addition, they extended his role as head of government and leader of the cabinet. On the other hand, they initiated different steps in order to force parliament to do its duties. Not only did they narrow its ways and means to depose a chancellor; they also wanted to prevent premature dissolutions of parliament so that MPs were forced to tackle the political questions of the day and find compromises without facing new elections. The great majority of these regulations which were seen as a remedy to stabilize parliamentary democracy had already been inserted into the constitutional laws of the 12 *Länder* in the 3 Western occupation zones and thus can be judged as characteristic features of constitutional innovation in the post-Second World War Germany.

Much discussion dealt with the federal order of the future West German state. A fierce debating point[21] focused on the type of second chamber to be created—an American-style Senate or traditional *Bundesrat*—the latter option which corresponded to German constitutional tradition was implemented eventually. The other point centred on different views concerning that chamber's political powers. Here, the Western Allies exerted their influence in favour of a strong position for the *Bundesrat* especially in financial questions, but found much support among parts of the Christian Democratic delegates whereas most Social Democrats favoured a powerful central government.

Two further innovations need to be mentioned. The first is the new Federal Constitutional Court modelled along its US prototype, which was created in order to guard the central regulations of the new constitution and to protect the individual rights of German citizens and can be seen as the central embodiment of Western Germany as a *Rechtsstaat*, a state based on the rule of law. The second was the adjustment of the electoral system.[22]

In the view of many contemporaries, the electoral law for the Weimar *Reichstag*, based on proportional representation, had been one of the gravest errors of the political system introduced in 1919. It had favoured the fracturing of the party system, had given fringe parties the chance to enter parliament and thus had hindered the formation of coherent coalitions. But the question regarding which voting system might be installed in its place produced a heated public debate. Here, the British system of majority vote had prominent advocates inside and outside the Parliamentary Council. In their view, this voting system favoured strong political parties able to integrate different social groups and interests among their followers whereas parties which represented only small social groups or regional interests would be marginalized and disappear from parliament. So, before long, a two-party system would emerge, as in the British case, where both sides competed for electoral predominance.

Their critics were not convinced that these effects would be in the best interests of the new political system of the Federal Republic. They argued that by introducing majority vote, considerable parts of the electorate were not represented in parliament and that the composition of the *Bundestag* did not reflect the political views of the voters, which might cause people to turn away from the newly installed democratic system. Instead, they preferred to improve the voting system by correcting its deficits. So, they wanted to preserve proportional representation, but to introduce a certain threshold for getting into parliament which all parties had to exceed so that fringe parties would be kept out of the future *Bundestag*.

In the end,[23] elements of both views found their way into the new electoral law. Each voter had two votes—one for a personal candidate in his own constituency and one vote for a party list. The personal candidates were chosen by simple majority, the list candidates according to proportional representation. Only parties which had gained at least 5% of the total second votes cast could be represented in the *Bundestag* at all. In addition, the danger of radical, anti-democratic parties threatening the new political system was made even more remote by a constitutional provision which enabled the government and the new Federal Constitutional Court to ban any political organizations which, by the aims or by the actions of their adherents, threatened the democratic political system. While the Weimar constitution had allowed its opponents to take actions to undermine and destroy it, the Basic Law created an 'alert' democracy, able to ward off its destruction.

In the West German case, the Allied Powers played a more decisive role in constitution-making than in the other countries studied here. When the Military Governors ordered the heads of the West German *Länder* governments to convoke a Constituent Assembly, they strictly underlined that the new state had to be a representative liberal democracy with guarantees of individual rights and freedoms.[24] In addition, during the work of the Parliamentary Council, Allied officers repeatedly intervened in its deliberations; the point already mentioned—the federal structure of the future West German state—was only one of the issues in question. But in general, the German side was willing to meet their demands so that they need not fall back on direct and harsh orders. Overall, the wishes of the Allies and the conceptions of the members of the Parliamentary Council tended to correspond.

In the West German case again, the founding fathers of the *Grundgesetz* looked back to German constitutional tradition. As in the Italian debate, this return to features in German history considered as worthy of remembering and imitation was a subtle way to erase the Nazi years and to show that Germany had democratic traditions to which the makers of the Federal Law could refer. If the invention of tradition can be seen as an eminent element of nation-building,[25] the invention of a 'democratic' tradition is a way to construct a better, an 'ideal' German history where the forces of emancipation and enlightenment fed into the new political order created by the *Grundgesetz*. It obtained much of its legitimation and esteem from this imagined 'tradition'.

But unlike their fellow constitution-makers in Italy and Austria, the members of the Parliamentary Council could not evade discussions of the reasons for Hitler's rise to power. This debate[26] accompanied their work up to its end, alluded to different topics and arguments and did not run along party lines, but was a serious and scrupulous dialogue. Even when the economic, social and ideological circumstances of the 1920s and early 1930s were mentioned as well, most speakers considered the Weimar constitution to have been the most decisive prerequisite for the rise of the National Socialist movement and for Hitler's chancellorship. So, they altered all those regulations which in their view had impeded the formation of a strong and stable government. In addition, they tried to take precautions against the rise of anti-democratic forces, left-wing as well as right-wing, and to concede to the future Constitutional Court the right and the means to ban anti-parliamentary elements from the political arena. This emphasis on creating an 'alert' democracy was a specific and characteristic feature of the Basic Law.

Even in East Germany, we find this return to German constitutional tradition. When the Communist Party (KPD) was founded again in Berlin in June 1945, its central committee called special attention to its conviction that it would be wrong to impose the Soviet system on Germany at this moment, that instead it was the task of the day to complete the bourgeois revolution started in 1848 and to set up an antifascist, democratic regime, a liberal parliamentary democracy with all democratic rights and freedoms for everybody. Only after this was achieved could further steps towards a socialist society and a Marxist-Leninist constitution be envisaged.[27] This reserved attitude concerning the implementation of a full-scale Soviet system in East Germany was induced by the general strategy of both the Soviet Union and the KPD[28] to not rule out by premature steps the formation of a united German state, comprising all four occupation zones, in which they hoped to be able to exert considerable political influence. They stuck to this strategy even when in their zone they initiated first measures towards a 'people's democracy' and a 'socialist' transformation of the economy.

After the forced unification of KPD and SPD in the Eastern zone, the new SED put itself at the head of this movement for national unity under Eastern perspectives. The main instrument for reaching this aim became the People's Congress Movement for Unity and a Just Peace, a nominated body representing political parties and other mass organizations. In May 1948, the Second People's Congress elected a *Volksrat*, a People's Council, which, afterwards, unanimously sanctioned a draft constitution for a (non-divided) German democratic republic, elaborated in one of its sub-committees along the lines mentioned above. A new People's Council repeated this step in May 1949. With the work of the Parliamentary Council in Bonn coming to its end and confronted with the perspective of a West German state being created, the SED and the Soviets changed course and decided to form an East German state as well. For propaganda reasons, they intended to wait for the proclamation of the Federal Republic in Bonn before they took the necessary steps in this direction. So, on 7 October 1949, the *Volksrat* changed his name into a provisional *Volkskammer*, proclaimed the foundation of the German Democratic Republic (DDR), put the draft constitution into operation and formed an East German government according to the provisions of this constitution.

The new constitution[29] referred in many points to the Weimar constitution of 1919. The DDR was defined as a representative democratic republic with a two-tiered parliament, the lower house, the *Volkskammer*, being its highest constitutional organ. A catalogue of basic and human rights was added, though an omnibus article against slander would give the future government rather unlimited powers to harass and persecute all those who had departed from the right way. In general, an independent judiciary was not provided for in the new constitution. The regulations which gave the SED an overriding hold on the political life of the DDR were those concerning the executive: all parliamentary groups had to participate in an all-party government, and the numerically strongest of them—which would always be the SED—had the legal claim to nominate the Head of Government. So, a central element of the Westminster model, the confrontation of government and opposition groups in parliament and their fight for the best solutions, was passed over and the predominance of the SED established. The provisions of the electoral law reinforced this tendency. According to Marxist-Leninist principles, elections were held on the basis of single lists of candidates, and each party had a previously determined number of allotted seats in the *Volkskammer*.

In East Germany, the impact of the occupation forces[30] was far more decisive for the process of state-building and constitution-making than in any other case referred to above. The KPD/SED conformed to this preponderant role of the Soviet Union and adapted its strategy to this situation. Political parties or organizations which opposed this course and proposed different constitutional concepts were attacked with harsh measures and were forced to comply. In addition, the timetable of promulgating a new constitution depended to a great degree on analogous steps being taken in the Western zones. Opting for a constitutional order along the model of 1848/49 and 1919 can't be seen as a sincere choice among different patterns, but was induced by other considerations, especially by the intention of the Soviet Union and its adjutant, the KPD/SED, to preserve and enhance their political influence in all four occupation zones. Irrespective of these calculations, they formed the draft constitution for the future German state in a way in which the long-term predominance of the SED would be established and dissident forces could be suppressed. Even if at first glance the resemblance of the constitution of October 1949 to its Weimar predecessor seems quite impressive, its substance and particularly the parts concerning the balance of power and the rule of law departed completely from the purported model.

## CONCLUSIONS

What conclusions can we draw from the fact that in all four countries a parliamentary democracy of the Western type was introduced after the Second World War—at least (with regard to East Germany) if we look at the letter of these constitutions, not at the reality behind them? There was no intense and controversial discussion about the type of constitutional order to be introduced in any country looked at. For most of the political parties involved in these discussions, the Christian Democrats, the Conservatives and the Liberals as well as the Social Democrats, a return to the Westminster model as it had been established in all countries after the First World War was the best option they could think of. Even if the parties involved, especially the Social Democrats, reckoned that for a happy future, the traditional liberal democracy of the nineteenth century had to be completed by steps towards social democracy and that economic redistribution and elite change were prerequisites for a viable political order, they were sure that Western-style parliamentary democracy gave enough freedom to reach these goals in future.

In a more general view, going back to the preceding constitutional laws, as was the case in all four countries, was a manifestation of national sovereignty and of abjuring Fascism and National Socialism. The dark period of Mussolini's and Hitler's rule was expelled from national history, the reasons for their rise and successful assertion more or less put aside, and a direct line was drawn from the happy transition to a democratic order in the *Risorgimento* or after the First World War to the creation of a parliamentary democracy after the Second World War. To be sure, the founders of the new constitutions insisted upon changes in the former constitutional order, even decisive ones, in order to correct its deficiencies, but the general trend was for the restoration of the former political system. In this endeavour, they wanted to integrate their countries into the general constitutional trends then current in Europe, to overcome their status as outlaws of the international order due to their Fascist or National Socialist past and to become respected and appreciated members of post-war Europe.

And, in short, they were successful.[31] Unlike after the First World War, the democratic political order in Italy, Austria and West Germany now persisted. The reasons for this success story are different in each country, but general trends can be ascertained. In all three countries, the main political parties supported the new constitutional order and were its strongest pillars. Anti-democratic groups which had been strong during the interwar period now became fringe phenomena. In addition, politicians looked upon with appreciation and esteem represented this new political order. The best example is Konrad Adenauer, in whose West German *Kanzlerdemokratie* people could see that strong political leadership could be reconciled with a parliamentary system. Relying on a coalition government with a coherent majority in the *Bundestag*, Adenauer was able to implement the reconstruction legislation necessary for social stability and economic growth and to pave the way for the integration of the Federal Republic into the Western community.

The emerging Cold War was the third factor to be mentioned in this context. When an impermeable antagonism divided Western liberal societies from 'totalitarianism', West Germany, Austria and Italy now could install themselves on the 'proper', the 'good' side of the new international order. In striving for membership in the 'West', the shaping and retaining of a democratic political system was an essential prerequisite for admittance to this club. This antagonistic interpretation of the post-war order was particularly prominent in countries like Italy, Austria and West Germany which bordered on the Iron Curtain running through Europe. The incorporation of Eastern Germany into the Soviet bloc, on the other hand, transformed the German Democratic Republic into a Stalinist puppet regime. So, in all cases analysed here, the notion of an 'ideal' political system depended to a great extent on which hemispheric order the country in question wanted to adhere to. Adjustment in the post-war international order and modelling the government system went hand in hand.

# NOTES

1. Cf. Marie-Luise Recker, 'Europäischer Parlamentarismus in der Zwischenkriegszeit zwischen Funktion und Dysfunktion' in Benjamin Conrad, Hans-Christian Maner and Jan Kusber (eds.), *Parlamentarier der deutschen Minderheiten im Europa der Zwischenkriegszeit* (Dusseldorf: Droste Verlag, 2015) 27–43.

2. Cf. Ian Kershaw, *Roller-Coaster. Europe 1950–2017* (London: Penguin, 2018).

3. Cf. Hans Woller, *Geschichte Italiens im 20. Jahrhundert* (München: C.H. Beck Verlag, 2010).

4. Cf. for details of these political developments Carlo Ghisalberti, *Storia costituzionale d'Italia 1848–1948* (Bari: Laterza, 1989) 395 f.

5. Cf. for more details Karl Dietrich Bracher, *Die Krise Europas 1917–1975* (Frankfurt am Main: Ullstein, 1982) 291 ff.

6. Cf. for this question Elena Aga-Rossi and Victor Zaslavsky, *Togliatti e Stalin. Il PCI e la politica estera staliniana negli archivi di Mosca* (Bologna: Il Mulino, 1997) esp. 55 ff.

7. Cf. Luisa Mangoni, 'Civiltà della crisi. Gli intellettuali tra fascismo e antifascismo' in Francesco Barbagallo (coordinatore), *Storia dell'Italia repubblicana*, vol. I (Torino: Einaudi, 1994) 615–718.

8. See the election results in Christian Jansen, *Italien seit 1945* (Göttingen: Vandenhoeck & Ruprecht, 2007) 34. The Liberals got 7%, the Republicans 4%.

9. See for these decisions Ghisalberti, *Storia*, 410 ff.; Francesco Barbagallo, 'La formazione dell'Italia democratica' in *Storia dell'Italia repubblicana*, vol. I, 3–128, esp. 110 ff.; Pietro Scoppola, *La repubblica dei partiti. Profilo storico della democrazia in Italia (1945–1990)* (Bologna: Il Mulino, 1991) 181 ff.

10. This uncertainty is underlined by Woller, *Geschichte Italiens im 20. Jahrhundert*, 214 f.

11. Cf. Ernst Hanisch, *Der lange Schatten des Staates. Österreichische Gesellschaftsgeschichte im 20. Jahrhundert* (Vienna: Ueberreuter, 1994) 399 ff.; Klaus Eisterer, 'Österreich unter alliierter Besatzung 1945–1955' in Rolf Steininger and Michael Gehler (eds.), *Österreich im 20. Jahrhundert*, vol. II (Vienna: Böhlau Verlag, 1997) 147–87.

12. Gertrude Enderle-Burcel and Rudolf Jerabek (eds.), *Protokolle des Kabinettsrates der Provisorischen Regierung Karl Renner 1945*, vol. I (Vienna, 1995) protocol No 14, 26 June 1945, p. 297.

13. Cf. Ibid., protocol No 5, 10 May 1945, p. 36 f.

14. Ibid., protocol No 6, 13 May 1945, p. 65.

15. Cf. Hanisch, *Schatten*, and Eisterer, *Österreich*.

16. Cf. Frank R. Pfetsch, *Ursprünge der Zweiten Republik, Prozesse der Verfassungsgebung in den Westzonen und in der Bundesrepublik* (Opladen: Westdeutscher Verlag, 1990) esp. 267 ff.
17. Cf. for these discussions Michael Feldkamp, *Der Parlamentarische Rat 1948–1949. Die Entstehung des Grundgesetzes* (Göttingen: Vandenhoeck & Ruprecht, 1998); Karlheinz Niclauß, *Der Weg zum Grundgesetz. Demokratiegründung in Westdeutschland 1945–1949* (Paderborn: Ferdinand Schöningh Verlag, 1998).
18. Cf. Sebastian Ullrich, *Der Weimar-Komplex. Das Scheitern der ersten deutschen Demokratie und die politische Kultur der frühen Bundesrepublik 1945–1959* (Göttingen: Wallstein Verlag, 2009) 165 ff.
19. Cf. Marie-Luise Recker, 'Westminster als Modell? Der Deutsche Bundestag und das britische Regierungssystem' in Gerhard A. Ritter and Peter Wende (eds.), *Rivalität und Partnerschaft. Studien zu den deutsch-britischen Beziehungen im 19. und 20. Jahrhundert. Festschrift für Anthony J. Nicholls* (Paderborn: Ferdinand Schöningh Verlag, 1999) 313–335.
20. Cf. for details Marie-Luise Recker, *Parlamentarismus in der Bundesrepublik Deutschland. Der Deutsche Bundestag 1949–1969* (Dusseldorf: Droste Verlag, 2018) 40 ff.
21. Cf. Karlheinz Niclaus, *Der Weg zum Grundgesetz*, 211 ff.
22. Cf. for this point Erhard H.M. Lange, *Wahlrecht und Innenpolitik. Entstehungsgeschichte und Analyse der Wahlgesetzgebung und Wahlrechtsdiskussion im westlichen Nachkriegsdeutschland 1945–1956* (Meisenheim am Glan: Verlag Anton Hain, 1975) esp. 329–408.
23. Cf. Recker, *Parlamentarismus*, 61 ff.
24. See Frankfurter Dokumente No 1, 1 September 1948, in *Der Parlamentarische Rat 1948–1949. Akten und Protokolle*, vol. I (Boppart: Harald Boldt Verlag, 1975) 30–6.
25. Cf. Benedict Anderson, *Imagined Communities. Reflections on the Origins and Spread of Nationalism* (London/New York: Verso, 2006).
26. See Ulrich, *Der Weimar-Komplex*, 93 ff.
27. See Aufruf des Zentralkomitees der KPD, 11 June 1945, in Hermann Weber (ed.), *DDR. Dokumente zur Geschichte der Deutschen Demokratischen Republik 1945–1985* (Munich: Deutscher Taschenbuch Verlag, 1986) No 4, p. 32–6.
28. Cf. for this strategy Hermann Weber, *Geschichte der DDR* (Munich: Deutscher Taschenbuch Verlag, 1989; 3rd ed.) 156 ff. and 186 ff.; Norman M. Naimark, *The Russians in Germany. A History of the Soviet Zone of Occupation 1945–1949* (Cambridge/Mass.: Belknap Press of Harvard University Press, 1997) 55 ff.
29. Reprinted in Weber, *DDR*, No 79, p. 156–163.
30. Cf. Naimark, *The Russians in Germany*, 318 ff.
31. Cf. For the German case Recker, *Parlamentarismus*, 689 ff.

# CHAPTER 11

# Too Ideal to Be a Parliament: The Representative Assemblies in Socialist Czechoslovakia, 1948–1989

*Adéla Gjuričová*

When thinking about the political systems and practices of Communist states in the Stalinist and the late-socialist eras, parliaments and legislations are not what first comes to mind. And yet, taking the example of Czechoslovakia, throughout the period of Communist Party dominance (1948–89), the institution of elections and elected legislatures formally never ceased to exist. People did elect deputies and the deputies did adopt laws and legitimize governments. Moreover, the constitutional and legal image was part of the foundation myth of socialist 'people's democracies' in these countries, along with the 'ruling working class' or the 'revolutionary energy' of the Communist Party. And although in practice the electoral and legislative processes remained under complete control of the Communist Party Central Committee, the state-funded Marxist theory developed a doctrine that claimed that 'representative bodies' of the socialist states were far better than bourgeois parliaments, if not ideal.[1]

A. Gjuričová (✉)
Institute of Contemporary History, Czech Academy of Sciences, Prague, Czech Republic
e-mail: gjuricova@usd.cas.cz

© The Author(s) 2019
R. Aerts et al. (eds.), *The Ideal of Parliament in Europe since 1800*, Palgrave Studies in Political History, https://doi.org/10.1007/978-3-030-27705-5_11

Parliaments under socialism have attracted relatively little scholarly attention. In the Czech case, we have only a number of published memoires and studies by veterans of socialist or revolutionary parliaments,[2] and an annotated edition of resources exists solely for the National Assembly in 1968.[3] This article, on the other hand, draws on extensive archival research and a number of interviews and memoirs. My historical analysis also takes into account German political-science research, especially the application of the neo-institutional approach as employed by Joachim Amm,[4] studying the processes by which schemes, rules, norms and routines become established as authoritative guidelines for social behaviour. When assessing the 'overall institutional performance', Amm concluded that the Federal Assembly had zero sovereignty performance, merely a minimum democratic performance and only some symbolic performance.[5]

This chapter takes a slightly different perspective. It seeks to explore the Czechoslovak National/Federal Assembly as a parliament that clearly lacked sovereignty and yet considered itself superb. First, it offers a brief summary of the Marxist view of parliaments as well as the Leninist, Stalinist and late-socialist theoretical re-interpretations that were applied in Czechoslovakia. The core of the article follows the country's history of socialist parliamentary practice and seeks to distinguish the main roles parliament played within the political and social system: has it been an institution with certain powers, a pure legitimization strategy of the regime, part of the system of representation, an expression of the federal structure of the state, or a political instrument sui generis? To what extent did this role change during the reform period of *perestroika*, which experimented with reformist electoral and legislative practices? These perspectives will be combined with the question of what public image the Communist Party wanted the parliaments to present and the expectations of the society, which it was supposed to mirror at different stages.

The Czechoslovak Velvet Revolution of 1989, with its proclaimed respect for peace and legality, found the *ancien régime*'s parliament at the centre of new politics. The concept, values and practices of socialist parliamentarism began to clash with new interests, and the nominally smoothly working parliament interacted with the new democratic public. On the other hand, the discredited MPs were practically the only experienced politicians and experts in parliamentary practice. Their interaction with the new democrats-to-be and the interface between the socialist experience and the expectations associated with democracy produced a striking conflict.

## Theory...

In their works, Karl Marx and Friedrich Engels were more than harsh towards the European parliamentarism of their time. 'Parliament of the rich'[6] was the label given by Marx to the eminent British legislature while elections in nineteenth-century Europe were generally referred to as 'deciding once in three or six years which member of the ruling class was to misrepresent the people in Parliament'.[7] The 'bourgeois parliaments' were yet another instrument of the ruling class, as opposed to the socialist representative bodies that would truly represent the working people. Along with the radically critical analysis of the capitalist system and its institutions, classical Marxism also defended at length its own position against social democrats and other moderate socialist thinkers. Along that line, the founders of Marxism rejected the idea that a socialist society could be achieved through parliamentary means: the socialist movement had to get rid of the incurable disease of 'parliamentary cretinism',[8] that is, the expectation that things are determined and directed by a majority of votes.

By 1948, as the Czechoslovak socialist dictatorship came to being, the original radical scepticism of Marx, tending to propose a complete break with the parliamentary system, had been abandoned. The Communist movement had adopted a more pragmatic Leninist interpretation that emphasized the Marxist requirement of the 'conversion of the representative institutions from talking shops into "working" bodies' that would be 'executive and legislative at the same time'.[9] The *Soviets*, that is, councils of representatives at all levels, were supposed to hold power and carry out the people's will. Following WWII, Stalin had clearly supported the Czechoslovak Communists in their 'parliamentary' quest for power, infiltrating other political parties, public administration and elected bodies. However, long before taking control of the Czechoslovak government and transforming its parliamentary institutions, he had suppressed the original self-administrative aspect of the *Soviets* and replaced it with complete bureaucratic control by the Party. Several decades later, in the mid-1980s, Mikhail Gorbachev referred to 'the democratic mechanism introduced by our socialist revolution', which had been later deformed. His *perestroika* project was supposed to 'fully renew the role of the Soviets, as the bodies of political power, as bearers and powerful carriers of socialist democracy'.[10]

The Communist Party was no post-war newcomer to the Czechoslovak political system. The party had been founded in 1921 and had suffered from police prosecution as well as internal purges and dramatic ideological upheavals since then. Despite all these factors, it was a successful representative of the radical working-class electorate, regularly winning 30–40 parliamentary seats out of the total 300. As a radical protest party, it was never considered as a potential partner in complex coalition governments. At the end of 1929, Klement Gottwald, the new young leader of the Communist fraction, addressed the House of Deputies, radically dismissing the capitalist system and its imperialist backing. The laughter of the other MPs provoked him to say: 'And we go to Moscow to learn, you know what? We go to Moscow to learn from the Russian bolsheviks how to wring your necks. And you know that the Russian bolsheviks are masters at it'.[11] The same man became Czechoslovak prime minister in 1946. By then such threatening had ceased. The Communist Party had been an active member of the National Front, a permanent coalition of the handful of legally existing parties carrying out far-reaching socialist reforms, including the nationalization of large manufacturers, mining and the film industry in 1945, as well as sweeping social transformations such as the expulsion of ethnic Germans from the country.

The Communists managed to win the 1946 elections and headed for full control. Within a few months following the cabinet crisis of February 1948, the doctrine changed substantially. Through the so-called action committees, the Communists and their agents had taken control of parties and parliamentary fractions, social associations, local government as well as the security forces. The parliamentary elections in May 1948 were carefully organized to produce a reliable body to pass revolutionary legislation, as we shall see further in this article, but also to transform itself into a representative body of the Stalinist type under direct Party control.[12] Dropping the denotation of 'parliament' and referring to it as a 'representative assembly' was only the surface indication of a much deeper change. This legal concept introduced completely new notions of representation, separation of powers and accountability.

Although several other political parties formally continued to exist, there was nothing like an open political competition between them; in reality, they were turned into pure satellites of the Communist Party. The composition of representative assemblies was no longer to be derived from party electoral support exclusively: the bodies needed to mirror the society in a more direct and, at the same time, more sophisticated sense. This system of so-called descriptive representation produced parliaments consisting of deputies who 'embodied' the society's professional, gender, ethnic and age segments—as opposed to mere political preference expressed by bourgeois parliaments. However, finding such a matrix of candidates, some of whom had to combine several categories, was a challenging task and, in fact, a substitute for the electoral process. In the actual election, voters only approved the names of candidates included on a single ballot of the National Front, adopted previously by the Communist Party Central Committee. Elections then served, as the *Dictionary of Socialist Deputy* puts it, 'to choose those thousands of officials' and 'to include the masses in political life and educate them'.[13]

The socialist concept rejected the 'bourgeois theory' of separation of powers—executive, legislative and judicial—and suggested there was only a single, unified power held by the working class that is the guarantee of the people's sovereignty in the state.[14] In this way Communist doctrine also abolished the exclusiveness of the parliament in the political system. The national parliament was 'merely' the supreme level of a united system of representative organs at local, municipal and district levels.[15]

The Leninist theory of a joint legislative and executive role was also expressed through a specific concept of the mandate. Members of parliament were understood to be 'elected political and state officials' required to work in the constituency, as well as in the representative body and other state institutions. They would bring the working people's input to the parliament, inform people about legislative work and monitor how the laws worked in their constituency. They were under direct control of their electorate: those who did not work as required could be dismissed by voters at any time.[16] This extreme focus on direct accountability obviously created a most feeble mandate, which allowed the Party to control the parliament.

## ... VERSUS PRACTICE

Thus the doctrine on parliaments and representative assemblies of the socialist states had a number of internal contradictions, and the bodies elected at the national level in particular occupied a highly ambiguous position in the state-socialist systems. They were supposed to be the highest organs of the people's power—whilst enjoying very limited autonomy not only in practice, but even in theory. Despite its inconsistency, the theory resisted change during the socialist era. Simultaneously, the practice and role of the actual bodies were changing, along with the social and political conditions and the current strategy adopted by the Communist Party. It seems that the parliaments were supposed to demonstrate very different or even opposing representations of state socialism, as the following examples illustrate.

During the coup of February 1948, the existing National Assembly did not play a key institutional role in the cabinet crisis through which the Communist Party took control of the executive. The parliament became a venue of intense talks with the Communists trying to persuade the deputies from other parties to follow their course. With much of the persuading proving successful, the National Assembly became a secondary stage for executing the takeover, with the Action Committee of the parliamentary National Front completing the neutering of non-communist parties and investigating the remaining anti-communist deputies.

And yet, the mere preservation of the same parliament at the dawn of a socialist dictatorship—and even keeping its name stemming from the 'bourgeois' period throughout the most radical phase of socialist restructuring—provided a pretence of continuity with the previous state of affairs. This seeming continuity, along with an exhibited legal image of the regime, had the potential of comforting some opponents as well as those lulled by the democratic rhetoric of the Communist Party. Evidence from the files of the Communist Party Politburo shows the leaders explicitly discussing 'who will appear in the National Assembly Presidium', on the one hand, while searching for candidates who 'make sure that nothing happens from the legal point of view'[17] on the other. The legality of the new system was an important value that the parliament was supposed to represent.

Informal bargaining led the parliamentary body to give a vote of confidence to the new Communist-dominated government and to adopt a new Constitution. Its initial declaration codified a critical view of interwar Czechoslovakia and other features of a Marxist historical interpretation, though the wording of the actual articles preserved a seemingly democratic character. It was largely based on drafts formulated by the Communist Party prior to February 1948, at a time when their proposals had to be moderated for a genuine coalition government.

The parliament, elected in 1946, belonged to the coalition period as well. Nevertheless, it no longer was one of the vertices of the power triangle formed by President, Government and Parliament. Disapproval could still be heard in the spring of 1948, although mostly within individual party fractions, that is, behind closed doors. Non-conformist deputies faced pressure, threats and accusations, and many resorted to 'taking holidays', resignation or secretly leaving the country.[18] The National Assembly was not really a collective actor, but an object of or a stage for infiltration, neutering and 'purification' of non-Communist parties. Organizing the general election was another challenge for the new government: once again, it had to pretend to be an election, to attract maximum participation, and yet confirm full support for the National Front. In that respect, the combination of propaganda, democratic and legalistic rhetoric and pressure was a great success: according to the official figures, a white ballot—the only form of opposition to the united ballot of the National Front—was cast by just slightly over 10 per cent of voters in 1948.

The following period, characterized by the militant Stalinist restructuring of the state and society, used the parliament to demonstrate the revolutionary spirit and its efficiency. Dozens of MPs had been swept away by political trials or deprived of their mandate. The parliament no longer gave voice to different opinions and to anti-government opposition. Party fractions were formally abolished, legislative work and the decision-making (or what was left of it) shifted to the Presidium and committees, that is, the bodies that worked in closed meetings.[19] The plenary sessions of the National Assembly became a platform for the Communist Party to announce plans and programmes, while the parliament as a whole was there to embody the powerful legislative machine carrying out the revolutionary transformation of the legal system. While the national economy was organized along the respective Five-Year Plans, the parliament had to meet its own Legislative Two-Year Plan announced by the Congress of Lawyers in 1949 in order to establish the 'new law' with 'an explicit class character'.[20]

Draft bills were prepared strictly outside the parliament.[21] It is obvious that the critical political bargaining took place elsewhere at this stage—within the Communist Party leadership or, to a much lesser extent, within the organs of the National Front. From 1954 on, the legislative activity diminished: 316 laws were adopted in 1948–54 as opposed to just about one-third of that number in the remaining six years of the decade.

## SELF-PARLIAMENTARIZATION

In the 1960s, the parliament was entrusted with—and itself embraced—a new task: to embody the rationalization of law and politics. The general doctrine was not challenged, though the focus of parliamentary work shifted to rational interventions in legislation, based on cooperation with expert communities and respect for the accuracy of the regulation as well as some humanization of law. This period lends itself to a reflection about the possibility of applying the concept of self-parliamentarization for the first time.[22] The Assembly began to be concerned with itself, its own working methods and responsibilities. It adopted new rules of procedure and sought to establish a certain distance from the government bills. It is remarkable that, within the overall sense of liberalization, which was immediately accompanied by a general atmosphere of dissatisfaction, among all state institutions, the National Assembly and its inactivity until then became the first target of public criticism.[23]

The 'deepening of parliamentary activity'[24] was announced officially as a new guideline and endorsed by the MPs elected in 1964. A wave of criticism was gradually creeping into the committees of the National Assembly. It targeted issues in the management of various economic sectors, problems in supply, residential construction and so on. The MPs lobbied massively against some ministers, even though unanimous voting always prevailed during plenary sessions.[25]

January 1968 brought a change in the leadership of the Communist Party and an acceleration of the democratization, which had, however, not been intended or even accepted by many prominent officials. The reform-minded Slovak Alexander Dubček replaced the previous hard-liner Antonín Novotný as the Party First Secretary. The National Assembly wanted to join the Prague Spring reforms by increasing their involvement in preparing the new Party manifesto and in their official meetings with the Government, and, above all, by adhering to the requirement for 'judicial rehabilitation', that is, clearing the sentences of some of the victims of the 1950s political trials.

This final proposal was deferred by a number of actors, but the reform movement in general was accelerating. In Czech politics and among the public, the focus of the reforms was on 'socialism with a human face', that is, liberalization and democratization of the originally Stalinist socialism. The Slovaks saw the aim of the reform movement elsewhere, namely, in the federalization of Czechoslovakia. The subordinate position of Slovakia within a country with a Czech majority and with all central institutions located in Prague was considered to be a Stalinist distortion of socialism.

Week after week, reforms were gathering momentum. The parliament was their important stage. In March 1968, the National Assembly Presidium held sessions as often as twice a week. In April, Josef Smrkovský, one of the voices of the reform, was elected the Chairman of the parliament, in what was far from the usual unanimous votes: 68 out of 256 voted against his election. In his inaugural address, for the first time since 1948, the National Assembly was described as representing all citizens of the country, not just certain categories or the working class.[26] The parliament distanced itself from the Government, tried to execute its control function and sought wider international contacts. On 25 June, the law on judicial rehabilitation was passed. The new Press Law followed the day after, withdrawing censorship of the media and book publishing.

The aforementioned self-parliamentarization reached a new level: Without a new election, that is, in the former political composition, the National Assembly achieved new leadership and internal organization and managed to extend its political influence in the control of state. This trend was to grow even more spectacularly: in the week following the Warsaw Pact invasion in August 1968, the National Assembly was meeting continuously in a dramatic setting, with MPs not leaving the parliament building in order not to be captured and issuing anti-invasion and reformist statements addressed to the parliaments of the occupying countries, Czechoslovak state institutions and the people of Czechoslovakia.[27]

## FEDERALIZATION

The Soviets demanded that the leadership of the Czechoslovak Communist Party put an immediate and resolute end to every aspect of liberalization other than federalization. The reason was that, unlike most other emancipation policies of the Prague Spring, the call for federalization did not fundamentally contradict Soviet doctrines. On the contrary, the Soviet Union was, at least in theory, an exemplary socialist federation. It was the Czechs' consent, however, that became more surprising.[28]

The term federalization first emerged in public in the spring of 1968 and, by the autumn of the same year, the radical constitutional transformation of the country was passed by the parliament, after very brief debate among both experts and the public. The Constitutional Law on Czechoslovak Federation—in fact a new Constitution[29]—was adopted by the National Assembly, symbolically, on 27 October 1968, on the eve of the 50th anniversary of the foundation of Czechoslovakia. As of 1 January 1969 two new republics, the Czech Republic and the Slovak Republic, their parliaments called National Councils, and governments, came into being on the territory of the previously unitary country. These institutions were subjected to the federal ones. The National Assembly was therefore transformed into a two-chamber Federal Assembly: the Chamber of

People mirrored the proportion between the populations of the two nations, while the Chamber of Nations contained equal numbers of Czech and Slovak MPs. There was a complex system of voting on important issues, which introduced the 'ban on majorization', a minority veto that protected Slovak MPs from being outvoted by their more numerous Czech counterparts.

Yet in the meantime, the parliaments grew tame and obedient again: for example, only four MPs voted against the Treaty on the Temporary Sojourn of the Soviet Army. The transforming parliament(s) were also more than willing to work without refreshing their mandate in any kind of popular election. For example, the National Assembly first elected members of the Czech National Council by hand-picking candidates among its own members and 'important figures of public life' in the summer of 1968. Later, the National Council chose, out of their own ranks, members of the newly established Chamber of Nations of the Federal Assembly.

After a series of anti-reformist purges in the parliaments, which replaced one-third of all MPs, and with hard-liners back in power, the postponed elections were held in 1971 and produced a quiet, stable and consensual parliament. The main role that the new regime expected the Federal Assembly to perform was to calm the situation, settle down the system and, especially, represent the new federal structure. Without the general liberalization and democratization of the Prague Spring reforms, it diminished the federal aspect of the structure to something similar to 'compulsory figures' that political actors had to practise on formal occasions.

The subsequent late-socialist parliaments worked at a stable pace, with little dynamism. Keeping a mandate for the full 18 years between 1971 and 1989 was by no means an exception. A working schedule was regularly set for the following year: four meetings of the committees, four sessions of the Presidium and four plenary sessions at which both chambers met for one or at most two days. The rigidly formalized meetings mostly elected the same chairmen of chambers and committees, referring to their experience and great achievements in the previous terms. Speakers for plenary sessions were selected, and their contributions were written and approved in advance. Committees approved, and plenary sessions passed, several laws each year, mostly minor amendments of the existing ones. Votes were unanimous, though preceded by a discussion. When assessing the sessions, parliament officials and the Communist Party leadership emphasized, inter alia, the criteria of 'thorough preparation' and 'successful coordination' of speeches, 'high quality' of the sessions and professional impressions made.[30] Close to ideal, it would seem.

## BACKUP LEGISLATURE

Within the two decades, the parliaments developed into well-oiled machines, which symbolized the existence of a parliamentary institution, exemplified the federal structure and were there, should their mobilization be needed. This 'backup' legislature was first called to duty during the *perestroika* period. Mikhail Gorbachev's course announced in the mid-1980s, calling for the return of power to the *Soviets*, was certainly a new impulse for the ossified Communist Party, devastated by the post-1968 purges. The problem for the Czechoslovak communists was that Gorbachev's programme seemed too close to the Prague Spring reforms for them to endorse it enthusiastically. It was only as late as in 1988, that the parliament was entrusted once again by the Communist Party to fulfil a new mission: to show the 'spirit of openness' and assist with the economic reforms. The parliament was under pressure by the government: it needed to pass reform regulations swiftly and smoothly and, at the same time, pretend democratic procedures and initiatives vis-à-vis the public. The volume of legislation was growing. In 1988, for the first time since 1971, a plenary session took as long as three days. Further pressure came from public opinion, since the deputies met immediate critique whenever they came to meetings in their constituencies.

On the other hand, however, the parliament itself used the new conditions to free itself from the government's automatic expectations, to seek its new presentation in the media and to enhance its status. Explicit criticism directed towards economic development and various ministers now regularly appeared in committee debates. Nonetheless, the principle that the parliament would be subjected to the Communist Party Central Committee and to 'the needs of the government' was never questioned. The parliamentarians' struggle to create an image different from the usual hands raised in unanimous votes found its expression in a series of two TV documentary films produced by the Czechoslovak Television in 1987. They embodied the contradiction: they showed the MPs' hard work in the committees, their highly critical speeches, lengthy expert discussions, perspiring government ministers, as well as human reactions, simply to share the image of the toil and professionalism preceding... a unanimous vote. As the title aptly put it: 'Before the MPs Agree'.[31]

In 1988, the Federal Assembly saw an unprecedented state-imposed resignation of nine MPs, due to long-term illness or diplomatic posts. Until then, mandates would change during a term only if a deputy died. The Communist Party Central Committee stated that the people wanted only active deputies in the legislature. The Party guidelines also suggested that 'some new elements that are not in contradiction with the electoral law' be tested, esp. choosing from more candidates.[32] Such by-elections took place in the spring of 1989, and several constituencies experienced competitive electoral campaigns and were allowed to freely choose from more candidates for the first time in several decades.

## THE DOWNFALL OF THE IDEAL PARLIAMENT

As the Velvet Revolution began in November 1989, the Federal Assembly was, physically speaking, situated right at its heart. The steel and glass construction at the upper end of Wenceslas Square was designed in the reformist era of the 1960s as an institutional counterweight to the Prague Castle. And yet, for many days, the parliament was absent from the symbolic topography of the revolution: the protesters instead turned their attention to the organs of the Communist Party and media headquarters.

In the 1970s and 1980s, opposition groups claimed the original sense of parliamentary autonomy by using the Federal Assembly as the official, non-Party addressee for their appeals, petitions and letters. By intentionally omitting the leaders of the Communist Party, they meant to draw attention to the formally existing democratic constitutional system. And yet, as it turned out in late 1989, it was just as difficult for the opposition itself, once it got into power, to respect the law and accept the parliament as an independent partner. Civic Forum at first did not take the parliament into account at all or played it down as a Communist 'voting machine'. Yet from a certain point, as constitutional and other legislative amendments were needed, the Federal Assembly was called into duty: Civic Forum requested that the legislature pass revolutionary legislation smoothly once again.

In between, however, Members of the Federal Assembly realized how important they were. After all, even through the parliament's symbolic performance, they became experts familiar with the political system and having experience in politics. The self-parliamentarized Communist-dominated legislature opposed Civic Forum by insisting on a democratic process: the constitutional amendments had to go through a proper legislative procedure and the Presidential vote should be popular, they argued, knowing that Václav Havel, unknown to the majority of Czechoslovak citizens at the moment, could not get enough support to rise to the Presidency. All in all, the revolutionary movement found itself confronted with a highly unpopular socialist parliament, which it did not control, but one that was desperately needed in order to pass any legislative amendments. Moreover, the Velvet Revolution came to face an established system of federal and sub-federal parliaments, which had strong formal powers and presented a major obstacle to what was dubbed as the 'articled revolution',[33] that is, a quick and negotiated régime change seeking to respect the country's legislation at the same time.

President Havel, elected by the Communist-dominated parliament at the very end of the year, after his Civic Forum rejected a popular vote and exerted pressure on MPs to vote to support him, provided a perfect example. By giving his first address to the parliament on 23 January,[34] Havel wanted to use his authority and dramatic talent to make the legislature promptly pass his proposed Constitutional amendment changing the country's name from the Czechoslovak Socialist Republic to Czechoslovak Republic. Yet he was unaware of the current struggle the chambers were engaged in and did not have the 'expert' knowledge of procedure either, expecting that he would be able to 'storm in and before they wake up, they will have passed my proposal'.[35] Yet no success followed. Not only was the President referred to the committees and the legal procedure, but in effect, he set in motion the 'hyphen war' between the Czech and Slovak political élites that lasted for months. The Slovaks expected a deeper change in the federal system than just dropping a word from the name of the state. They explicitly demanded a hyphen and a capital S in the word Czecho-Slovak.

To get the legislature under control, a special law was adopted in late January 1990, which allowed the removal of the mandate of about half of all members of the federal parliament, if they were not willing to resign on their own, 'in light of their previous activity' or 'in the interest of a balanced distribution of political powers'. New MPs, who supposedly provided 'better guarantees of developing political democracy', were co-opted.[36] This provisional parliament was to downplay its own autonomy and serve the public. The new leaders, including President Václav Havel, did not approach the MPs as people carrying a mandate or representing certain political organizations or programmes, but as citizens fulfilling their respective duties, 'who care for the future of their country rather than about their own comfort'.[37]

The revolution's democratic ideal was the first one to collapse. Yet many other standards and expectations—all in fact associated with the unpopular socialist parliament—were falling apart. For example, continuity and stability, no matter how ridiculed it was before, seemed entirely out of reach for the revolutionary parliament. When half of the deputies were replaced by new ones through co-opting in January 1990, the first free elections in June changed three quarters of deputies, while after the election of 1992, half the MPs were newcomers. The continuity of parliamentary work—which involved immense legislative tasks of re-introducing democratic procedures in state administration as well as numerous elements of retribution—was more or less provided by the existing parliamentary administration. But here, historical legitimacies made things even more complicated: first, employees expelled from the administration after 1968 were accepted back, and then, if things were not going well, conspiracy by the Communist Secret Service was cited as the reason and alleged collaborators of the Secret Service were found among the employees.

The socialist parliament had created the ideal of politics as an unpaid, honorary office. In 1990, being an MP became a regular paid job. However, the salary that the parliamentarians approved for themselves was about three times the average wage. This became one of the first instances of income inequality that the post-Communist public was exposed to and caused a wave of criticism in the media.[38] While the public expressed their expectation that the parliament do a professional job for a professional salary, it also seemed that, in order to cut the links with the Communist era, the political sphere needed people with no political experience, leadership or legal education, people who were willing to temporarily sacrifice themselves for the good of others. Such an intersection was difficult to reach. The previous, artificially constructed system of representation, replicating the social structure, had collapsed as well. Workers and farmers that the Communist government sent to the parliament completely disappeared. The previous 30 per cent representation of women dropped to less than 10 per cent.

The most substantial disappointment concerned Czecho-Slovak relations. The tension between Slovak and Czech political representatives of revolutionary publics could be felt from the very outset of the 1989 revolution. Soon the Slovaks insisted that redistribution of powers between the federal and republics' institutions was a primary issue of a democratic transformation, while the Czechs, surprised, saw this as an obstacle to more urgent tasks of democratization and eradication of Communism. The existing federal system, originally created only to formally express equality between the Czechs and Slovaks, could not handle democratic practice. No matter what sophisticated processes of constitution-making and negotiating the federal parliament created, for the reasons described above, the simultaneous emancipation of the parliament(s) from other institutions, rebuilding the party spectrum and creating new political élites involved different strategies on the part of the Czech and Slovak political élites and were never shared by the two national political communities. The Federal Assembly remained isolated from Slovak politics—and aversion to bargaining arose on both sides. The new constitution was never adopted, and Czecho-Slovak bargaining proved inconclusive.

## The Last Task

In 1992, the federal parliament found itself to be the only remaining federal institution in an increasingly fractionalized Czechoslovakia. And it also turned out to be the only institution that could once again legalize what had been decided elsewhere, namely, at meetings of new election winners behind closed doors. The last thing that the federal parliament was asked to do was to validate the dissolution of the Czechoslovak federation, including a dissolution of the parliament itself.

This chapter exploring the Czechoslovak parliament since the World War II pursued a number of stages and manners in which a—nominally identical—legislative body was utilized for very different ends. In the realm of symbolic performance, it had reached dissimilar, or even contradictory, effects: once it represented a democracy that no longer existed, later it stood for revolutionary energy, then rationality, pro-reform ethos, calm settlement or the spirit of openness. In the perspective we followed, it was not the democratic revolution that brought the ideal, but rather the opposite: it represented discontinuity, chaos and endless discussions in front of TV cameras, just to name a few effects. Through this specific lens, we could see that concepts of parliamentary work and policies were perceived, practised and accepted in conflicting manners by the Czech and Slovak publics as well as by political representatives. Some of these differences turned out to be irreconcilable, and the federal parliament eventually played a key role in administering and legitimizing the break-up of the Czechoslovak federation in 1992.

Parliaments are often criticized for being inefficient, impotent, excessively verbose or permanently quarrelling. In the story of the Czechoslovak socialist parliament we saw several stages in which it might seem that the ideal was met: these parliaments were highly consensual, constructive and accountable; there was a system of speeches, and political will was effectively translated into laws. Except that…

There was a reason behind making this chapter provocative. Perhaps it might help us look at previous but also current European parliaments with more indulgence. Since whenever one approaches an ideal, there is a price to pay. A body like a parliament, in fact, in such a case ceases to be a democratic parliament.

## NOTES

1. This chapter was written as part of a research project supported by the Czech Science Foundation (GAČR, GA15-14271S).
2. Zdeněk Jičínský, *Vznik České národní rady v době Pražského jara 1968 a její působení do podzimu 1969* [The Foundation of the Czech National Council during the Prague Spring of 1968 and its Activities until the Fall of 1969] (Prague: Svoboda, 1990); František Cigánek, 'Předlistopadový parlament ve světle archivní dokumentace' [Pre-November parliament through the lens of archival documents] in Emanuel Mandler, *Dvě desetiletí před listopadem 89* [Two Decades prior to November 89] (Prague: Maxdorf–Ústav pro soudobé dějiny AV ČR, 1993); František Cigánek, *Kronika demokratického parlamentu 1989–1992* [The Chronicle of Democratic Parliament 1989–1992] (Prague: Cesty, 1992); Zdeněk Jičínský, *Čs. parlament v polistopadovém období* [Czechoslovak Parliament in post-November era] (Prague: Nadas-Afgh, 1993).
3. František Cigánek (ed.), *Národní shromáždění 21.-28. srpna 1968* [The National Assembly, 21–28 August 1968], Prameny k dějinám československé krize 1967–1970 [Sources on the History of the Czechoslovak Crisis 1967–1970], vol. 3. Brno, ÚSD AV ČR–Doplněk 1995.
4. Joachim Amm, *Die Föderalversammlung der CSSR. Sozialistischer Parlamentarismus im unitarischen Föderalismus 1969–1989* (Wiesbaden: Westdeutscher Verlag, 2001).
5. Amm, *Die Föderalversammlung*, 141–5. Werner Patzelt came to similar pessimistic conclusions when discussing the case of the East German Volkskammer, yet he saw it as a stage for conflicts within the ruling party. Werner J. Patzelt and Roland Schirmer, *Die Volkskammer der DDR: Sozialistischer Parlamentarismus in Theorie und Praxis* (Wiesbaden: Westdeutscher Verlag, 2002).

6. Karl Marx, *Letter to the Labour Parliament* (1854). English translation by https://www.marxists.org/archive/marx/works/1854/03/09.htm
7. Karl Marx, *Civil War in France*, Chapter 5 [The Paris Commune], English translation by https://www.marxists.org/archive/marx/works/1871/civil-war-france/ch05.htm
8. Karl Marx, *The Eighteenth Brumaire of Louis Bonaparte*, 1852 https://www.marxists.org/archive/marx/works/1852/18th-brumaire/ch06.htm
9. Karl Marx, *Civil War in France*, Chapter 5 [The Paris Commune], accessed 30 October 2015, https://www.marxists.org/archive/marx/works/1871/civil-war-france/index.htm. Cf. Vladimir Ilyich Lenin, *The State and Revolution: Experience of the Paris Commune of 1871. Marx's Analysis*, Chapter 3, accessed 30 October 2015, https://www.marxists.org/archive/lenin/works/1917/staterev/ch03.htm
10. Michail Sergejevič Gorbačov, *Přestavba a nové myšlení pro naši zemi a pro celý svět* [*Perestroika and New Thinking for Our Country and the Whole World*] (Praha: Svoboda, 1987) 96–7.
11. *Společná česko-slovenská digitální parlamentní knihovna* [*Common Digital Czecho-Slovak Parliamentary Library*], National Assembly 1929–1935, The House of Deputies, Stenographic records, 7th session, 21 December 1929, accessed 30 October 2015 http://www.psp.cz/eknih/1929ns/ps/stenprot/007schuz/s007003.htm. Cf. Jacques Rupnik, *Histoire du parti communiste tchécoslovaque* (Paris: Presses de la Fondation nationale des sciences politiques, 1981).
12. Karel Kaplan, *Národní fronta 1948–1960* [The National Front 1948–1960] (Prague: Academia, 2012) 100–1.
13. František Koranda et al., *Slovník socialistického poslance* [The Dictionary of Socialist Deputy] (Prague: Svoboda, 1985) 408–9.
14. Jan Bartuška, *Státní právo Československé republiky* [The State Law of the Czechoslovak Republic] (Prague: Státní nakladatelství učebnic, 1952) 39, cf. 75.
15. Ibid., 39, 74–5. Cf. Koranda, *Slovník*, 152–156 and 436–7.
16. Koranda, *Slovník*, 225–6.
17. Kaplan, *Národní fronta*, 476.
18. Ibid., 387–414.
19. For details see Jan Winter's sections in Jiří Kocian (ed.), *Slovníková příručka k československým dějinám 1948–1989* [Dictionary Handbook on Czechoslovak History 1948–1989] (Prague: ÚSD AV ČR, 2006) 5 ff.
20. Jaromír Císař and Vladimír Kindl, 'Vývoj zákonodárství na území ČSR 1945–1990' in Ladislav Soukup (ed.), *Příspěvky k vývoji právního řádu v Čs. 1945–1990* [Contributions to the Development of Legal System in Czechoslovakia 1945–1990] (Prague: Karolinum, 2002) 79–96, esp. 84–5.

21. Curiously enough, some of the bills were largely inspired by the earlier, pre-1948 drafts. The famed Act on Family Law of 1949 serves as the best example: at the time it was passed, it was one of the most progressive statutes in Europe introducing full gender equality and abolishing many traditional patriarchal institutions. However, its wording was directly derived from a draft prepared by Milada Horáková, international women's movement activist, former Member of National Assembly, by then, however, political prisoner of the Communist régime. As an anti-communist politician, she was convicted and sentenced to death in 1950.

22. The team of the author used the concept to describe the socialist parliaments in democratic transitions. See, for example, Adéla Gjuričová and Tomáš Zahradníček, *Návrat parlamentu: Češi a Slováci ve Federálním shromáždění* [The Return of Parliament: Czechs and Slovaks in the Federal Assembly, 1989–1992] (Prague: Argo–Ústav pro soudobé dějiny AV ČR, 2018). It was inspired by Bettina Tüffers, *Die 10. Volkskammer der DDR. Ein Parlament im Umbruch. Selvstwahrnehmung, Selbstparlamentarisierung, Selbstauflösung* (Düsseldorf, Drost 2016).

23. Císař and Kindl, *Vývoj zákonodárství*, 79–96.

24. Quoted in Cigánek, *Národní shromáždění*, 7.

25. Ondřej Felcman, *Československý parlament na prahu Pražského jara: Národní shromáždění na cestě k reformě (1964–duben 1968)* [Czechoslovak Parliament at the Dawn of the Prague Spring: The National Parliament on the Way to reform (1964–April 1968)] (Prague: NLN, 2015).

26. Cigánek, *Národní shromáždění*, 8.

27. Cigánek, *Národní shromáždění*, 287–300.

28. Tomáš Zahradníček, 'Federalization–the Path to Demise' in *Aspen Review Central Europe*, vol. 2, No 1 (2013) 25–30.

29. The Constitutional Act on the Czechoslovak Federation was adopted in October 1968. It amended the Constitution of Czechoslovakia from 1960, formally placing many of the former roles of the central government under the jurisdiction of the two national governments.

30. See, for example, the speech by Richard Nejezchleb, Minutes of the Defense and Security Committee 4th meeting, 4 February 1987, Federal Assembly 5th term Collection, Archives of the Parliament of the Czech Republic. Cf. speech by Dalibor Hanes, Minutes of the 2nd meeting Presidium, 24 June 1986, Ibid.

31. *Než poslanci souhlasí* [Before the MPs Agree], 2 parts, 1987. The Archives of the Czechoslovak Television preserved them, along with documents on their 'approval screenings'.

32. Cigánek, *Předlistopadový parlament*, 57–85.

33. Petr Roubal, *Starý pes, nové kousky: kooptace do Federálního shromáždění a vytváření polistopadové politické kultury* (Prague: Ústav pro soudobé dějiny AV ČR, 2013) 27–32.
34. 'President's Speech in the Federal Assembly, 23 January 1990' in Václav Havel, *Projevy z let 1990–1992. Letní přemítání (Spisy sv. 6)* [Speeches from the period of 1990–1992. Summer Meditations (Collected works Vol. 6)] (Prague: Torst, 1999) 25–43.
35. For further analysis of Havel's entry into parliament, see Jiří Suk, *Konstituční, nebo existenciální revoluce? Václav Havel a Federální shromáždění 1989–1990* [Constitutional or Unconstitutional Revolution? Václav Havel and The Federal Assembly 1989–1990] (Prague: Ústav pro soudobé dějiny AV ČR, 2014) 36.
36. Act No 4/1990 Coll., on dismissing deputies of representative bodies and on electing new deputies of the National Committees, Art. I.
37. 'The President's Speech in the Federal Assembly, 9 May 1990' in Havel, *Projevy*, 133. Cf. 'President's Speech in the Federal Assembly, 23 January 1990' in Havel, *Projevy*, 26.
38. For example, Petr Hájek, 'Prázdniny na omdlení' [Holidays to die for] in *Reflex*, vol. 1, No 21 (21 August 1990) 8; Zdeněk Hrabica, 'Pošta "Parlament"' [Post 'Parliament'] in *Verejnosť*, vol. 1, No 62 (26 July 1990) 2; Marie Borůvková, 'Otevřený dopis poslancům FS' [An Open Letter to the Deputies of the FA] in *Reflex*, vol. 1, No 25 (18 September 1990) 54.

# CHAPTER 12

# The Transfer of Parliamentary Ideals to Civil Society in the Netherlands in the 1970s

*Wim de Jong*

In the summer of 1966, Dutch prime minister Jo Cals called on parliament and government to create an atmosphere to 'prevent clashes between youth and government'.[1] It was a remarkable year in the usually peaceful Netherlands. A royal wedding had been disturbed and riots had ensued between the Amsterdam police and sympathizers of the anarchist youth movement 'provo'. Cals, in an effort to prevent further violence, attended a debate with provos and invited one of their representatives to his official residence. The youngster, however, expressed disappointment in the meeting. Still it was a sign that indeed 'the times they were a-changing'. Parliamentary politics had kept a dignified distance from society since the Second World War. Now the clamour of the street had reached the political establishment.

In the years to come, there would be much talk of a 'gap' between politics and an alienated society. Parliament's hegemony as the institution par excellence of modern democracies was challenged by movements like provo. Progressive forces looked for democratization outside of parliament. The old republican idea of direct participation in demonstrations, universities and corporate governance was revitalized. Parliament's representative

W. de Jong (✉)
Open University of the Netherlands, Heerlen, The Netherlands

© The Author(s) 2019
R. Aerts et al. (eds.), *The Ideal of Parliament in Europe since 1800*,
Palgrave Studies in Political History,
https://doi.org/10.1007/978-3-030-27705-5_12

legitimacy was called into question for its failure to respond to social developments and for representing a politics based on deliberation and compromise.

Literature on the history of political representation views this period as important due to what Manin calls the transition from a party democracy to an 'audience' democracy, from a system in which political parties had a strong grip on society and parliament to a situation in which voter preferences became more volatile and at the same time passive due to the personalization and mediatization of politics.[2] Rosanvallon analyses in a more historical fashion the dissemination of representation across society beyond, and contestation of, the electoral-representative system in institutions of oversight through which civil society actors create a 'counter'-democracy.[3]

Both downplay parliament. Manin's schematic model describes parliament in party democracies as completely immersed in party discipline[4]; audience democracy gives more freedom to representatives, but politicians use the media rather than parliament as a platform. Dialogue between government and parliament is less important than dialogue with interest groups. Parliament's heyday was the nineteenth century, before party democracy came along.[5] Rosanvallon's emphasis on the pluralization of political sovereignty leads him to de-emphasize parliament as well, which comes as no surprise considering the demise of parliamentary democracy in France in 1958. Since the 1970s, parliamentarism for Rosanvallon has been 'in decline' everywhere, in part because it fails to hold government to account.[6]

In the Netherlands, however, parliament retained a more central role. Partly in response to criticism, politicians sought to sustain its relevance. As a result, in the 1970s parliament's representative claim was strengthened, not only as an institution, but also as a repertoire of political values and practices. Democratization within civil society took a parliamentary form. Representative 'claims' (Saward) involve an understanding of representation as a process, a performance focusing on how representation works in practice. Political actors make representative claims, by which they seek to constitute an audience.[7]

In this period politicians had to do something to sustain parliament's claim to be the central stage for democratic representation. The resulting picture of the institution leads us to qualify narratives of parliamentary decline, strongly present in this period as well as in twenty-first-century Western political and academic commentary. Indeed, like E.P. Thompson's middle class, parliament appears to be always in decline. As the Dutch historian Aerts argues, these nostalgic decline narratives often mainly reflect contemporary normative assumptions about politics.[8]

This contribution lays out three vectors of a contextualized history of parliament: receptivity, assertiveness and dissemination. First, the perceived crisis induced MPs to develop an open, receptive attitude towards the representation of new societal interests within parliament. In some respects, parliament became a battleground for social movements during the 1970s. Secondly, the ambivalent response of political actors to rival representative claims will be examined, focusing on the introduction of the ombudsman. Finally, it will show how democratization in student and works councils in practice amounted to expanding parliamentarism and its values of deliberation and majority decision-making.

The story ends in the early 1980s: the realignment of Dutch politics and the end of polarization led to a more pragmatic parliamentary debate; the extra-parliamentary movements fuelling the challenge to parliament were broadly institutionalized. Soon the 1970s were remembered as the high-tide mark of political engagement. As I hope to make clear, this was true of parliamentary as well as extra-parliamentary politics.

The penetration of extra-parliamentary movements in the Netherlands is perhaps exceptional in a West European context; the West German Ausserparlamentarische Opposition was aimed more at building a new society than at influencing parliament.[9] The West German SPD, the French PS and the British Labour Party were never as deeply influenced by the 'new' social movements as were progressive Dutch parties, heavy internal debate notwithstanding.[10] Dismissing the 1968 insistence on identity of governors and governed and the supposed need for a reform agenda in this direction as 'profound illusions and misinterpretations' of political representation in a media democracy, Biefang and Schulz show how the Bundestag's parliamentary reforms emphasized transparency of its proceedings and communication with society, in contrast with the Dutch tendency to indeed increase the identity of representatives and their constituents explored here.[11]

Comparative research, however, would also yield many similarities: institutions such as the ombudsman posed a challenge to parliaments everywhere, with different solutions adopted, some following a more British and others a more Scandinavian model. The democratization of Dutch student councils had few rivals, but the development of works councils in the FRG is broadly comparable; across the English Channel, there were similar tendencies concerning the professionalization and self-assertion of parliament in the 1960s.[12]

## THE EXTRA-PARLIAMENTARY CHALLENGE

Parliament made a comeback on the continent after the Second World War in the context of a disciplined democracy, with nightmarish recollections of interwar mass dynamism.[13] Popular participation in strikes and demonstrations was restricted. A discourse of reconstruction supported governments based on a broad range of parties and an ethos of cooperation.[14]

In the beginning of the 1960s, expectations of parliament shifted, leading to a narrative of decline. An unhealthy entanglement with capitalism supposedly led to a technocratic mentality and failure to hold government to account.[15] Sociologist P. Thoenes in 1962 wrote that 'formally, power lies with parliament, but this does not mean much when experts have so much authority'.[16] The critique of parliament was connected with a general 'crisis of democracy'.[17] Real opposition and clear political alternatives were seen as necessary to combat voter apathy. As prominent Social-Democrat Jaap Burger summarized in 1971: 'One cannot expect this democratic technique to appeal to the fantasy of citizens, whatever its use. The credit of the parliamentary system has been impaired'.[18] A golden age was invoked of independent, rhetorically skilled MPs, not hemmed in by lobbies and political parties. An extensive survey by the popular magazine *Revu* in 1966 showed that 75 per cent of the respondents thought MPs lacked understanding of popular sentiments. It fuelled proposals across the board for direct democracy and monitory devices.[19]

Furthermore, protest movements heavily criticized parliamentary values of deliberation and majority decision-making, for which they substituted direct action. Parliament was deemed susceptible only to capitalist pressure groups and 'old' movements such as trade unions; hence movements confronted authorities, multinationals and landlords directly. The radical variants of these movements did not seek dialogue: they felt the establishment had lost moral authority, in part because of the ongoing Vietnam War. These developments came to the Netherlands comparatively early in the form of the Pacifist Socialist Party, which upon entering parliament in 1959 fiercely criticized its outmoded language and its addressing issues no longer of concern to the population.[20]

The connecting node of parliament, government and lobby groups was the political party.[21] The PSP was the first sign of the party-system crisis that swept Dutch politics from the mid-1960s onward. The proportional voting system gave easy access to political newcomers and breakaway factions. The erosion of the 'pillarized' system of Catholic, Protestant and Social Democratic identity-based organizations in every social field meant parliament was opened up.[22] Party discipline disintegrated, leading to fragmentation of parliament and a reorientation process of most parties, which after 1967 struggled to maintain their profile when the dominant denominational parties found themselves challenged by groups such as the Pacifist Socialist Party (PSP), Farmers, Democrats '66 (D'66, 1967) and Politieke Partij Radicalen (PPR, 1969). An atmosphere of political polarization materialized at the end of the 1960s.

The political turbulence made politics in general more interesting. The rise of the parliamentary press brought parliament into the living rooms of more citizens. Mass media faced the same problems as political parties, in that their former denominational base was eroding. Parliament and the press became more mutually dependent.[23] The press focused on the political process and personal backgrounds, which, however, evolved around parliament.[24] MPs who understood television gained a strong profile.

This age of progressive and conservative 'polarization' in Dutch politics would be dominated by skilled politicians like Joop den Uyl (Social-Democrat) and his adversaries Dries Van Agt (Christian-Democrat) and Hans Wiegel (Liberal). With the help of the parliamentary press, they successfully conveyed the impression that politics happened in and around parliament, no small feat in an age of extra-parliamentary activity. They succeeded in suggesting that social conflicts were basically resolved in parliament. In general, this contributed to a more assertive parliament, with sharper and more critical debating, a process encouraged as Member of Parliament (MP) became a full-time job in 1968. The deferential attitude was abandoned in both parliament and society. Due to the unstable political constellation, parliamentary debate was more unpredictable and publicly exciting in the 1970s than in the subsequent Christian-Democrat-dominated era.[25]

The contemporary perception, however, was different, fuelled by the crisis discourse. In 1969 the Genootschap voor Reclame (Advertising Association), backed by Unilever, published a major survey on the public 'image' of parliament. Dutch MPs failed the test: yes, the public found them to be intelligent, smooth talkers, but also dishonest liars without moral reservations, people who put party interests above the common good. Sixty-five per cent of the 'lower' and 56 per cent of the 'higher' working class' saw them as unapproachable, against only 28 per cent of the higher classes; Unilever director A. Bol said parliament should work on its image by demonstrating its quantitative achievements over the past ten years, in order to convince the 'consumer' of its 'product'. All that 'dull banter' should be seen as actually leading to something.[26]

Speaker of the Dutch lower chamber F. van Thiel rejected the idea that parliament should sell itself to the public, which he also thought impossible because parliament was always divided between majority and opposition. Education could help the public understand what parliament was doing, but it could not reverse that fact that government had become more complex and that the language of MPs had become more specialized.[27] Thanks to detailed surveys among MPs in 1972 and 1979, it is possible to get a picture of MPs' views on their relationship with the public. MPs both in 1972 and 1979 had a highly negative view of citizens, who were seen as having a faulty view of parliament's task and as regarding MPs merely as representing interests. MPs saw themselves as trustees, not delegates mainly working *for* the public.[28]

MPs nonetheless in 1972 also described their most important task as representing and keeping in regular contact with different groups in society, and they underlined autonomy within the party. Influential Social-Democrat Ed van Thijn said in 1976 that a well-functioning MP had a close connection with society, constituency and media.[29] In 1979 on the contrary, MPs emphasized representation of their constituency and party discipline more than that of society as a whole. Political scientist H. Daemen explained this by pointing to the erosion of the traditional political parties and ideological segmentation, which at the end of the 1960s may have caused MPs to find contacts with society more important than party politics. Writing at the end of the decade, he pondered whether the clearer and calmer waters Dutch politics had reached by then had caused a return to traditional party politics.[30] The attitude of MPs in 1972, however, can also be seen as a response to the criticism of a 'gap' with society.

The contemporary perception was also that the integration of new social movements in parliament was rather problematic. Environmental action groups for instance had a hard time getting a hearing from within the 'iron ring'.[31] 'Unconventional participation' of citizens did not easily fit in with representative democracy. Radical progressives saw the representative system as an obsolete obstacle to democratization.[32] It was never receptive enough to social demands.[33] Parliamentary decentralization was needed to solve this problem, political scientist J. van Putten argued.[34] His colleague A. Lijphart noted that while many saw strengthening parliament as the wrong approach, citizen apathy made direct democracy a poor solution. He argued for a stronger parliament.[35]

Within the largest left-wing party, the highly influential social democratic PvdA, the question was whether to reform a declining parliament or to concentrate on democratizing society.[36] PvdA politician Jos van Kemenade claimed in 1979 that the broadening of politics, expressed in the catchword 'the personal is political', had reduced parliament's importance.[37] The radicals thought parliament would wither away and a democratized society would take over. The social-democrats developed a post-materialist profile. Since 1973 the PvdA was even characterized as an 'action party' for democratization in institutions like the school and the workplace.[38] Den Uyl, however, stressed the 'small margins' of democratic politics and the need to defend parliament, while acknowledging the need for democratization.[39] The action committees in his party circumscribed his room for manoeuvring.[40] In 1977 the Party Council, with representatives of social movements such as Piet Reckman (social work) and Ien van den Heuvel (peace movement), even prevented the formation of Den Uyl's second government.[41]

## RECEPTIVITY AND ASSERTIVENESS

The narratives of democratization of society and decline of parliament made contemporary progressive forces somewhat blind to the rather successful integration of new trends and movements in parliament. A closer look reveals that extra-parliamentary movements were present in parliament and not limited to the small PSP, Farmers and Communist groupings. They captured important positions within the PvdA; Members of pressure group Nieuw Links (New Left), which claimed the party chairmanship in 1969, had ties to the new social movements.

MPs were quite receptive to social movements. In 1972 MPs, primarily from the progressive wing and a new generation of MPs since 1967, told political scientist R. van Schendelen that 'action- and protest groups provide me with better information'. He linked this response to their self-image as more that of popular tribunes and to their search for points of political conflict as opposition MPs at that moment.[42] During the 1970s Social-Democrat seats were filled with sympathizers or representatives of movements of international solidarity with Angola or Chile (Jan Pronk), feminism (frontwoman Hedy D'Ancona), the peace movement, social welfare and the environmental movement (Meiny Epema-Brugman,

1970, and Rie de Boois in 1972). MP Gerda Brautigam (1963–72) represented a new consumer awareness.[43] Movements on environmental issues, social work and international solidarity benefitted from the visibility of MPs who promoted them, like Anneke Goudsmit of D'66.

Public hearings, advocated by reform-minded groups like Nieuw Links and D'66, became more frequent.[44] From 1969 onwards, action committees in environmental and other issues testified at such hearings, along with traditional interest groups such as trade unions. One of the most dramatic hearings took place in 1972. The hearings concerned the potential release of three Nazi war criminals, the 'Breda Three', and provoked a controversy that led to a reduction in televised hearings. This response was possibly one of the reasons why the parliamentary committee for the contentious issue of abortion opposed holding a public hearing in 1975[45]; the strong, feminist, pro-abortion movement had allies in parliament, notably Anneke Goudsmit of D'66, whose acts of civil disobedience famously helped prevent the closing of an abortion facility in 1976. The attitude towards hearings hence can be characterized as ambivalent: hearings were used to respond to social developments, but contested issues also caused parliament to treat them with caution.

The interplay of intra- and extra-parliamentary forces thus strengthened parliament as an arena where battles over social issues were played out. Parliament was receptive both in recruitment and in the issues it addressed. These factors contributed to a parliament that responded much more to social issues than the decline narratives of the 1960s implied. It was by and large representative of societal problems; by becoming more ideological, opening up to social concerns and creating a closely followed media cycle, parliamentary politics stayed relevant.

Parliament also showed an assertive attitude when its representative monopoly was challenged. Since the 1920s parliament had been sharing its powers of oversight with some institutions like the Central Bureau of Statistic, notably in the socio-economic sphere, in a kind of functional representation. The critique of parliament strengthened reform proposals for watchdog institutions such as the ombudsman, directly representing individual citizens.[46] Politicians, political and legal scientists and commentators saw this 'monitory democracy' (Keane) as complementing a far from ideal parliament, which did not exercise its powers of oversight satisfactorily.[47] These institutions unlike parliament derived legitimacy not from aggregating sectional interests within society, but from their impartiality and proximity to citizens (Rosanvallon).[48]

The ombudsman is an official who investigates administrative malpractice in the name of citizens who issue complaints through him. It is thus a challenge to parliament as the institution par excellence to call government to account. Conservative Protestant MP Van de Wetering in 1960 called it a guarantee against 'excessive administrative mastery'; he sat on a commission which after a journey to Sweden recommended introducing the ombudsman.[49] Sweden is the modern originator of the Parliamentary Ombudsman, set up as a representative of the citizens towards the king in 1809. Partly inspired by Montesquieu, it was an institution independent from the executive which was intended to supervise the King, his offices and courts on behalf of the *Riksdag*. Appointed by parliament, he is completely independent of parliament to which he reports.[50] In Sweden, and in the Nordic countries to which the ombudsman spread during the twentieth century, the ombudsman was tasked with ensuring that authorities and courts observed impartiality and objectivity and that the public sector respected civil rights. The Swedish ombudsman can not only issue statements about public matters, but can also act as special prosecutor which can initiate legal proceedings against officials which have committed criminal offences and report negligent civil servants. The Swedish ombudsman with his strong prerogatives was transferred initially only to Finland in 1919 and after the Second World War to Denmark in 1953 and Norway in 1962.[51] West European countries subsequently implemented the office in diverse ways, sometimes in a specific domain such as the army.

A Social-Democrat report preferred an ombudsman with close proximity to parliament, which should remain the Dutch citizens' guardian against administrative malpractice. For this reason it felt the parliamentary Committee of Petitions should be strengthened, as its members argued.[52] Advocates, notably from liberal parties, however, feared a British-style parliamentary commissioner would be an 'ombudsmouse'[53] and effectively prevented extending the Committee of Petitions; just as legal scholars who had recommended its introduction in 1964 to combat the alienation of citizens in complex bureaucracies, they argued for an ombudsman appointed by but independent from parliament.[54] Government feared the hollowing out of parliament. But Liberal MP Rietkerk (VVD) thought the ombudsman's investigations and frequent reports would help parliament, but only if he were truly independent and could be approached directly, as in the Danish model.[55]

The lack of consensus hindered the proposal. The slow process led Marcel van Dam, a New Left Social-Democrat, in 1969 to start the successful television show *Geachte (Dear) Ombudsman*, which featured complaints of citizens against government.[56] Ultimately a compromise was struck: the conservative Van Agt government saw the ombudsman as an independent official along Danish lines. Ironically it wanted the ombudsman to be 'independent, not only of the Crown but also of parliament', to prevent its politicization. A broad parliamentary majority, however, claimed the prerogative to appoint and impeach the ombudsman,[57] a proposal ultimately adopted in 1983 in the revised Constitution.

The ombudsman example shows the ambivalence of politicians faced with rival representative claims. This was not necessarily approached as a zero-sum game: many MPs wanted to improve government accountability and felt that an independent official would strengthen parliament; a parliamentary commissioner would never have sufficient public authority. Parliament did not reinforce its own petition committees because by the end of the 1960s the introduction of the ombudsman was considered inevitable: it was just a question of time. Speaker of the House Van Thiel thought the ombudsman could enhance parliament's communication with the public.[58]

At the same time, the relationship between parliament and the ombudsman was closely guarded; it could not be allowed to undermine parliament as the TV Ombudsman had done, which is why it insisted on parliament's right of appointment. The protection of parliamentary prerogatives thus went hand in hand with the wish to bridge the gap between parliament and society.

## Parliamentarizing Society in the 1970s

A third and final dynamic was the expansion of parliamentarism into society. A parliamentary 'repertoire' of democracy includes key elements such as public deliberation between equals; discussion on the basis of agreeing to disagree; representatives of different persuasions or stakeholders, chosen or otherwise selected; striking compromises and majority decision-making; accountability of leaders to those represented.

A metaphor often used in this connection is that of 'sportsmanship' and the 'political game'.[59] The notion of playing by the rules is connected to the parliamentarization of society.[60] The above-mentioned elements set the parliamentary repertoire apart from conceptions of democracy based, for example, on unity of a group versus an oppressor (in certain radical repertoires), anarchist versions or direct democracy. The parliamentary repertoire would seem to have had a hard time in the 1970s, when these more radical participatory forms were popular. How is it then that parliamentary forms were actually disseminated during this period? The Dutch political and administrative elite struck a compromise with social movements calling for democratization. This compromise boiled down to introducing a type of parliamentarism in institutions like universities as the most obvious way to gratify their representative claims.

In imitation of May 1968, students occupied Amsterdam University in May 1969, demanding *one man one vote* democracy, claiming the university board was not willing to seriously consider their radical proposals for direct democracy. Although there was public support for the occupations, most politicians supported the decision of the board to remove the students, because the students by overriding representative procedures and claiming the decisive say did not accept 'parliamentary' rules in their dealings with the university board. PSP representative B. van der Lek was quite alone in arguing that democratic procedures were nice when everything went smoothly, but not when protesters had no other means to accomplish their goals.[61] Den Uyl, who had to deal with aforementioned tensions within his party, defended parliamentary rules: emancipation and democratization had never been accomplished by illegal and violent means. By 'legal' he meant civil disobedience was allowed only when an 'unreasonable opponent' refused to deliberate, as at Tilburg College, the first site of student occupations.[62]

The Amsterdam University board also had far-reaching plans for democratization, but drew the line at participation in a university parliament, claiming that students could not claim an exclusive say; they were only one of the legitimate stakeholders.[63] In the aftermath of the occupations, Dutch authorities quickly reduced the tension by introducing a comparatively far-reaching role for students in the administration of universities, for example, in the appointments of professors, a change that went into effect in 1972.[64]

One can describe this new development as a university parliament: participation was organized along representative lines. Students, board, academic and non-academic personnel and members appointed by the government were represented in university and college (hogeschool) councils; university councils had largely the same powers vis-à-vis the board as the Dutch parliament and were instituted on faculty and university-wide levels. Ultimately, there were too many stakeholders in the university to give students an exclusive direct democratic say. The expansion of the parliamentary repertoire to the sphere of education, a spill-over of parliamentarism in democratization processes beyond parliament, was not deemed a success by all. Radical students saw the cup as half-empty and lost interest in university elections and tried to form an extra-parliamentary opposition within the university. Parliamentarism would work as 'inkapseling' (encapsulation) of radical protest.[65]

In practice the university reform act (the WUB) did not always work satisfactorily. The law poorly delineated the balance between academic personnel and students within the council. In this age of polarization, the conflict-oriented approach of students did not accord well with the 'parliamentary' values of deliberation, majority decision-making and legitimate diversity.[66] They nevertheless were forced into the mould of 'government by discussion'; in Utrecht, complaints arose that the system was too harmony-driven and the dualism between board and council did not develop.[67] The 'council university' (a phrase used in analogy to the socialist council republic) conflicted with the simultaneous wish for a professional and productivity-oriented university, which led to its demise in 1997, when a more hierarchical and technocratic system was introduced.[68]

The WUB was only one reform which introduced a parliamentary repertoire, famous because the student movement was well covered by the media. Another example was works councils, which in the 1950s were still advisory and quite parochially organized.[69] Based on harmony and cooperation, they operated as a corporate community chaired by the director. The Catholic Employers advised directors to stay calm when criticized and contemplate what employees 'really meant'.[70] In the beginning of the 1970s, a much more conflict-oriented climate emerged in the social-economic sphere, with strikes and occupations of corporations. Analogous to the WUB, progressive legislation regarding works councils was introduced in 1971. As a result of Den Uyl's tenure, works-council legislation became more radicalized in 1979, awarding more prerogatives to the works council, including the right of approval for corporate decisions. All council members were to be elected. Crucially however, consultations with corporate administrators separate from the works council were still compulsory, which was why this compromise was not applauded by some radicals, but still the prerogatives of the council were quite extensive.[71]

In the reform debate over the works councils, the parliamentary analogy arose. The emphasis on mutual understanding and cooperation was replaced with holding corporate leadership to account.[72] Although they acknowledged that democracy in works councils was different from political democracy because those involved in corporations were not equals, reformers saw this difference as exactly the reason the council should be made a kind of parliament and provided with more equal relations to the executive, popularizing the notion that the council represented the interests of the employees.[73]

With the democratization of works councils, representatives had to learn successful 'medezeggenschap' (co-decision) practices such as deliberation and consensus-building. Parliament was the model for this, sometimes referred to as corporate parliamentary democracy.[74] The debate on works councils mirrored that on the 'monistic' or 'dualistic' role of parliament versus government.[75] D'66 and the conservative CDA members stressed 'consultation' as the modus operandi of the works council against a 'model of conflict', when the worker representation became overly dualistic in character. This stress on consultation also affirmed the 'parliamentary' repertoire, but instead of accountability underlined deliberation and compromise. This, CDA MP Van Zeil emphasized, was not a 'harmony model', because it did not rule out conflict.[76]

The analogy between works councils and parliament also provoked criticism: both created a small bureaucratic power elite, claimed organizational theorist M. Mulder in 1978. The left described the de facto parliamentary character of works councils in terms of *autogestion*, direct worker power. The progressive demands for reform of the works councils, however, went in the direction of making them more akin to parliaments. Social-Democrat MP Stan Poppe, for example, described the works council as 'representatives of the people themselves. The Works council will have to develop into an organ which determines policy, appoints the quotidian administrators and holds them to account, and is accountable to the corporate employees and society'.[77] He was quite unhappy with the weakening of the reform by the conservative government succeeding Den Uyl in 1977, which reduced transparency and accountability to the personnel, while keeping the provision that the leadership could bar people from the works council. Poppe compared this to a situation where 'the government would claim a right to bar MPs who in its judgment hinder the functioning of parliament and consultations with government'.[78]

From the employer's point of view, Shell manager P.J.M. Theunissen claimed completely transparent negotiations between employer and workers would make it harder for works councils to account for their actions to the 'kiezersvolk' (the electorate). This implicit parliamentary metaphor was used in a negative way: treating councils as parliaments was not a good thing.[79] In the same vein, the board of Internatio-Müller called criticism useful, but only at 'the appropriate time'. The works council was 'not a parliament and the board not a government'.[80]

What about the international context of this parliamentarization of society? Within the space of this study, I can only point to the FRG, where some developments are comparable, such as the extent to which worker *Mitbestimmung* had developed by the 1970s. University reform, however, was not as extensive there as in the Netherlands.[81]

## CONCLUSION

The 'decline of parliament' became a commonplace of the 1960s critique of parliament, supporting an ideal of popular representation by a parliament that critically interrogated government, concerned itself with general questions of political ideology instead of technocratic problem-solving and had a close and active connection with its constituents, thus bridging the famous 'gap' between political system and citizenry. Extra-parliamentary opposition in the 1960s broadened the scope of democratic politics, calling into question the hegemony of the parliamentary model in the Netherlands.

Partly in response to the omnipresent decline narrative, Dutch MPs and political parties worked to make parliament a relevant political arena in the 1970s, even though the contemporary focus was on extra-parliamentary activity. With the help of mass media, skilful politicians bridged the gap with society, successfully conveying the impression that socio-political battles were decided in parliament. A comparatively quite responsive political establishment created a parliament open to extra-parliamentary influence, in its recruitment as well as in the issues it addressed, a venue for social movements, instead of being rendered irrelevant by them. The increase in public hearings attested to the development of a more open parliament. There was also assertiveness in response to the extra-parliamentary challenge. Parliament defended its prerogatives, as the ombudsman case makes clear. Through the lengthy negotiations about this institution, MPs made sure it became an independent office, supporting parliament instead of undermining it.

Finally, there was a spill-over in the other direction: parliamentary values of deliberation, dialogue and majority decision-making became the model for democratization of society in student and works councils. There was a touch of irony to this development, because the *autogestion* rhetoric of the time was distinctly unparliamentary. Ultimately this nonetheless proved the only practicable way to implement participatory democracy.

The Dutch parliament in the 1970s was far from ideal, at least not according to its contemporaries. Haunted by narratives of its own decline and irrelevance in the face of extra-parliamentary activity, MPs secured its relevance, helped by a frantic political atmosphere. Perhaps this is why in Dutch political memory the 1970s stand out as the high-tide mark of politics, when the epic battles of 'Joop' and his opponents were a soap opera with dedicated followers. The theatre of this soap opera was parliament. In the 1980s, Dutch politics as elsewhere took a pragmatic turn. Parliament became less exciting, due to clear and stable majorities and the waning of polarization. The new generation of politicians was less convinced of the ability of parliament to structure the development of society. Again a perception of the declining power of parliament compared to that of government led to changes in its daily routines, aimed at more efficiency and an increasing use of its investigative powers.[82]

Although the catalogue of complaints remains unchanged, even increasing in vehemence after the turn of the century, parliament has retained its relevance in Dutch politics, absorbing and lending voice to new movements, whether of a progressive-Animal-party or a right-wing-populist-Freedom-Party variety. In this way, the Dutch parliament lends a voice to its own fiercest critics.

## NOTES

1. Handelingen Tweede Kamer (Proceedings Dutch House of Representatives, here further: HTK) 1965–1966, p. 1894.
2. B. Manin, *The Principles of Representative Government* (Cambridge: Cambridge University Press, 1997) 218–34.
3. Viz. Rosanvallon, *Counter-Democracy. Politics in an Age of Distrust* (Cambridge: Cambridge University Press, 2008) 83.
4. Manin, *The Principles*, 196 and 213.
5. Ibid., 235.
6. Rosanvallon, *Counter-Democracy*, 83 and 227.
7. M. Saward, *The Representative Claim* (Oxford: Oxford University Press, 2010) 28.
8. R. Aerts, 'Iemand moet het doen. Tweehonderd jaar beeld en zelfbeeld van de Tweede Kamer' in R. Aerts et al. (eds.), *In dit huis. Twee eeuwen Tweede Kamer* (Amsterdam: Uitgeverij Boom, 2015) 439–67 and 440.

9. M. Vogel, 'Ausserparlamentarisch oder antiparlamentarisch? Mediale Deutungen und Benennungskämpfe um die APO' in U. Frevert and Heinz-Gerhard Haupt (eds.), *Neue Politikgeschichte: Perspektiven einer historischen Politikforschung* (Frankfurt: Campus Verlag, 2005) 140–65, 148 and 164.

10. Viz. J-W. Duyvendak, R. Koopmans and K. Hanspeter, *Understanding European Movements: New Social Movements, Global Justice Struggles, Anti-Austerity Protest* (London and New York, 2013/1995) 64–5; H. Nehring, 'Great Britain' in M. Klimke and J. Scharloth (eds.), *1968 in Europe: A History of Protest and Activism, 1956–1977* (New York: Palgrave Macmillan, 2008) 125–36; H. Nehring, *Politics of Security. British and West German Protest Movements and the Early Cold War, 1945–1970* (Oxford: Oxford University Press, 2013) 252.

11. Andreas Biefang and Andreas Schulz, 'From Monarchical Constitutionalism to a Parliamentary Republic' in Pasi Ihalainen, Cornelia Ilie and Kari Palonen (eds.), *Parliaments and Parliamentarism. A Comparative History of a European Concept* (New York: Berghahn, 2016) 62–80 and 76–77.

12. M. Rush, *Parliament Today* (Manchester: Manchester University Press, 2005); C.J. Kam, *Party Discipline and Parliamentary Politics* (Cambridge: Cambridge University Press, 2009) 4.

13. J-W. Müller, *Contesting Democracy. Political ideas in Twentieth Century Europe* (Yale: Yale University Press, 2011) 128.

14. P. de Rooy, *Ons stipje op de waereldkaart. De politieke cultuur van modern Nederland* (Amsterdam: Wereldbibliotheek, 2014) 216–20.

15. For example, J. Cals, 'Democratie, nieuwe tijden, nieuwe vormen' (Lecture St. Jacobskring, The Hague 1964) 1; P. Thoenes, *De elite in de verzorgingsstaat* (Leiden: H.E. Stenfert Kroese, 1971/1962) 187–188; A.L. Constandse, 'Onbehagen in de politiek' in *De Gids* 130 (1967) 208–14 and 212.

16. Thoenes, *De elite in de verzorgingsstaat*, 189.

17. As voiced by a.o. Wright Mills in the United States and echoed endlessly in Great Britain and the Netherlands. Müller, *Contesting Democracy*, 128; C. Wright Mills, *The Power Elite* (New York: Oxford University Press, 1956); D. Bell, *The End of Ideology. On the Exhaustion of Political Ideas in the Fifties* (Boston: Harvard University Press, 1988/1960). In the United Kingdom, for example, B. Crick, *The Reform of Parliament* (London: Weidenfeld and Nicolson, 1964) and A. Hill and A. Whichelow, *What's wrong with parliament?* (Harmondsworth: Penguin Books, 1964).

18. J.A.W. Burger, 'De PvdA en de democratie' in *Socialisme en Democratie* 28 (1971) No 3, 115–20, esp. 116.

19. For example, *De Tijd*, 23 December 1966; for example, A.D. Belinfante, *De burger en zijn staat* (Alphen aan den Rijn: Samson 1966); *Een stem die telt* (Werkgroep PvdA 1967).

20. K. Vossen, 'De andere jaren zestig. De opkomst van de boerenpartij (1963–1967)' in G. Voerman (ed.), *Jaarboek 2004: Documentatiecentrum Nederlandse Politieke Partijen* (Groningen: Rijksuniversiteit Groningen, 2005) 245–66.
21. The expression 'iron ring' was coined by J. van den Berg and H. Molleman, *Crisis in de politiek* (Alphen aan den Rijn: Samsom, 1973) 184.
22. A. Bos and J. van Merriënboer, 'Van het dorp van Romme naar het grote bedrijf van Vondeling' in R. Aerts et al. (eds.), *In dit huis. Twee eeuwen Tweede Kamer* (Amsterdam: Boom, 2015) 383–407, esp. 404.
23. R. Koole, 'Hijgende vragen, vlotte babbels. De symbiose van politiek en media' in Jo Bardoel (ed.), *Journalistieke cultuur in Nederland* (Amsterdam: Amsterdam University Press, 2002) 101–14, esp. 103.
24. I. van den Broek, 'Engagement als deugd' in Ibid., 69–84.
25. Bos and Van Merriënboer, 'Van het dorp van Romme naar het grote bedrijf van Vondeling', 389.
26. *De Tijd*, 21 March 1969; *Algemeen Handelsblad*, 20 March 1969.
27. *Het Vrije Volk*, 20 March 1969.
28. H. Daemen, 'Gekozenen over kiezers' in R. van Schendelen et al. (eds.), '*Leden van de Staten-Generaal,...*' (Den Haag: Vuga, 1963) 273–88, esp. 275; Aerts, 'Iemand moet het doen', 459.
29. E. van Thijn, 'Overleeft de parlementaire democratie 1984?' in *Socialisme en Democratie* 33 (1976) No 3, 103–113, esp. 112.
30. Daemen, 'Gekozenen over kiezers', 276.
31. Van den Berg and Molleman, *Crisis in de Nederlandse politiek*, 163–4.
32. Aerts, 'Iemand moet het doen', 461.
33. H.M. Jolles, *De poreuze demokratie. Een sociologisch onderzoek naar het inspraakverschijnsel* (Alphen aan den Rijn: Samsom, 1974) 46.
34. J. van Putten, *Demokratie in Nederland* (Utrecht/Antwerpen: Het Spectrum, 1975) 232.
35. A. Lijphart, 'Hervorming van het parlement in vergelijkend perspectief' in *Socialisme en Democratie* 30 (1973) No 7/8, 311–18, esp. 315.
36. For example, G. van Benthem van den Bergh, 'Democratie en socialisme' in *Socialisme en Democratie* 25 (1968) No 11/12, 567–74, esp. 572; Th. Van Lier, 'Grenzen aan democratie' in *Socialisme en Democratie* 26 (1969) No 2, 99–103, esp. 100–1.
37. Bos and Van Merriënboer, 'Van het dorp van Romme naar het grote bedrijf van Vondeling', 406.
38. Viz. B. Tromp, 'Socialisme, organisatie en democratie' in *Socialisme en Democratie* 33 (1976) No 4, 155–172, esp. 155.
39. J. den Uyl, 'De smalle marge van democratische politiek' in *Socialisme en Democratie* 27 (1970) No 7, 299–321; Van Thijn, 'Overleeft de parlementaire democratie 1984?', 103–13.

40. Ph. Van Praag, *Strategie en illusie. Elf jaar intern debat in de PvdA (1966–1977)* (Amsterdam: Het Spinhuis, 1990).
41. A. Bleich, *Joop den Uyl 1919–1987. Dromer en doordouwer* (Amsterdam: Uitgeverij Balans, 2015).
42. M. van Schendelen, *Parlementaire informatie, besluitvorming en vertegenwoordiging* (Rotterdam: Universitaire Pers Rotterdam, 1975; dissertation) 122–4.
43. Information on Dutch MPs can be found on the excellent website www.parlement.com, Parlementair Documentatiecentrum, Leiden University.
44. H. Kummeling and P. Bovend'Eert, *Het Nederlandse parlement* (Deventer: Wolters Kluwer, 2000) 371; From 6 in 1966/67 to 30 in 1971/72, in the period until 1975 on average 15 per year, viz. W. Veenstra, 'Openbare hoorzittingen in het parlement (1 januari 1967–1 januari 1975)' in *Acta Politica* 11 (1976) 383–405, esp. 387.
45. Veenstra, 'Openbare hoorzittingen', 15: they voted 11 to 7 against holding a public hearing.
46. I. de Haan, 'Verplaatste democratie? Politieke representatie in functionele organen' in R. Aerts en P. de Goede (eds.), *Omstreden democratie. Over de problemen van een succesverhaal* (Amsterdam: Boom, 2013) 89–107.
47. J. Keane, *The Life and Death of Democracy* (London: Simon and Schuster/W. W. Norton and Company, 2009) 728.
48. P. Rosanvallon, *Democratic Legitimacy. Impartiality, Reflexivity, Proximity* (Princeton: Princeton University Press, 2011) 5.
49. HTK 1959–1960, p. 1131, 28 June 1960; Appendices HTK 1959–1960, No 5450, Verslag van de Commissie Onderzoek Militair Aankoopbeleid, No 3, p. 34.
50. Joachim Stern, 'Sweden' in Gabriele Kucsko-Stadlmayer (ed.), *European Ombudsman-Institutions. A comparative legal analysis regarding the multifaceted realisation of an idea* (Vienna/New York: Springer, 2008) 409–416, esp. 411–12; Stig Jägerskiöld, 'The Swedish Ombudsman' in *University of Pennsylvania Law Review* 109 (1961) 1077–1099, esp. 1078.
51. Linda C. Reif, *The Ombudsman, Good Governance and the International Human Rights System* (Leiden: Martinus Nijhoff, 2004) 4 and 6.
52. Appendices HTK 1966–1967, No 9027, Nota van de Commissie voor de Verzoekschriften inzake haar taak, werkwijze en bevoegdheden, No 2, p. 4.
53. For example, Goudsmit (D'66), HTK OCV/UCV, 1967–1968, p. C29; and Diepenhorst (ARP), HTK 1967–1968 pp. 682–83; and Beernink (CHU), Handelingen Eerste Kamer (Proceedings Dutch Senate) 1967–1968, p. 128.
54. J.G. Steenbeek, *De parlementaire ombudsman in Zweden, Denemarken en Noorwegen* (Haarlem: Tjeenk Willink, 1963) 74.

55. HTK 1970–1971, p. 2602.
56. Interview with M. Van Dam in *Nieuwsblad van het Noorden*, 4 October 1969.
57. J. Talsma, *Vijf historische en rechtshistorische studies over het recht van petitie, verzoekschriften aan de Tweede Kamer en het ombudsmanvraagstuk. Nederland, 1795–1983* (Arnhem: Gouda Quint, 1989) 266.
58. *Het Vrije Volk*, 20 March 1969.
59. H. te Velde, 'Spelers en spelbrekers. De beschaving van de Tweede Kamer' in *De negentiende eeuw* 30 (2006) No 1, pp. 35–47.
60. N. Elias and E. Dunning, *Quest for Excitement: Sport and Leisure in the Civilising Process* (Dublin: University College Dublin Press, 2008/1986) 173.
61. HTK 1968–1969, p. 2929.
62. Den Uyl, 'De smalle marge van democratische politiek', 303.
63. A.D. Belinfante, '*Preadvies*' *Congres medezeggenschap mei 1970. Nederlands Katholiek Vakverbond* (Utrecht, 1970) 23.
64. Wet Universitaire Bestuurshervorming (WUB), 1970.
65. J. Janssen and P. Voestermans, *Studenten in beweging. Politiek, universiteit en student* (Baarn: Ambo, 1984) 262.
66. An example was the 'case Daudt' at Amsterdam University: H. Daalder, 'De zaak Daudt' in H. Daudt, *Over echte politicologie. Opstellen over politicologie, democratie en de Nederlandse politiek Amsterdam* (Amsterdam: Bert Bakker, 1995) 40–86.
67. L.J. Dorsman, 'Professionalisering als probleem. De val van een college van bestuur' in L.J. Dorsman and P.J. Knegtmans (eds.), *Het universitaire bedrijf. Over professionalisering van onderzoek, bestuur en beheer* (Hilversum: Uitgeverij Verloren, 2010) 53–72, esp. 65.
68. In 1997 the WUB was replaced by the MUB (Wet Modernisering Universitaire Bestuursstructuur).
69. J. van Drongelen and S.F.H. Jellinghaus, *Wet op de ondernemingsraden* (Zutphen: Paris, 2008) 26.
70. *Het leiden van een ondernemingsraad* (Algemene Katholieke Werkgevers Vereniging, 1955) 19.
71. J. Ramakers, 'Strijd om de zelfstandige ondernemingsraad. De herverdeling van macht' in J. Ramakers, G. Voerman en R. Zwart (eds.), *Illusies van Den Uyl? De spreiding van kennis, macht en inkomen* (Amsterdam: Het Spinhuis, 1998) 49–59, esp. 58.
72. This is still the case in the 1960s, for example, J.A.M. Engelen, *De betekenis van de ondernemingsraad* (Nijmegen: Dekker & Van de Vegt, 1961) 17–32; *De ondernemingsraad in Nederland* (Contactgroep Opvoering Productiviteit van de Sociaal-Economische Raad, 1966) 112.

73. B.W.M. Hövels and P. Nas, *Ondernemingsraad en medezeggenschap* (Nijmegen: Instituut voor Toegepaste Sociologie, 1976) 4–5.

74. *Het Vrije Volk*, 5 May 1978; Vondeling in *NRC Handelsblad*, 19 January 1978.

75. I. van Haren, *De ondernemingsraad. Een handleiding voor de praktijk* (Deventer: Kluwer, 1975) 30.

76. HTK 1977–1978, pp. 3553–6.

77. HTK 1977–1978, p. 3541.

78. HTK 1977–1978, p. 3544.

79. M. Mulder, 'Het werk van de ondernemingsraad in de jaren tachtig: moeilijkheden en mogelijkheden', S. Poppe, 'Veranderingen maken de mensen zélf' and P.J.M. Theunissen, 'De nieuwe ondernemingsraad. Het standpunt van een manager' in *De zelfstandige ondernemingsraad* (Leiden: Stenfert Kroese, 1978) 16, 45 and 87.

80. 'Internatio-Müller: Ondernemingsraad is geen parlement' in *Leeuwarder Courant*, 7 June 1973.

81. O. Bartz, 'Expansion und Umbau. Hochschulreformen in der Bundesrepublik Deutschland zwischen 1964 und 1977' in *Die Hochschule* 2 (2007) 154–70, esp. 165.

82. C. Hoetink, 'Tussen traditie en modernisering. De Tweede Kamer op het breukvlak van de eenentwintigste eeuw' in Aerts et al. (eds.), *In dit huis*, 413.

# CHAPTER 13

# Change and Continuity: Implementing Parliamentary Democracy in Eastern Europe After 1989 with a Focus on Slovenia

## *Jure Gašparič*

*It seems as if all the columns supporting the Parliament have collapsed; that nobody thinks anymore about what is obvious to every other legislative represen- tation: that it has to safeguard the conditions of its existence by itself. As it is, the parties act as if their principal intention was to kill parliamentarianism, although it is only the Parliament that gives them power and validity; by its destruction, they would be left with nothing.* (Novice, 22 February 1901)

These words were written by a journalist at the Slovenian newspaper *Novice* in 1901, at the beginning of a tumultuous century when it still seemed as if the Habsburg Monarchy would last forever. At that time the journalist's conclusion that the Austrian Parliament in Vienna was on the verge of suicide was not particularly insightful or original; he merely wrote down what was being discussed at every local coffeehouse table. The very much desired parliament, a great acquisition of the constitutional era, often ended up as a great disappointment.

J. Gašparič (✉)
Institute of Contemporary History, Ljubljana, Slovenia
e-mail: jure.gasparic@inz.si

© The Author(s) 2019                                                           239
R. Aerts et al. (eds.), *The Ideal of Parliament in Europe since 1800*,
Palgrave Studies in Political History,
https://doi.org/10.1007/978-3-030-27705-5_13

Today, more than a century later, when Slovenian deputies no longer hold seats in the Austrian Reichsrat nor in the National Assembly of the Kingdom of Serbs, Croats and Slovenes/Yugoslavia or in the (federal or republican) Socialist Assemblies of the Second (Tito's) Yugoslavia, the dilemma seems to remain the same. The classic parliament—the goal of the majority of the population in the early 1990s, when Yugoslavia was falling apart—soon became one of the least trustworthy institutions in the eyes of the citizens. People wish for a parliament, but eventually they are not happy with it; they perceive it merely as a political theatre, a democratic decoration, whereas the true decisions that affect citizens' lives are taken by the representatives of political parties behind the closed doors, as in the times of the Habsburg Monarchy.

Nevertheless, after half a century of state socialism, in the early 1990s, classic parliamentarianism was 'resurrected' all over East-Central Europe. Almost all the countries east of the Iron Curtain became parliamentary democracies after 1989–1990 (some of them with elements of semi-presidentialism). It is therefore appropriate to ask why and how parliamentarianism initially was so attractive in East-Central Europe because the current lack of confidence in parliament is a characteristic not only of Slovenia, but can be observed throughout East-Central Europe.[1]

*Tables 1 and 2: In the spring of 1991, researchers from Central and Eastern Europe conducted joint research on public opinion entitled 'Political culture and political and economic orientations in Central and Eastern Europe during transition.' The survey was repeated in most of the same places in 1999. The findings, which emerged out of the research, highlighted the gap between first expectations and later reality. A historian, confronted with these figures, faces numerous challenges, interpretative doubts and questions.*

*If you consider things from the viewpoint of their usefulness, do you believe that we need the parliament in order to ensure everything runs smoothly, or do you think we could do as well without it?*

| Democratization in Eastern Europe | | We need a parliament | We could do without a parliament |
|---|---|---|---|
| Belarus | 1999 | 85,6 | 14,4 |
| Bulgaria | 1991 | 96,0 | 4,0 |
| | 1999 | 72,7 | 27,3 |
| Czech Republic | 1991 | 87,5 | 12,5 |
| | 1999 | 63,0 | 37,0 |
| Estonia | 1991 | 94,0 | 6,0 |
| | 1999 | 84,9 | 15,1 |
| East Germany | 1991 | 89,9 | 10,1 |
| | 1999 | 88,8 | 11,2 |
| West Germany | 1999 | 90,7 | 9,3 |
| Hungary | 1991 | 93,5 | 6,5 |
| | 1999 | 93,0 | 7,0 |
| Latvia | 1999 | 76,5 | 23,5 |
| Lithuania | 1991 | 90,2 | 9,8 |
| | 1999 | 62,6 | 37,4 |
| Poland | 1991 | 83,2 | 16,8 |
| | 1999 | 82,0 | 18,0 |
| Romania | 1991 | 93,8 | 6,2 |
| | 1999 | 85,1 | 14,9 |
| Russia | 1999 | 64,6 | 35,4 |
| Slovakia | 1991 | 83,9 | 16,1 |
| | 1999 | 77,1 | 22,9 |
| Slovenia | 1991 | 90,3 | 9,7 |
| | 1999 | 79,9 | 20,1 |
| Ukraine | 1991 | 85,6 | 14,4 |
| | 1999 | 69,3 | 30,7 |

Source: *Values in Transition VIII. Slovenia in Central- and East-European Comparison 1991–2011* (*Vrednote v prehodu VIII. Slovenija v srednje in vzhodnoevropskih primerjavah 1991–2011*), p. 324

Toš, N., Grizold, A., Bruszt, L., Simon, J. in Barnes, S. (2000). *Slovensko javno mnenje 1999/1: Demokratizacija v vzhodno-evropskih državah (mednarodna raziskava) in Nacionalna varnost* [Podatkovna datoteka]. Ljubljana: Univerza v Ljubljani, Arhiv družboslovnih podatkov. ADP – IDNo: SJM991. Accessible at http://www.adp.fdv.uni-lj.si/opisi/sjm991/ and Toš, N., Bruszt, L., Simon, J. in Barnes, S. (2000). *Slovensko javno mnenje SJM 1991/1: Demokratizacija v Vzhodnoevropskih državah* [Podatkovna datoteka]. Ljubljana: Univerza v Ljubljani, Arhiv družboslovnih podatkov. ADP – IDNo: SJM911. Accessible at: http://www.adp.fdv.uni-lj.si/opisi/sjm911/ and Simon, J. *Demokratizacija v vzhodnoevropskih državah 1990–92* [Podatkovna datoteka]. Ljubljana: Univerza v Ljubljani, Arhiv družboslovnih podatkov. ADP – IDNo: TD92. Accessible at: http://www.adp.fdv.uni-lj.si/opisi/td92/

To what degree do you trust the parliament?

| Democratization in Eastern Europe | | Completely | To a considerable degree | A little | Not at all |
|---|---|---|---|---|---|
| Belarus | 1999 | 6,1 | 21,5 | 40,1 | 32,3 |
| Bulgaria | 1991 | 9,7 | 32,0 | 35,1 | 23,2 |
| | 1999 | 6,8 | 25,8 | 28,5 | 38,9 |
| Czech Republic | 1991 | 2,7 | 36,7 | 49,3 | 11,4 |
| | 1999 | 1,4 | 18,4 | 51,2 | 29,0 |
| Estonia | 1991 | 4,0 | 29,2 | 46,2 | 20,5 |
| | 1999 | 1,8 | 17,5 | 52,3 | 28,3 |
| East Germany | 1991 | 2,3 | 33,3 | 41,0 | 23,4 |
| | 1999 | 2,9 | 38,9 | 41,3 | 16,8 |
| West Germany | 1999 | 5,2 | 58,2 | 28,5 | 8,1 |
| Hungary | 1991 | 11,7 | 37,5 | 37,6 | 13,2 |
| | 1999 | 5,2 | 35,9 | 40,6 | 18,3 |
| Latvia | 1999 | 0,3 | 18,5 | 47,5 | 33,7 |
| Lithuania | 1991 | 16,4 | 45,6 | 21,8 | 16,3 |
| | 1999 | 0,9 | 16,0 | 44,2 | 38,9 |
| Poland | 1991 | 6,1 | 32,4 | 49,0 | 12,5 |
| | 1999 | 0,9 | 19,8 | 53,9 | 25,4 |
| Romania | 1991 | 23,0 | 36,6 | 23,5 | 16,9 |
| | 1999 | 4,2 | 17,1 | 42,8 | 35,9 |
| Russia | 1999 | 0,8 | 5,3 | 19,4 | 74,4 |
| Slovakia | 1991 | 3,0 | 34,6 | 48,3 | 14,1 |
| | 1999 | 1,0 | 20,6 | 44,9 | 33,4 |
| Slovenia | 1991 | 7,0 | 34,3 | 45,3 | 13,4 |
| | 1999 | 2,0 | 13,7 | 52,9 | 31,4 |
| Ukraine | 1991 | 4,5 | 18,4 | 45,3 | 31,8 |
| | 1999 | 0,9 | 6,6 | 35,5 | 57,0 |

Source: *Values in Transition VIII. Slovenia in Central- and East-European Comparison 1991–2011* (*Vrednote v prehodu VIII. Slovenija v srednje in vzhodnoevropskih primerjavah 1991–2011*), p. 302

Toš, N., Grizold, A., Bruszt, L., Simon, J. in Barnes, S. (2000). *Slovensko javno mnenje 1999/1: Demokratizacija v vzhodno-evropskih državah (mednarodna raziskava) in Nacionalna varnost* [Podatkovna datoteka]. Ljubljana: Univerza v Ljubljani, Arhiv družboslovnih podatkov. ADP – IDNo: SJM991. Accessible at http://www.adp.fdv.uni-lj.si/opisi/sjm991/ and Toš, N., Bruszt, L., Simon, J. in Barnes, S. (2000). *Slovensko javno mnenje SJM 1991/1: Demokratizacija v Vzhodnoevropskih državah* [Podatkovna datoteka]. Ljubljana: Univerza v Ljubljani, Arhiv družboslovnih podatkov. ADP – IDNo: SJM911. Accessible at: http://www.adp.fdv.uni-lj.si/opisi/sjm911/ and Simon, J. *Demokratizacija v vzhodnoevropskih državah 1990–92* [Podatkovna datoteka]. Ljubljana: Univerza v Ljubljani, Arhiv družboslovnih podatkov. ADP – IDNo: TD92. Accessible at: http://www.adp.fdv.uni-lj.si/opisi/td92/

Could it be that people, gripped by euphoria and enthusiasm in 1989–1990, opted for something they did not actually want, as it was inefficient and corrupt? Let us have a look at the initial phase of transition.

## RAPID REBIRTH OF PARLIAMENTARIANISM

During the fall of the single-party regimes in these countries, one of the main goals was to establish a Western parliamentary democracy. There were no major objections raised about that; when doubts appeared, they mainly stemmed from the existing political situation (and were mostly manifested in the efforts to strengthen the presidential function rather than that of the parliament). Therefore, a rapid and almost uncritical rebirth of parliamentarianism, regardless of minor variations in individual countries, seemed almost logical. Why was that so?

Presumably, it was in the first place because parliamentarianism in its rudimentary institutional form already existed during the fall of the socialist regimes. The Socialist parliaments, which were, in their substance, by no means classic parliaments, became important elements of the democratization process: they were institutional elements that could not be circumvented. This was mainly the case in Poland and Hungary, the two countries that went through what is known as 'negotiated' transition.[2] In Poland the representatives of the communist authorities held roundtable talks with the Solidarity trade union and agreed, in 1989, that Solidarity would become a legal organization allowed to publish its own newspaper (Adam Michnik's famous *Gazeta Wyborcza*). Even more importantly, the communist authorities agreed that semi-free elections to the Sejm would be held. In addition, a new second chamber of the parliament was established: the Senat. The parliamentary elections on 4 June thus represented the watershed of the epoch, which was rather naively but clearly symbolized on the opposition's pre-election flyer showing Gary Cooper from the movie *High Noon* holding in his hand a ballot instead of a gun.[3] Roundtable talks were also held in Hungary,[4] where in the summer of 1989 the representatives of the reformist branch of communists and the opposition agreed on the revision of the constitution. They did not destroy existing institutions, but gave them new substance instead. Parliament was elected at the first free elections in the spring of 1990. In Czechoslovakia,[5] where the regime was overthrown much more rapidly than in Hungary and Poland, the central and symbolic point of the Velvet Revolution was encompassed in the Občanské fórum (OF) slogan 'Havel na Hrad' ('Havel to the castle'), meaning that Vaclav Havel should become the president. However, this demand in fact implied a fight for control of the federal parliament (in addition to which there were also separate Czech and Slovak parliaments). Since the federal 'shromáždeni' was responsible for electing the president, starting in November 1989 demonstrations took place in front of its building every day. The key dilemma for the OF was how to gain control of the parliament—where they did not have a single seat—without recourse to the classic revolutionary methods of disbanding the parliament and causing a constitutional crisis. The OF did not want to destroy the state institutions or the parliament: they wanted parliament to be involved as an actor in the transition, and they wanted the changes to be constitutional. Eventually, the parliament elected Havel as president, co-opted the new deputies from the democratic movement and adopted the basic legislation assuring free society (the laws governing elections, parties, association, etc.). This represented the first time since 1968 that the federal parliament found itself at the forefront of political developments.[6]

After the fall of the Berlin Wall, the East German *Volksversammlung* also became an important political factor. Its 10th convention was very specific and unusual. After its MPs were, for the first (and last) time since the end of World War II (WWII), elected in free and democratic elections (the parliament of the German Democratic Republic was constituted on 5 April 1990), in only six months the *Volksversammlung* carried out the East German part of what was legally and economically an extremely demanding project of the reunification of the two Germanies. The goal was achieved by MPs who lacked classic parliamentary experience, although they were assisted by Bonn. Thus the interpretation soon asserted itself that the 10th Assembly of the GDR was nothing but an 'eager pupil', 'colonized' by its Western tutors, who used it as a tool for their reunification project. However, we should not overlook the fact that the last East German Assembly was never in a completely subordinate position.[7]

In the countries of the former Yugoslavia, we cannot speak of negotiated transition. Here the dissolution of the country and the system was violent and at the same time specific due to its unique socio-political system.[8] The system was based on the Constitution of 1974, which represented the culmination of the 'Yugoslav experiment'. It introduced the delegate system (parliamentary deputies were replaced by delegates with an imperative mandate), which was a non-transparent, anachronistic, indirect form of self-management. The Assembly of the SFRY (Socialist Federal Republic of Yugoslavia) became bicameral and consisted of two equal chambers: the Federal Assembly and the Assembly of Republics and Provinces to which delegates were sent from the Assemblies of the six republics and two autonomous provinces. The Republican Assemblies, including the Slovenian Assembly, became tricameral, consisting of the Chamber of Associated Labour, Chamber of Municipalities and the Socio-Political Chamber (!). Thus the political system distanced itself from the principles of classic parliamentarism even further. The importance of delegates declined, in comparison with members of the Assembly, and the Assembly of delegates frequently gave the impression that it was merely a 'ratification body'.[9]

Like its monarchic predecessor, the second Yugoslavia was faced with constant internal crises, which culminated in the late 1980s. In this multifaceted crisis (i.e. economic, social and political), many political solutions were proposed, but they were very diverse and clearly linked to the individual republics' elites. Given the federal structure of the state, this divergence eventually escalated into a major conflict. The strongest and the most aggressive elite gathered around Slobodan Milošević (at first the president of the Central Committee of the League of Communists of Serbia, and later the president of the Presidency of the Socialist Republic of Serbia). This Serbian elite and its allies (the leaderships of Montenegro, Kosovo and Vojvodina) argued for increased powers for the central federal authorities. This actually implied a reduction of federalism and reinstatement of the classic socialist system, which had been in place in Yugoslavia before the constitutional reforms of 1971–1974. On the other hand, a loose integration of Slovenia, Croatia, Bosnia and Herzegovina, and Macedonia came about primarily through fear of the centralist and nationalist offensive of Milošević's circle. The strongest views within this group were advocated by the leadership of the League of Communists of Slovenia, which supported the democratization of society, the establishment of non-communist political groups, a greater role for the republics and the introduction of a market economy.[10]

The already loose federal system became even looser, and political control in the individual republics diminished. No monolithic party with its accompanying organizations existed in Slovenia, but rather a dispersed authority, which was disintegrating (the Socialist Youth League of Slovenia was one of the first opposition 'parties'). The demands for pluralism and systemic changes became increasingly forceful and directed at the Slovenian Delegate Assembly. In its final term in the period 1986–1990, the Assembly thus became one of the key actors in a peaceful and evolutionary transition to a multi-party parliamentary system and independence. In September 1989 it adopted several amendments to the Slovenian Constitution and thus formed the basis for gaining gradual independence and establishing a multi-party system. Later it adopted the necessary electoral legislation and called the first post-war democratic elections.[11]

Several new parties took part in the elections of April 1990. They formed a coalition called Demos, without the participation of former socialist organizations, which had been transformed into political parties. The Demos coalition won the majority of votes and formed the government. Political life was overwhelmed by the spirit of multi-party parliamentarianism, although the former system of a tricameral Delegate Assembly still existed. The newly elected deputies (still officially called delegates) were eagerly but often ineptly trying to perform their new functions. Particularly at the beginning, the new Assembly faced procedural complications and often ended up in awkward and helpless situations.

The delegates initially wanted the first session to appear like a celebration—a historical spectacle celebrating the return of democracy, but they failed to fulfil their plan. It turned out totally different. 'The session looked like a tragedy and comedy', the newspaper *Delo* wrote. Technical complications were common: the delegates had problems using electronic voting devices, while the chairing of the sessions was chaotic. A lack of trust was omnipresent. The newly elected Demos delegates felt that they were under surveillance and repeatedly convened in so-called secure locations. Above all, journalists were making fun of the new democratic political elite.[12]

However, the parliament nevertheless asserted itself as a classic representative body and played a central political role in the preparations for independence. On 25 June 1991, it adopted the key independence documents, on the basis of which Slovenia became an independent and sovereign state.

Elections were also held in the other republics, which consequently formally established a classic parliamentary democracy, although an authoritarian style prevailed in their political practices, which could be termed democratic in form but authoritarian in reality. The Croatian President Franjo Tuđman, who was also the president of the strongest political party HDZ (Croatian Democratic Union), openly modelled himself after Tito, and the Serbian (Yugoslav) President Slobodan Milošević constituted a specific family-based sultanate system. The Yugoslav Wars broke out; these wars resulted not from centuries of ethnic hatred but rather from the meticulous plans of the political centres, which used nationalism as a transitional ideology for attaining their political goals.

## Historical Legacy?

A certain form of parliamentarianism therefore already existed in the late 1980s (and it became an 'institutional' actor of reforms/revolutions); it was also an established system in the West, in the part of Europe from which—quoting Milan Kundera—its Eastern part had been torn apart, kidnapped. Following the example of the West, in particular Germany, was therefore not unusual, and this additionally explains the decision to adopt parliamentary democracy. Last but not least, classic parliamentarianism was a system that had already existed before in East-Central Europe (before WWII and/or earlier). People in this part of Europe felt that they were the part of the Western cultural-civilization circle, whose values included parliamentary democracy. Nevertheless, no general references were made to the historical legacy, as different nations regarded (and still do) their pasts very differently. In Slovenia nobody referred to the Habsburg Monarchy (in the late 1980s, the Monarchy was still considered the 'prison of nations' and was painted very negatively, although the romantic features of the Habsburg fin de siècle were often favourably cited), nor to the Kingdom of Serbs, Croats and Slovenes/Yugoslavia, which also had a bad reputation. As Hungary had not experienced true democracy in its k.u.k. and Horthy's periods, it did not try to revive the old Hungarian Assembly. On the other hand, it is apparent that, in an ideological sense, parts of the Slovenian as well as Hungarian societies looked back to their 'parliamentary past', as some political parties clearly referred to their historical legacy. In Hungary these were the FKGP (Hungarian Smallholders Party) and the KDNP (Christian Democratic People's Party),[13] while the Slovenian example was the SLS (Slovenian People's Party), which was the strongest Slovenian political party from its establishment in the 1890s until 1941. Although the 'new' SLS, which emerged during the process of democratization at the end of the 1980s, had no connection whatsoever (except a virtual one) with the 'old' SLS, it continuously kept referring to its namesake—one of its presidents even claimed to be a proud successor of Anton Korošec, the most prominent Slovenian politician in interwar Yugoslavia (and the only non-Serbian president of the Belgrade government).[14]

In East-Central Europe, only the Czech Republic looked back to the past while forming the new system. The interwar Czechoslovak Republic, led by the charismatic philosopher T. G. Masaryk, became a historical point of reference for Czech parliamentary democracy (though not in Slovakia). Vaclav Havel was proclaimed as Masaryk's successor, and politicians asked themselves how the 'president–liberator' would have acted in similar situations.[15] The Czech constitutional system is (was) thus largely a replica of the First Republic: a bicameral parliament with a chamber of deputies and a directly elected senate as well as a president, elected by the parliament (later this was changed: now the President of the Republic is elected directly).[16]

## A Time of Disappointment

The course towards the institutional and substantive formation of parliamentary democracy was in fact set immediately at the first signs of the collapse of the socialist regimes. The wishes of the populace were clear. According to public opinion polls, in Slovenia a large majority of people believed that the country should follow the example of the West European countries. The consensus was that Slovenia's democracy had not yet attained Western standards, despite the democratically elected Delegate Assembly and that a multi-party system was required. Therefore the country and its citizens clearly needed a parliament.

On this basis we could easily conclude that the degree of confidence in parliamentary democracy in Slovenia at the beginning of the new era of Slovenian parliamentarianism was high. However, views were at the same time wracked by distrust and often contradictory. On the one hand, people supported the parliament as an institution, while on the other hand, they believed that politicians did not want the public to interfere in political affairs, that ordinary people were in fact kept away from power, that politicians became interested in the people's opinion only when problems arose and that (consequently?) a strong state executive could be more useful than all the discussions in the parliament.[17] Great expectations were mixed with the legacy of the old system.

The formation and understanding of parliamentary democracy by the electorate as well as by the elected representatives stemmed from its political-historical legacy and the specific features of the transitional development and structural formation of the political space, as well as from established theories and practices abroad (particularly in the West).

It has been a product of a ready-made political-cultural pattern, which is still being formed today. While the new political institutions of parliamentary democracy developed relatively quickly, the shift in people's mentality has been slower, and this is characteristic of all of East-Central Europe.[18] It seems that the statement from the nineteenth-century British Parliament still applies: 'Rules were copied, culture was not.'[19]

A time of disappointment with parliamentary democracy soon followed, not only in Slovenia but also in other countries in Central Europe. It became obvious that this form of government had often been idealized and overly romanticized, while barely anyone truly understood its essence. It is even questionable whether all of the substantive conditions for its enforcement were met. The countries of the former East (in the opinion of some researchers)[20] thus began to face nationalism, the lack of a culture of compromise, the lack of confidence in politics, an ideological vacuum, transience and so on, which do not offer a favourable ground for the development of parliamentary democracy, which has by definition been unstable.

Everybody is critical, 'ordinary people' as well as those who have helped dissolve the one-party systems. In Slovenia, Evald Flisar, the president of the Slovene Writers' Association, a member of what was formerly a strong opposition elite, was explaining to his colleagues back in 1997 that the centre of political development 'was now the Parliament, as in all other democratic countries ... Writers were no longer "chosen" to articulate the needs of the nation.'[21]

## Conclusions

Everywhere, the parliaments emerged 'too quickly', almost by inertia, mainly because of three reasons:

- They already existed in the late 1980s in a rudimentary socialist form and became actors of reform.
- Parliamentarianism was an established system in the West.
- Historical political legacy also played an important role.

We can claim that parliaments were 'getting ahead' of their surroundings. Dissatisfaction with parliamentary democracy, which (also) stems from a lack of understanding of its premises and workings, has soon spread across all spheres of society. Moreover, the perception of the parliaments has been disastrously affected by numerous political scandals, eagerly pursued by the media. The former Slovenian Deputy Ciril Ribičič wrote back in 1995 that 'only bad news is good news' when it came to the question of parliamentarians, that a parliament is generally an expensive, inefficient and privilege-seeking 'gang of lazy spendthrifts'.[22] Also the former Slovak Deputy Jozef Banáš, who published the widely read 'report from the study visit to politics', came to a similar conclusion. In a likeable, satirical style he described how

> the politicians' standard of living does not differ depending on whether they belong to the socialist left or conservative right, but rather hinges on whether they had been rich before they went into politics or gained their wealth after that. Socialists who grew rich in politics became conservatives. If socialists were rich when they entered politics, they were conservatives even though they were members of a socialist party. A politician who was poor before entering politics and remained poor when exiting politics, is neither a socialist nor a conservative, but an idiot.[23]

With these words Banáš humorously expressed what the readers wanted to read. One of the Slovenian public opinion polls revealed that people do not know exactly what parliamentarians do: they remember only their lapses, failures and affairs, which accompany the work of the parliament.[24] As in the past, actual practice has compromised the ideal form of parliamentary democracy.

However, we should point out that in the first 20 years the parliaments did carry out their basic task: as elected representatives they adopted legislation, built new political and economic systems and brought them in line with EU legislation in a more or less consensual manner.[25] The legislative workload has often been impressive (in the 20-year period, the Slovenian Parliament adopted, on average, more than 300 parliamentary acts per year), even if the parliamentary culture—at least in the Czech Republic and Slovenia—was improvised (there has been no regular division into frontbenchers and backbenchers, only a few deputies are capable of inspiring rhetoric as they usually simply read their speeches drearily, the sequence of pro–contra–pro–contra argumentation is merely accidental, etc.).[26] It seems that the parliamentary culture[27] largely affects the relationship between the parliament and the public as well as the people's perception of the parliament. Naturally, we should not overlook the role of the media and the omnipresent 'medialization' of politics, which has thoroughly changed the relationships between the voters and MPs, especially in the age of digital technologies. The attitude towards politics and parliaments is mostly formed through the prism of the media.[28]

During a bitter budgetary debate in the autumn of 1993, the young Slovenian Parliament was visited by the Czech president Vaclav Havel. The former dissident addressed the Slovenian parliamentarians in a short speech that revealed his thoughts about 'anti-political politics'. Havel, who was greatly admired in Slovenia as elsewhere, symbolized a romantic, 'velvet' image of the transition. In politics, Havel was mostly afraid of the role of parties, and he also warned the Slovenian Parliament about it:

> One of the things that we definitely have in common is the fact that we are both building a parliamentary democracy. A new political spectrum is emerging, new political subjects, which are seeking their own identity and their place. These subjects are seeking avenues for cooperation, also as regards the ways of representation. To put it simply, we are building a political system. And we are building this system along with another difficult task of parliaments: the transformation of the entire legal and the economic system.
>
> But in this dramatic, interesting and exciting situation, there are many hidden dangers to which we should pay special attention. In my opinion, one of these dangers is that the parties in this area could obtain an overrated role. It seems as if countries now belong to political parties. As if the parties were not supposed to serve their countries, but rather that countries should serve the parties. This danger is of course related to the electoral system. I believe this is one of the dangers posed to the emerging of new parliamentary democracies which I have mentioned before. I wholeheartedly wish that your Parliament as well as ours would be safe from these dangers, which have been preying on us in this difficult period.[29]

As the most recent research of our Czech colleagues emphasizes, in Havel's opinion the Czech Parliament was not 'safe' from danger. As president, Havel constantly criticized it for being hesitant and slow and reproached it for having only the party interests in mind. He would often exert pressure against it and attempt to increase his powers as president. Furthermore, Havel's attitude was quite openly anti-parliamentary (which has until now been overlooked by those who have studied his work), and he even mobilized the people against the parliament (although he had been elected by this very body).[30]

We can therefore conclude that parliamentary democracy is the desired and idealized form, even though almost nobody—neither ordinary citizens nor most of the political and social elites—is satisfied with its actual practice in the European East. New parties—more determined, more 'honest' and more 'efficient'—are not a rarity, and the political arena east of the former Iron Curtain is still being restructured.[31]

## NOTES

1. Jure Gašparič, *Državni zbor 1992–2012. O slovenskem parlamentarizmu* (Ljubljana: Inštitut za novejšo zgodovino, 2012) 295–301.
2. Sabrina P. Ramet and F. Peter Wagner, 'Post-Socialist Models of Rule in Central and South-Eastern Europe' in Sabrina P. Ramet (ed.), *Central and Southeast European Politics since 1989* (Cambridge: Cambridge University Press, 2010) 17–18 and 23–6.
3. Konstanty Gebert, 'Poland since 1989: Muddling Through, Wall to Wall' in Ibid., 139–61.
4. András Bozóki and Eszter Simon, 'Hungary since 1989' in Ramet (ed.), *Central and Southeast European Politics*, 204–32.
5. Jiří Suk, *Labyrintem revoluce. Aktéři, zápletky a křižovatky jedné politické krize* (Prague: Prostor, 2003) 24–30.
6. Adéla Gjuričová, 'Coming to (a Short) Life: The Czechoslovak Parliament 1989–1992' in *Prispevki za novejšo zgodovino*, LV, 2015, No 3 (Complex Parliaments in Transition: Central European Federations Facing Regime Change) 9–23; Tomáš Zahradníček, 'Debates Were to be Held in the Parliament, but it Proved Impossible: The Federal Assembly and the Velvet Revolution in Czechoslovakia in 1989' in Ibid., 105–21; Petr Roubal, 'Revolution by the Law: Transformation of the Czechoslovak Federal Assembly 1989–1990' in Ibid., 60–83.
7. Bettina Tüffers, 'The 10th Volkskammer of the GDR: Just a Keen Student or a Parliament with Its Own Culture?' in Ibid., 24–40; Bettina Tüffers, *Die 10. Volkskammer der DDR. Ein Parlament im Umbruch: Selbstwahrnehmung, Selbstparlamentarisierung, Selbstauflösung* (Dusseldorf: Droste Verlag, 2016).
8. See paper by Attila Agh, 'Parlamenti v vzhodni in srednji Evropi–deset let kasneje' and comments by Matevž Krivic and Božo Repe to his theses, in T. Krašovec (ed.), *Razvoj slovenskega parlamentarizma. Kolokvij ob 10. obletnici parlamentarizma v Sloveniji. Zbornik referatov, koreferatov in razprav* (Ljubljana: Državni zbor Republike Slovenije, 2000) 11–25 and 89–91.
9. Jure Gašparič, 'Slovenian Socialist Parliament on the Eve of the Dissolution of the Yugoslav Federation: A Feeble "Ratification Body" or Important Political Decision-Maker?' in *Prispevki za novejšo zgodovino*, LV, 2015, No 3, pp. 46–7.

10. Božo Repe, *Jutri je nov dan. Slovenci in razpad Jugoslavije* (Ljubljana: Modrijan, 2002) 63–73 and 232–5; Stefano Lusa, *Razkroj oblasti. Slovenski komunisti in demokratizacija države* (Ljubljana: Modrijan, 2012).
11. Miran Potrč, 'The Legal Basis for the First Democratically Elected Assembly of the Republic of Slovenia was Provided by the Legislation Adopted on 27 December 1989 in the Assembly of the Socialist Republic of Slovenia' in *Prihodnost parlamentarne demokracije. Zbornik strokovnega srečanja ob 20. obletnici prvih večstrankarskih volitev*, November 2010 (Ljubljana, 2010) 26–32.
12. Blaž Babič, 'Vzpostavitev parlamentarizma v polnem pomenu besede: "Parlamentarna demokracija vrača udarec"' in *Prihodnost parlamentarne demokracije*, 48–58; Stefano Lusa, *Razkroj oblasti. Slovenski komunisti in demokratizacija države* (Ljubljana: Modrijan, 2012) 225–7 and 230–2.
13. András Bozóki and Eszter Simon, 'Hungary since 1989' in Ramet (ed.), *Central and Southeast European Politics*, 214–16.
14. Jure Gašparič, 'Menjava političnih elit na Slovenskem po drugi svetovni vojni' in *Čas. zgod. Narodop.*, 2008, letn. 79, zv. 3/4, pp. 114–27.
15. Cf. a documentary movie 'Občan Havel'.
16. Carol Skalnik Leff, 'Building Democratic Values in the Czech Republic since 1989' in Ramet (ed.), *Central and Southeast European Politics*, 162–81.
17. Gašparič, *Državni zbor*, 42–4.
18. Michal Kopeček, 'Historická paměť a liberální nacionalismus v Česku a střední Evropě po roce 1989' in *Kapitoly z dějin české demokracie po roce 1989* (Prague/Litomyšl: Paseka, 2008) 259.
19. See Chap. 2 in this book, Henk te Velde, 'Between National Character and an International Model: Parliaments in the Nineteenth Century', and Tagungsbericht 'The Ideal Parliament: Perception, Interpretation and Memory of Parliaments and Parliamentarism in Europe', 30 May 2013–1 June 2013, The Hague, in H-Soz-u-Kult, 20 September 2013, http://hsozkult.geschichte.hu-berlin.de/tagungsberichte/id=5029 by Juliane Brandt.
20. Piotr S. Wandycz, *Cijena slobode. Povijest Srednjoistočne Europe od srednjega vijeka do danas* (Zagreb: Srednja Europa, 2004) 339–40.
21. Aleš Gabrič, 'Lahkotnost rušenja starega in težavnost vzpostavljanja novega' in A. Gabrič (ed.), *Slovenska pot iz enopartijskega v demokratični sistem* (Ljubljana: Inštitut za novejšo zgodovino, 2012) 11–32.
22. Ciril Ribičič, *Siva tipka 074* (Ljubljana, 1995) 124.
23. Jozef Banáš, *Idioti v politike* (Bratislava, 2010) 31.
24. Gašparič, *Državni zbor*, 295–301.
25. Also the parliaments in Croatia and Serbia have been following the same path after 2000, after the death of the first president Franjo Tuđman and

defeat of HDZ in Croatia and after 5 October and overthrowing of the vožd Slobodan Milošević in Serbia. The same cannot be said about Bosnia and Herzegovina, as it remains unstable and quite chaotic following the Dayton Accords.

26. Gašparič, *Državni zbor*, and Jan Wintr, *Česká parlamentní kultura* (Prague: Auditorium, 2010).

27. Wintr, *Česká parlamentní kultura*, 5–7.

28. See Andreas Schulz and Andreas Wirsching, 'Parlamentarische Kulturen in Europa – das Parlament als Kommunikationsraum'in Andreas Schulz and Andreas Wirsching (eds.), *Das Parlament als Kommunikationsraum* (Berlin/Dusseldorf: KGParl/Droste Verlag, 2012) 20–1.

29. 'Dokumentacijsko-knjižnični oddelek Državnega zbora RS. Dobesedni zapis 13. seje I. mandata DZ (9. 11. 1993)' accessible at: http://www.dz-rs.si/wps/portal/en/Home

30. Adéla Gjuričová, 'Anti-Politics vis-a-vis Parliamentary Democracy. Vaclav Havel and the Czechoslovak Parliament in the 1990s' in Marie-Luise Recker and Andreas Schulz (eds.), *Parlamentarismuskritik und Antiparlamentarismus in Europa* (Berlin/Dusseldorf: KGParl/Droste Verlag, 2018) 281–290.

31. Furthermore, deputies have frequently switched parties, and new parties keep emerging. In Hungary, 50 out of total 386 deputies switched parties 45 times (!) in the period 1990–1994, and 54 deputies switched them 68 times in the next parliamentary mandate. In Poland, 131 deputies switched parties in the period 1989–1991 and 65 deputies in 1991–1993; in the Czech Republic two governments (in 1996 and 2006) depended on non-attached deputies; in Slovakia 44 deputies switched parties in the period 1990–1992 and then another 28, only 5 deputies in the period 1994–1998 and 37 deputies in 1998–2002. In Slovenia, 29 out of 90 deputies switched parties in the first term (1992–1996), the second term was quite stable, the third and fourth terms were again more dynamic, while the fifth terms (2008–2011) was the most stable. Svetozár Krno, Jozef Lysý and Martin Krno, 'Národná rada od zániku Česko-Slovenska a vzniku Slovenskej republiky po súčasnosť in M. Pekník (ed.), *Slovenské národné rady a cesta k parlamentarizmu* (Bratislava: Veda, vydavateľstvo Slovenskej akadémie vied, 2008) 280–1; Gašparič, *Državni zbor*, 237–40.

# CHAPTER 14

# Postscript

*Henk te Velde*

As the introduction to this volume explains, this book is about parliament as an idea, as a specific culture of doing politics and as a practice of representation, deliberation and procedure. It belongs to a recent tradition of parliamentary history that does not concentrate on ministerial responsibility and the power of parliaments, but rather on what a parliament actually was and what contemporaries thought that its purpose was or should be. This still rather new tradition studies debating practices as well as the culture of parliament and parliament as a concept.[1] Although the new tradition is certainly not the exclusive focus of the present volume, it has helped the authors to further 'historicize' parliaments and to see interesting sides of parliaments that previously seemed to be insignificant or meaningless. Consequently, the 'Ideal of Parliament' appears in a new light. To start with, the ideal itself has changed over time; in the way we understand it now, it developed only fully during the nineteenth century. Jens Späth, writing about one of the earliest examples of a parliament in this book, the Cádiz Cortes (Chap. 3), says that 'parliamentary discussion [at that time, still] served to persuade rather than to give account of measures'. The meaning and evaluation of parliamentary debates has

H. te Velde (✉)
Leiden University, Leiden, The Netherlands
e-mail: H.te.Velde@hum.leidenuniv.nl

© The Author(s) 2019
R. Aerts et al. (eds.), *The Ideal of Parliament in Europe since 1800*,
Palgrave Studies in Political History,
https://doi.org/10.1007/978-3-030-27705-5_14

changed—even though both persuasion and accountability have to a certain extent always been part of most debates. Parliamentary discussion has always had many purposes, and open discussion and representation of the people have always had to be balanced.

The ideal of parliament has always been a rather practical ideal, too. Therefore, one of the key phrases of this book is the title of the chapter about communist Czechoslovakia: 'too ideal to be a parliament'. Of course, we already knew that the Czechoslovakian parliament was mostly a parliament in appearances only. However, Adéla Gjuričová (Chap. 11) has studied it more seriously than happened in previous overviews of the history of parliaments, and she is arguing that this parliament was, in fact, 'highly consensual, constructive and accountable'. There was even 'a system of speeches, and political will was effectively translated into laws', but still: it was too ideal to be true. It did not bode well for the institution, that, instead of a parliament, it was called a 'representative assembly', a word that was used in the nineteenth century for parliaments that were still quite far removed from large parts of society. In order to fulfil the functions of a proper parliament, parliaments need real disagreement about the political issues at stake, and criticism of the always imperfect way in which they represent the country. In short, parliaments need critics who are dissatisfied with the way they operate, otherwise parliaments petrify, cease to be responsive or become complacent. It is true, the ideal of parliament can lead to disaffection and disillusion (Remieg Aerts and Joop Th.J. van den Berg, Chap. 1) and has even led to a persistent 'Parliament Decline Thesis' (cf. Kálmán Pócza, Chap. 8), but these sentiments do not necessarily hamper parliaments, let alone threaten their existence. They *could*, as happened in the case of Weimar, but, as Thomas Raithel writes (Chap. 9), in Germany there was already 'very little enthusiasm for parliamentarism' to start with. Of course, a parliament can disappear, but until now, the most common development has been gradual change. Even the onslaught on parliamentarism by Nazism and fascism led, indirectly, after 1945 to almost two decades of unprecedented belief in an austere parliamentary democracy, also in Italy and, in particular, in Germany (Marie-Luise Recker, Chap. 10). More in general, disaffection may also directly lead to beneficial changes, as the democratization of the end of the nineteenth century shows. If no disaffection had existed, things would not have changed, or at least not as quickly.

The creative tension between deliberation and representation is perhaps the central puzzle of the history of parliaments. In some ways related is the fascinating paradox of parliaments as symbols of the nation. More often than not, the emerging nineteenth-century institutions chose indigenous names such as Cortes or States General for their representative assemblies which they presented as national organizations surrounded by national ritual. However, they also called or started to call these institutions parliaments, as a sign that they realized that they belonged to a new species of institutions, in fact a transnational phenomenon that was increasingly having many things in common. Parliaments were also following the same examples: less than some would think, the British Parliament—which was always invoked as prestigious beacon—and more French or even German examples. One would perhaps expect that, as a result, the national elements would retreat to the background, but they have not disappeared, and for good reasons. For one, the national element helped to underline the 'agreement' in the 'agreement to disagree', or, as Marnix Beyen (Chap. 4) puts, the 'non-partisan past'. Also, it demonstrated that a parliament should represent a concrete polity or political community. It was one of the less conspicuous ambitions of the time-consuming debates of the German National Assembly of 1848 'to forge the nation together by creating a common political language' (Andreas Schulz, Chap. 6). Quite recently, the European 'Assembly', on the other hand, struggled to gain legitimacy as a parliament, despite already choosing the name of parliament as early as 1962 in all the languages of the European Community, because it was not conceived as a democratic and national representation in the first place.

At the time of writing, the national issue is complicating the discussion about Brexit in Parliament. 'Taking back control' has been the slogan of the Leave campaign. But what does this mean for the British Parliament? The phrase conveniently lacks a subject, but the implicit subject is the 'British people' who 'have spoken'. But what about the majority of the 'Scottish people' who voted in majority against Brexit? And, more complicated still: suppose Parliament really wants to listen to the wishes of the majority, how should they do so?

These are clearly questions of our time. In the nineteenth century, commentators were more worried about issues such as the 'dignity' of parliamentarians and their 'civilized, respectful way of speaking' (Jens Späth, Chap. 3), today they are occupied with the responsiveness to the population. However, in the two cases, the nature of both deliberation as well as representation was and is at stake. It shows the striking flexibility of an institution that was designed in a different age with different goals in mind. This flexibility is not a guarantee that the institution will exist forever, let alone that it will develop in the 'right' direction, but, notwithstanding the decline thesis, there is some reason for optimism about the future of parliaments. It is a challenge, though, to keep alive the *ideal* of a parliament in times when the really existing parliaments are omnipresent.

## NOTE

1. Examples from different national traditions: Nicolas Roussellier, *Le Parlement de l'éloquence. La souveraineté de la délibération au lendemain de la Grande guerre* (Paris: Sciences Po 1997); Thomas Mergel, *Parlamentarische Kultur in der Weimarer Republik. Politische Kommunikation, symbolische Politik und Öffentlichkeit im Reichstag* (Düsseldorf: Droste 2002), Andreas Schulz and Andreas Wirsching eds., *Parlamentarische Kulturen in Europa. Das Parlament als Kommunikationsraum* (Düsseldorf: Droste 2012) and other books in the same series; Pasi Ihalainen, Cornelia Ilie and Kari Palonen, eds, *Parliament and Parliamentarism. A Comparative History of a European Concept* (New York and Oxford: Berghahn 2016); Remieg Aerts, Carla van Baalen, Joris Oddens, Diederik Smit and Henk te Velde eds, *In dit Huis. Twee eeuwen Tweede Kamer* (Amsterdam: Boom 2015); Henk te Velde, *Sprekende politiek. Redenaars en hun publiek in de parlementaire Gouden Eeuw* (Amsterdam 2015).

# Index[1]

---

[1] Note: Page numbers followed by 'n' refer to notes.

© The Author(s) 2019

R. Aerts et al. (eds.), *The Ideal of Parliament in Europe since 1800*,
Palgrave Studies in Political History,
https://doi.org/10.1007/978-3-030-27705-5

Printed by Printforce, the Netherlands